Positive Tourism in Africa

T0290068

Positive Tourism in Africa provides a crucial counter-narrative to the prevailing colonial and reductionist perspective on Africa's tourism trajectory and future. It offers a uniquely optimistic outlook for tourism in Africa whilst acknowledging the many challenges that African countries continue to grapple with. By examining broad and localised empirical studies, conceptual frameworks, culturally centred paradigms, and innovative methodological approaches for African contexts, this book showcases the many facets of tourism in Africa that illustrate hope, resilience, growth, and survival.

This volume explores themes such as community-based tourism, wildlife tourism, tourism governance and leadership, crisis recovery, regional integration, the role of indigenous knowledge, event tourism and the impact of smart technologies. It acknowledges the challenges and opportunities for growth that exist in these various contexts and explores how tourism creates value for the spectrum of its participants.

Including a wide selection of contributions from diverse authors, many of them African, this book offers an Afro-centric interpretation of tourism phenomena. It will be of great interest to students, researchers and academics in the field of Tourism and African Studies, as well as Development Studies and Geography.

Mucha Mkono is an Australian Research Council (DECRA) Fellow at the University of Queensland Business School. Her research focuses on a range of issues in tourism, especially pertaining to Africa, including wildlife conservation and trophy hunting, social movements, and representations of Africa.

Contemporary Geographies of Leisure, Tourism and Mobility
Series Editor: C. Michael Hall
Professor at the Department of Management,
College of Business and Economics, University of Canterbury,
Christchurch, New Zealand

The aim of this series is to explore and communicate the intersections and relationships between leisure, tourism and human mobility within the social sciences. It will incorporate both traditional and new perspectives on leisure and tourism from contemporary geography, e.g. notions of identity, representation and culture, while also providing for perspectives from cognate areas such as anthropology, cultural studies, gastronomy and food studies, marketing, policy studies and political economy, regional and urban planning, and sociology, within the development of an integrated field of leisure and tourism studies.

Also, increasingly, tourism and leisure are regarded as steps in a continuum of human mobility. Inclusion of mobility in the series offers the prospect to examine the relationship between tourism and migration, the sojourner, educational travel, and second home and retirement travel phenomena.

The series comprises two strands:

Contemporary Geographies of Leisure, Tourism and Mobility aims to address the needs of students and academics, and the titles will be published in hardback and paperback. Titles include:

Positive Tourism in Africa
Edited by Mucha Mkono

Routledge Studies in Contemporary Geographies of Leisure, Tourism and Mobility is a forum for innovative new research intended for research students and academics, and the titles will be available in hardback only. Titles include:

Tourism in Iran
Challenges, Development and Issues
Edited by Siamak Seyfi and C. Michael Hall

Tourism Policy and Planning Implementation
Issues and Challenges
Edited by Konstantinos Andriotis, Dimitrios Stylidis and Adi Weidenfeld

For more information about this series, please visit: www.routledge.com/Contemporary-Geographies-of-Leisure-Tourism-and-Mobility/book-series/SE0522

Positive Tourism in Africa

Edited by Mucha Mkono

Routledge
Taylor & Francis Group

LONDON AND NEW YORK

First published 2019 by Routledge

2 Park Square, Milton Park, Abingdon, Oxon OX14 4RN

605 Third Avenue, New York, NY 10017

*Routledge is an imprint of the Taylor & Francis Group,
an informa business*

First issued in paperback 2022

British Library Cataloguing-in-Publication Data
A catalogue record for this book is available from the British Library

Library of Congress Cataloging-in-Publication Data
Names: Mkono, Mucha (Muchazondida), author.
Title: Positive tourism in Africa / Mucha Mkono.
Description: Abingdon, Oxon ; New York, NY : Routledge, 2019. |
   Includes bibliographical references and index.
Identifiers: LCCN 2018058391 (print) | LCCN 2019001883 (ebook) |
   ISBN 9780429428685 (eBook) | ISBN 9781138369405 (hardback : alk. paper)
Subjects: LCSH: Tourism—Africa. | Tourism—Social aspects—Africa.
Classification: LCC G155.A35 (ebook) | LCC G155.A35 M56 2019 (print) |
   DDC 338.4/7916—dc23
LC record available at https://lccn.loc.gov/2018058391

ISBN: 978-1-138-36940-5 (hbk)
ISBN: 978-1-03-233851-4 (pbk)
DOI: 10.4324/9780429428685

Typeset in Times New Roman
by Apex CoVantage, LLC

Contents

Figures

Tables

Contributors

David Adeloye, PhD Candidate in the Department of Tourism, University of Otago, New Zealand. Email: david.adeloye@postgrad.otago.ac.nz

Ogechi Adeola, Associate Professor in the Operations, Information Systems and Marketing Division of Lagos Business School (LBS), Lagos, Nigeria. Email: oadeola@lbs.edu.ng

Krishnee Appadoo, Lecturer in the Department of Law, University of Mauritius, Mauritius. Email: ka.appadoo@uom.ac.mu

Jim Ayorekire, Senior Lecturer in the Department of Forestry, Biodiversity & Tourism, Makerere University, Kampala, Uganda. Email: jayorekire@caes. mak.ac.ug

Bineswaree Bolaky, Economic Affairs Officer in the Africa section, Division for Africa, Least Developed Countries and Special Programmes at the United Nations Conference on Trade and Development. Email: bineswaree.bolaky@ unctad.org

Michael Bruce Byaruhanga, PhD fellow at Copenhagen University, Denmark, and Assistant Lecturer in Tourism in the Department of Forestry, Biodiversity & Tourism, Makerere University, Kampala, Uganda. Email: mbyaruhanga@ chuss.mak.ac.ug

Neil Carr, Professor and Head of the Department of Tourism, University of Otago, New Zealand. Email: neil.carr@otago.ac.nz

Olaniyi Evans, Lecturer in the School of Management & Social Sciences, Pan-Atlantic University, Lagos, Nigeria. Email: oevans@pau.edu.ng

Sheereen Fauzel, Senior Lecturer in the Faculty of Law and Management, University of Mauritius, Réduit, Mauritius. Email: s.fauzel@uom.ac.mu

Sanette Ferreira, Professor in the Department of Geography and Environmental Studies, Stellenbosch University, Stellenbosc, South Africa. Email: SLAF@ sun.ac.za

Robert Ebo Hinson, Professor and Head of the Department of Marketing and Entrepreneurship, University of Ghana Business School, Legon-Accra, Ghana. Email: hinsonrobert@gmail.com

Bernard Kitheka, Assistant Professor at Missouri State University, United States. Email: bkithek@g.clemson.edu

Tom Kwanya, Professor in the School of Information and Communication Studies, Technical University of Kenya. Email: tom.kwanya@gmail.com

Roopanand Mahadew, Senior Lecturer in the Department of Law, University of Mauritius, Mauritius. Email: r.mahadew@uom.ac.mu

Garry Marvin, Professor of Human-Animal Studies in the Department of Life Sciences, University of Roehampton, London, United Kingdom. Email: G.Marvin@roehampton.ac.uk

Joseph E. Mbaiwa, Professor of Tourism Studies and Director of the Okavango Research Institute, Maun, Botswana. Email: JMbaiwa@ub.ac.bw

Tsholofelo Mbaiwa, Co-Director of Felojoe Research Services, Botswana. Email: tshologabs@gmail.com

Mucha Mkono, Australian Research Council DECRA Fellow in the Business School, University of Queensland, Brisbane, Australia. Email: m.mkono@uq.edu.au; muchajosie@gmail.com

Takaruza Munyanyiwa, Lecturer in the Department of Tourism and Hospitality Management, Midlands State University, Gweru, Zimbabwe. Email: munyanyiwat@staff.msu.ac.zw

Regis Musavengane, Postdoctoral Research Fellow in the School of Tourism and Hospitality, University of Johannesburg, South Africa. Email: regmuss2000@yahoo.com

Cleopas Njekerai, Senior Lecturer in the Department of Tourism and Hospitality Management, Midlands State University, Gweru, Zimbabwe. Email: njerekaic@staff.msu.ac.zw

Shepherd Nyaruwata, Senior Lecturer in the Department of Tourism and Hospitality Management, Midlands State University, Zimbabwe. Email: scnyaruwata@gmail.com

Joseph Obua, Professor of Environmental Forestry and Ecotourism, Makerere University, Kampala, Uganda. Email: jobua09@gmail.com

Chloe Rooks, BSc Graduate, University of Roehampton, London, United Kingdom. Email: rooksc@roehampton.ac.uk

Caroline Ross, Reader in Evolutionary Anthropology and Head of the Department of Life Sciences, University of Roehampton, London, United Kingdom. Email: c.ross@roehampton.ac.uk

Boopen Seetanah, Associate Professor in the Faculty of Law and Management, University of Mauritius, Réduit, Mauritius. Email: b.seetanah@uom.ac.mu

Gladys Siphambe, PhD candidate in the Faculty of Business, University of Botswana, Gaborone, Botswana. Email: bsiphambe@gmail.com

Agnes Sirima, Lecturer and Head of the Department of Tourism and Recreation at Sokoine University of Agriculture (SUA), Morogoro, Tanzania. Email: agnes@sua.ac.tz

Jonathan Skinner, Reader in Social Anthropology in the Department of Life Sciences, University of Roehampton, London, United Kingdom. Email: Jonathan. Skinner@roehampton.ac.uk

Lesego S. Stone, research scholar at the Okavango Research Institute, University of Botswana, Maun, Botswana. Email: stonel@ub.ac.bw

Moren T. Stone, Senior Lecturer of Environmental Science and Tourism Studies at the University of Botswana, Gaborone, Botswana. Email: Moren.Stone@ mopipi.ub.bw

Zibanai Zhou, Lecturer in the Department of Tourism and Hospitality Management, Midlands State University, Gweru, Zimbabwe. Email: zhouz@staff. msu.ac.zw

Acknowledgements

I would like to express my deep gratitude to the many contributors who submitted their diverse and insightful chapters to this volume. They embraced my vision for a book that would tell a positive story on tourism in Africa. Their patience and good humour throughout the process is not lost on me. I should also acknowledge the interest of so many others who submitted proposals but could not be accommodated due to the limited space. No doubt, there are plenty more positive stories to tell about Africa still.

The Taylor & Francis team, who guided the effort from the start to its completion – Emma Travis, Lydia Kessell, and Carlotta Fanton, in particular, thank you. I would also like to thank the reviewers who provided feedback on the project. Their feedback was invaluable and their enthusiasm for the project to be commissioned spurred me on.

I am indebted to my colleagues at the University of Queensland, who have provided a collegial and nurturing environmental for my academic pursuits. Kevin Markwell (Southern Cross University) and Lisa Ruhanen (University of Queensland) have been generous mentors.

Finally, I thank my family and friends for their love, support and encouragement. My late grandmother, Blessing Mashego, my late mother, Salome Mpho Moyo, my father, Douglas Moyo, my sisters, Tsitsi, Ruzie and Bongi, and my late brother Tafara, you have all been my biggest cheerleaders through the years. My Aussie friends, Mye, Aimee and Jules, thank you for being there always on this journey.

1 Positive tourism in Africa

Resisting Afro-pessimism

Mucha Mkono

Introduction

Tourism in Africa is an ever-evolving tale of communities and economies striving to deliver memorable tourist experiences while optimising the gains, in the face of many challenges. Nonetheless, the 21st century signals a new *Africa rising* turn, which recognises progress on the continent, on various levels (Bunce, Franks, and Paterson, 2016; Hofmeyr, 2013; Johnson, 2016; Pillay, 2015; Taylor, 2014). While many challenges remain, more positive stories need to be told, as a way of creating a timely, new discourse – an 'Afro-positive' discourse, in tourism studies (and indeed in other fields of study). As Taylor (2014) argues, a change from the old, reductionist narratives of Africa is necessary, although it is important to caution that the new narrative should not just veer in the opposite direction without the necessary critical reflection.

This book presents critical studies that advance a more optimistic outlook for Africa, in various formats, including broad and localised case studies, conceptual frameworks and culturally centred interpretations of tourism phenomena. In doing so, it adds to the growing body of work on 'positive tourism' (Filep et al., 2016) – a way of understanding tourism in relation to the value it creates for tourists, hosts communities, economies and other elements of the tourism system. Such an approach is not intended to portray tourism as some sort of utopia, but rather to showcase the many facets of tourism in Africa that illustrate hope, resilience, growth and survival.

In its many forms – community-based tourism, wildlife tourism, nature tourism, adventure/adrenaline tourism, pro-poor tourism, cultural tourism, among others – tourism in Africa at this point in time presents an ideal setting in which to explore 'positive tourism'. In the next section, I define and contextualise the notion of 'positive tourism'.

Defining and contextualising 'positive tourism'

The idea of 'positive tourism' is broached by Filep et al. (2016, p. 10) who define it as follows:

> positive tourism is, broadly, a study of hedonic and eudaimonic human well-being and conditions (or various circumstances) for flourishing as they relate

to individual tourists, members of host communities and tourism workers in diverse sectors of the tourism industry.

Thus positive tourism draws on a range of disciplines and approaches to unpack the experience of tourism. Of course, the perspective of tourism as enriching to individuals and communities is not new. But it is fair to state, as Filep et al. point out, that dystopian views of tourism dominate academic research. A more balanced and nuanced view of tourism is necessary.

More than that, as already pointed out, in this book, positive tourism acquires added significance and meaning in terms of the deliberate endeavour to advance a positive representation of Africa itself, that is, the *Afro-positive* thrust which also entails resisting and undermining *Afro-pessimism* (I turn to this later). Nonetheless, in Filep et al.'s (2016, p. 4) conception, positive tourism is underpinned by humanistic philosophy, a framework which deals with the existential 'questions of the good life, individual growth and achievements, authenticity, personal responsibility', aspects of Being which have been investigated by numerous illustrious philosophers such as Maslow and Heidegger. Filep et al. make use of the tenets of humanistic and positive psychology to locate the positive in tourism. In this book, however, the interest is less on the psychological dimensions of touristic experience and more on the African cultural contexts of positive tourism.

Crucially, investigating positive tourism in Africa requires a multi-perspective approach that voices the wide spectrum of participants in the tourism system. It is worth re-emphasising that positive tourism is not about ignoring the many challenges and ills that tourism often brings into places and spaces. Rather, it is about understanding the conditions under which the tourism system and its participants can and have flourished, as Filep et al. (2016) put it. It is about recognising the potential for tourism to add value (and not just in monetary or economic terms) to individual lives, communities and economies. In this book, it is *particularly* about recognising the progress African countries have made in their tourism systems, *in spite of* the odds. I turn now to the state of knowledge on tourism in Africa, to solidify the rationale for this book.

Tourism in Africa: the state of knowledge

Tourism studies as a field of research has created an impressive body of knowledge on Africa. The themes are innumerable: wildlife/safari tourism (Baker, 1997; Mbaiwa, 2017), slum tourism (Chege and Mwisukha, 2013; Kieti and Magio, 2013; Rogerson, 2014), volunteer tourism (Alexander, 2012; Benson and Seibert, 2009; Stoddart and Rogerson, 2004), sustainable/ethical tourism (Akama and Kieti, 2007; Baker, 1997; Mbaiwa, 2005, 2011; Novelli, Barnes, and Humavindu, 2006; Saarinen, Becker, Manwa, and Wilson, 2009; Snyman, 2012; Spenceley, 2008b), pro-poor tourism (Akyeampong, 2011; Hill, Nel, and Trotter, 2006; Rogerson, 2006), community-based tourism (Manyara and Jones, 2007; Sebele, 2010; Spenceley, 2008a), among many others. It is, however, not necessary or possible to regurgitate all of the existing research here. The diversity of the continent and its tourism scenarios precludes that possibility. This disclaimer notwithstanding, a perusal of the top tourism journals, including *Annals of Tourism Research, Journal of Travel Research, Tourism Management, Current Issues in Tourism* and *Tourism Analysis*, reveals three key patterns which capture the state of tourism knowledge on Africa.

First, a sizeable proportion of (published) tourism research on Africa has been, and continues to be, conducted by outsiders, who are typically Western, or are living and/or studying in the West. As such, a Western-centric approach is implicitly and explicitly projected on the various 'findings' that emerge. While such knowledge must not be undermined simply because it is 'etic', it is important to recognise the limitations and biases that attend these outsider-gaze-based explorations. For example, the tourist who has been studied is largely Caucasian and wealthy. Increasingly, though, more studies of Asian tourists are being conducted. African tourists, on the other hand, are largely a non-existent category in research. What does this tell us about the nature of theorising in tourism?

Second, locals' opinions are often not meaningfully represented in tourism studies. Here I will use the example of the recent trophy hunting controversy that erupted after the shooting of Cecil the lion in 2015 (Mkono, 2018). When the lion was shot, the public discourse in the news and in social media was dominated by the West's outrage. Similarly, the studies which have been published in connection with the incident and the broader conservation debate have almost exclusively originated from the West (for example, Macdonald, Jacobsen, Burnham, Johnson, and Loveridge, 2016; Nelson, Bruskotter, Vucetich, and Chapron, 2016).

Third, there is typically an underlying but unmistakable *Afro-pessimistic* tone that runs through the studies. The resulting literature does not engender much hope or optimism, as Africa is invariably compared to the developed world and is – surprise, surprise! – found to be lagging behind in technology, climate change adaptation, meeting the challenges of poaching, alleviating poverty – the list goes on and on. In short, if tourism studies are to reflect a more balanced representation of the African continent, then the lens for viewing African countries needs to be adjusted and diversified. Africans themselves must have more page space in scholarly works. Afro-pessimism must be replaced by Afro-optimism, where and when appropriate. It is not good enough to make claims about plural voices when epistemic singularity persists. It is also problematic if the story of Africa, whether it is a tourism focused one or otherwise, is told of the same themes over and over again. It is therefore this book's quest to provide page space to African and Africa-interested scholars of various backgrounds, who have close communion with the African continent and its tourism stories. By striking a more hopeful note, these scholars play a part in resisting Afro-pessimism, a theme which I will now unpack briefly.

Resisting Afro-pessimism

The view that Africa is unfairly represented in Western scholarly works (and in the media) is long-standing (Nothias, 2016). Postcolonial Africa continues to be defined by colonial discourses through metaphors of darkness, innocence, emptiness, crisis, a basket case and notions of being in need of imperial saving (Grant, Djomo, and Krause, 2016). This Afro-pessimistic portrayal, with its influence on destination image, bears on Africa's desirability as a tourist destination, among other tourism implications. Yet the subject of Afro-pessimism has not yet been broached within tourism scholarship. It is therefore pertinent to investigate the ways in which tourism research and theorising could be implicated in the oversimplified representation of Africa.

In response to the hegemonic discourses of 'Afrique Noire', or Black Africa, Afro-positive/Afro-optimist scholars across disciplines are advocating more complex images of Africa (Grant et al., 2016). As Grant et al. (2016, p. 324) put it, Afro-optimism 'involves a break from the simplistic and neo-colonial nature of Afro-pessimism and introduces multiple, complex images of Africa'. Grant et al. provide the example, for instance, of scholars who seek to undermine the Afro-pessimist image of Africa by presenting photographs and quotations depicting 'everyday images' entitled 'Humans of Ghana', a project which showcases beauty, resilience and hope, which a group of researchers encountered during a recent field visit to Ghana.

Afro-pessimism is thus best countered with Afrocentrism, which, Momoh (2003) also cautions, should not be viewed as the flip side of Eurocentricity. Rather, Momoh asserts, it should be understood as a recognition of a humanist approach to building knowledge about Africa; one that investigates Africa from a sensitive, measured, sober and political point of view. It pays attention to social location, context, as well as material and cultural differences that influence social production. Such an Afrocentric approach is conspicuously lacking in tourism scholarship.

Structure of the book

The book is divided into four parts which together provide an extensive assessment of Africa's status quo and trajectory in tourism. Part I, 'Tourism and community livelihoods', focuses on the interactions between tourism and participant communities, with particular focus on the impacts on tourism active communities. In Chapter 2, Joseph E. Mbaiwa, Tsholofelo Mbaiwa and Gladys Siphambe evaluate community-based natural resource management programmes in the case of Botswana. Next, Regis Musavengane explores the role of land reform in promoting sustainable livelihoods through collaborative community-based ecotourism. This is followed by Moren T. Stone and Lesego T. Stone's chapter. They apply a systems thinking approach to examining the linkages between protected areas, tourism and community livelihoods. Part I concludes with Takaruza Munyanyiwa, Shepherd Nyaruwata, and Cleopas Njerekai's chapter on how community-based tourism ventures can survive in turbulent environments, based on a Zimbabwean CAMPFIRE project case study.

The second part of the book, 'Positive Afro-identities and indigenous cultural resources', weaves together issues of African identity, tourism development and indigenous resources, in the context of a postcolonial Africa. Postcoloniality is explicitly interrogated in Chapter 6, where I examine the role of digital counter-narratives in undermining Afro-pessimism, a bias that is indeed challenged by the overall positioning of this book. In the next chapter, Jim Ayorekire, Joseph Obua and Michael Bruce Byaruhanga's contribution considers the potential for innovative cultural tourism products for Uganda. In Chapter 8, Chloe Rooks, Garry Marvin, Caroline Ross and Jonathan Skinner delve into the personal dimensions of experience in their study of wildlife tourism as educational transformation. Joseph E. Mbaiwa, Gladys Siphambe and Tsholofelo Mbaiwa continue on the cultural theme in Chapter 9, exploring the strategies used by a community-based tourism project in Botswana to build cultural resilience, thus resisting the commodifying influences of tourism development. The final chapter of Part II, written by Tom Kwanya, engages with African indigeneity, in his analysis of opportunities for diversifying Kenya's tourism industry through packaging indigenous knowledge.

Part III of the book, 'Governance, integration and synergies', commences with Binaswaree Bolaky's discussion of regional integration as a lever for tourism development. Zibanai Zhou's chapter then assesses tourism development milestones in the SADC region in the postcolonial era. In Chapter 13, Ogechi Adeola, Olaniyi Evans and Robert Hinson evaluate the interaction between tourism and economic wellbeing in Africa. This broader perspective is complemented by Boopen Seetanah and Sheereen Fauzel's examination of the nexus between tourism development and human development, using evidence from Mauritius. Bernard Kitheka and Agnes Sirima then explore, in Chapter 15, tourism governance and organisational infrastructure across East Africa. The last contribution in Part III is Roopanand Mahadew and Krishnee Appadoo's evaluation of the contribution of the law to tourism development in Mauritius.

The final part of the book, Part IV, begins with David Adeloye and Neil Carr's chapter, a dual case study of Tunisia and Egypt, where they discuss the globally topical issue of terrorism and tourism recovery. In Chapter 18, I delve into the equally topical and very controversial subject of trophy hunting. The chapter examines how trophy hunters rationalise their pastime in social media, in response to the criticism directed at them, particularly in the aftermath of 'Cecilgate' (Mkono, 2018). The penultimate chapter by Sanette Ferreira follows, critically evaluating the challenges of managing a mature destination, using the case of South Africa's world-renowned Kruger National Park. The concluding chapter contemplates the future of tourism in Africa and identifies the key issues on which that future is predicated, before ending with recommendations for future research directions.

References

Akama, J. S., and Kieti, D. (2007). Tourism and socio-economic development in developing countries: A case study of Mombasa Resort in Kenya. *Journal of Sustainable Tourism*, *15*(6), 735–748.and

Akyeampong, O. A. (2011). Pro-poor tourism: Residents' expectations, experiences and perceptions in the Kakum National Park Area of Ghana. *Journal of Sustainable Tourism*, *19*(2), 197–213.

Alexander, Z. (2012). International volunteer tourism experience in South Africa: An investigation into the impact on the tourist. *Journal of Hospitality Marketing and Management, 21*(7), 779–799.and

Baker, J. E. (1997). Trophy hunting as a sustainable use of wildlife resources in southern and eastern Africa. *Journal of Sustainable Tourism, 5*(4), 306–321.

Benson, A., and Seibert, N. (2009). Volunteer tourism: Motivations of German participants in South Africa. *Annals of Leisure Research, 12*(3–4), 295–314.

Bunce, M., Franks, S., and Paterson, C. (2016). *Africa's media image in the 21st century: From the 'heart of darkness' to 'Africa Rising'*. New York: Routledge.

Chege, P. W., and Mwisukha, A. (2013). Benefits of slum tourism in Kibera slum in Nairobi, Kenya. *International Journal of Arts and Commerce, 2*(4), 94–102.and

Filep, S., Laing, J., and Csikszentmihalyi, M. (2016) (eds). *Positive tourism*. New York: Taylor and Francis.

Grant, J. A., Djomo, A. N., and Krause, M. G. (2016). Afro-optimism reinvigorated? Reflections on the glocal networks of sexual identity, health, and natural resources in Africa. *Global Change, Peace and Security, 28*(3), 317–328.and*and*

Hill, T., Nel, E., and Trotter, D. (2006). Small-scale, nature-based tourism as a pro-poor development intervention: Two examples in Kwazulu-Natal, South Africa. *Singapore Journal of Tropical Geography, 27*, 163–175. Wiley-Blackwell.and

Hofmeyr, J. (2013). Africa rising? Popular dissatisfaction with economic management despite a decade of growth. *Afrobarometer Policy Brief, 2*.

Johnson, S. (2016). Slowdown calls 'Africa rising'narrative into question. *The Financial Times. Retrieved, 2*.

Kieti, D. M., and Magio, K. O. (2013). The ethical and local resident perspectives of slum tourism in Kenya. *Advances in Hospitality and Tourism Research (AHTR), 1*(1), 37–57. and

Macdonald, D. W., Jacobsen, K. S., Burnham, D., Johnson, P. J., and Loveridge, A. J. (2016). Cecil: A moment or a movement? Analysis of media coverage of the death of a lion, panthera leo. *Animals, 6*(5), 26.and

Manyara, G., and Jones, E. (2007). Community-based tourism enterprises development in Kenya: An exploration of their potential as avenues of poverty reduction. *Journal of Sustainable Tourism, 15*(6), 628–644.

Mbaiwa, J. E. (2005). The problems and prospects of sustainable tourism development in the Okavango Delta, Botswana. *Journal of Sustainable Tourism, 13*(3), 203–227.

Mbaiwa, J. E. (2011). Changes on traditional livelihood activities and lifestyles caused by tourism development in the Okavango Delta, Botswana. *Tourism Management, 32*(5), 1050–1060. doi:10.1016/j.tourman.2010.09.002

Mbaiwa, J. E. (2017). Effects of the safari hunting tourism ban on rural livelihoods and wildlife conservation in Northern Botswana. *South African Geographical Journal*, 1–21.

Mkono, M. (2018). The age of digital activism in tourism: Evaluating the legacy and limitations of the Cecil anti-trophy hunting movement. *Journal of Sustainable Tourism*, 1–17.

Momoh, A. (2003). Does pan-Africanism have a future in Africa? In search of the ideational basis of Afro-pessimism. *African Journal of Political Science, 8*(1), 31–57.

Nelson, M. P., Bruskotter, J. T., Vucetich, J. A., and Chapron, G. (2016). Emotions and the ethics of consequence in conservation decisions: Lessons from Cecil the Lion. *Conservation Letters, 9*(4), 302–306.and

Nothias, T. (2016). How western journalists actually write about Africa: Re-assessing the myth of representations of Africa. *Journalism Studies*, 1–22.

Novelli, M., Barnes, J. I., and Humavindu, M. (2006). The other side of the ecotourism coin: Consumptive tourism in Southern Africa. *Journal of Ecotourism, 5*(1/2), 62–79.and

Pillay, D. (2015). The global economic crisis and the Africa rising narrative. *Africa Development, 40*(3), 59–75.

Rogerson, C. M. (2006). Pro-poor local economic development in South Africa: The role of pro-poor tourism. *Local Environment, 11*(1), 37–60.

Rogerson, C. M. (2014). Rethinking slum tourism: Tourism in South Africa's rural slumlands. Bulletin of Geography. *Socio-economic Series, 26*(26), 19–34.

Saarinen, J., Becker, F. O., Manwa, H., and Wilson, D. (2009). *Sustainable tourism in southern Africa: Local communities and natural resources in transition.* Bristol: Channel View Publications.

Sebele, L. S. (2010). Community-based tourism ventures, benefits and challenges: Khama rhino sanctuary trust, central district, Botswana. *Tourism Management, 31*(1), 136–146.

Snyman, S. L. (2012). The role of tourism employment in poverty reduction and community perceptions of conservation and tourism in southern Africa. *Journal of Sustainable Tourism, 20*(3), 395–416.

Spenceley, A. (2008a). Local impacts of community-based tourism in Southern Africa. *Responsible Tourism: Critical Issues for Conservation and Development,* 159–187.

Spenceley, A. (2008b). Requirements for sustainable nature-based tourism in transfrontier conservation areas: A Southern African delphi consultation. *Tourism Geographies, 10*(3), 285–311.

Stoddart, H., and Rogerson, C. M. (2004). Volunteer tourism: The case of habitat for humanity South Africa. *GeoJournal, 60*(3), 311–318.

Taylor, I. (2014). Is Africa rising. *Brown Journal of World Affairs, 21,* 143.

Part I
Tourism and community livelihoods

2 The community-based natural resource management programme in southern Africa – promise or peril?

The case of Botswana

Joseph E. Mbaiwa, Tsholofelo Mbaiwa and Gladys Siphambe

Introduction

The Community-Based Natural Resource Management (CBNRM) programme in eastern and southern Africa is viewed as a panacea for the livelihoods and biodiversity challenges affecting the sub-continent (Mbaiwa, 2004). The CBNRM is a participatory and community-based approach to natural resource management initiatives (Twyman, 2000). These participatory approaches began in the late 1980s. Scholars of CBNRM (e.g. Leach, Mearns, and Scoones, 1999; Tsing, Brosius, and Zerner, 1999; Twyman, 2000) argue that CBNRM aims at achieving conservation and rural economic development through local community participation in natural resource management. The CBNRM paradigm is built upon common property theory, which argues that common-pool resources can be sustainably utilised provided certain principles are applied. According to Ostrom (1990) and Bromley (1992), these principles include the autonomy and the recognition of the community as an institution, proprietorship and tenurial rights, rights to make the rules and viable mechanisms to enforce them, and ongoing incentives in the form of benefits that exceed costs.

The adoption of CBNRM in southern and eastern Africa, particularly in countries like Botswana, is based on these principles of common property theory (Mbaiwa, 2004; Thakadu, 2005). Central to the CBNRM paradigm are the theory and assumptions underlying the political decentralisation of natural resources (Boggs, 2000). Decentralisation of natural resource management implies a process of redistribution of power and the transfer of responsibilities from the central government to rural communities in resource management (Boggs, 2000; Thakadu, 2005). This is a shift from the so-called top-down to a bottom-up approach in natural resource management. The CBNRM paradigm thus reforms the conventional 'protectionist conservation philosophy' and 'top-down' approaches to development (Mbaiwa, 2004). The decentralisation of resources to local communities is assumed to have the potential to promote conservation and rural development (Blackie, 2006; Mbaiwa, 2005b; Taylor, 2000; Thakadu, 2005). Conservationists and scholars perceive the decentralisation of natural resources as a remedy for the chronic wildlife decline resulting from the central government's failure in resource management (Boggs, 2000). Local institutions, where local people have a role to play in resource management and derive benefits from such resources around them, are essential for CBNRM to achieve its goals. As such, CBNRM is based on the premise that local populations have a greater interest in the sustainable use of natural resources around them than do centralised or distant government or private management institutions (Taylor, 2000; Tsing et al., 1999; Twyman, 2000). CBNRM credits local institutions and people with having a greater understanding of, as well as a vested interest in, their local environment (Leach et al., 1999; Tsing et al., 1999; Twyman, 2000). The underlying assumption of CBNRM is that once rural communities participate in natural resource utilisation and derive economic benefits, this will cultivate the spirit of ownership and the development of positive attitudes towards resource use and ultimately lead communities to the use of natural resources found around them sustainably (Leach et al., 1999; Tsing et al., 1999; Twyman, 2000).

Botswana adopted CBNRM in the late 1980s. During this period, the management of natural resources, particularly wildlife, by the central government was in serious and chronic decline (Moganane and Walker, 1995; Mordi, 1991; Perkins, 1996). The centralisation of natural resources by the national government in Botswana alienated local communities from resource management. Gibson and Marks (1995) argue that traditional approaches to nature protection were viewed by governments and conservationists as insufficient and ineffective at protecting biodiversity in Africa. Local communities were excluded from resource management in favour of centralisation and privatisation of resources. Centralisation of natural resources in Botswana began during British colonial rule and continued under postcolonial governments (Mbaiwa, 1999). CBNRM in Botswana is designed to reverse problems caused by the centralisation of natural resources, which include wildlife resource decline.

Studies by Bolaane (2004), Kgathi, Ngwenya, and Wilk (2007), Magole and Gojamang (2005), Mbaiwa (2003, 2004), Swatuk (2005), Taylor (2000), Thakadu (2005) and Twyman (2000) criticise CBNRM for several issues. Blackie (2006) and Swatuk (2005) argue that CBNRM has not achieved its objectives of conservation and rural development, instead it is used as a tool used by donor conservation agencies and governments from developed countries to perpetuate the global domination of developing countries; Taylor (2000) writes of the marginalisation of minority groups like the Basarwa of Gudigwa from benefiting from CBNRM. Twyman (2000) argues that CBNRM in the Kalahari region is not fully developed to yield significant benefits to residents. Mbaiwa (2005a) also argues that tourism in Botswana is largely enclave in nature and is dominated by foreign companies, with the result that the majority of local people derive insignificant benefits from tourism in the Okavango Delta. Mbaiwa (2005a) further argues that local community attempts to benefit from tourism development either through CBNRM or by citizen companies are characterised by a host of problems (e.g. lack of capital, entrepreneurship and marketing skills), which make such attempts achieve lower benefits when compared with those of their foreign company competitors. Despite these criticisms, CBNRM is introducing local participation and benefits from tourism development, particularly in rich wildlife habitats like the Okavango Delta (Arntzen et al., 2003; Kgathi et al., 2007; Mbaiwa, 2004; Thakadu, 2005). While this is the case, existing research on CBNRM (for example, Arntzen et al., 2003; Magole and Gojamang, 2005; Mbaiwa, 2005b; Thakadu, 2005) has not adequately shown the extent to which individual CBNRM projects in the Okavango Delta have improved rural livelihoods or alleviated poverty. This limitation in the literature occurs at a time when related studies, for example by Fidzani, Mlenga, Atlhopheng, and Shatera (1999) and North West District Council (2003), argue that most people in the Okavango Delta live in poverty.

The literature highlights many of the challenges facing CBNRM implementation. However, Wilshusen, Brechin, and West (2002) argue that critics of CBNRM largely make their arguments in isolation of the political, social and economic context of a particular project. It is important to assess projects on an individual and contextualised basis. This chapter, therefore, analyses the impacts of CBNRM on livelihoods and biodiversity conservation using the villages of Khwai, Sankoyo and Mababe in the Okavango Delta, Botswana.

The sustainable livelihood framework

Improved livelihoods in rural settings such as the Okavango Delta can be measured using the sustainable livelihoods framework (SLF). Some studies (for example, Kgathi et al., 2007; Mbaiwa and Sakuze, 2009; Taylor, 2000) in the Okavango Delta have used the livelihoods framework. Taylor (2000) argues that the San or Basarwa of Gudigwa and Khwai have their access to livelihoods opportunities restricted by centralisation of natural resources, particularly through the establishment of the Moremi Game Reserve. Mbaiwa and Sakuze (2009) used the framework to analyse how the Basarwa of XaiXai can use their culture to derive economic benefits from tourism development. Mbaiwa (2004) analysed how basket production contributes to household livelihoods; Kgathi et al. (2007) describe different livelihoods options found in the Okavango Delta as well as related challenges, shocks and adaptation made by rural communities. Kgathi et al. (2007) argue that natural-resource-based activities in the Okavango Delta can be arable farming, livestock farming, collection of rangeland products, basket-making, fishing and community-based tourism. Mbaiwa et al. (2007) studied lack of access to natural resources by rural communities and how this affects their livelihoods. These studies have, however, not adequately examined how wildlife-based tourism through CBNRM can improve rural livelihoods.

The SLF recently became central to the discourse on poverty alleviation, rural development and environmental management (Ellis, 2000; Scoones, 1998). According to Chambers and Conway (1992, p. 7), 'a livelihood comprises the capabilities (stores, resources, claims and access) and activities required for a means of living'. Ellis (2000, p. 19) also points out that 'a livelihood comprises the assets (natural, physical, human, financial and social capital), the activities, and the access to these (mediated by institutions and social relations) that together determine the living gained by the individual or household'. Chambers and Conway (1992, p. 5) also note that 'a livelihood in its simplest sense is a means of gaining a living'.

The SLF is a suitable tool for analysis of livelihoods in this study because it links the broader socioeconomic components of household assets, livelihood activities, outcomes of livelihood activities and factors mediating access to livelihood activities (Ellis, 2000; Scoones, 1998). Activities are strategies or various ways in which households generate their livelihoods (Ellis, 2000; Kgathi et al., 2007). The SLF therefore seeks an accurate understanding of people's assets and capital endowments and the processes and conversion of these into desirable livelihood outcomes (Mubangizi, 2003). The SLF shows how in different contexts and through different strategies people support themselves through access to a range of resources or assets such as natural, economic, human and social capitals (Chambers and Conway, 1992; D'Hease and Kirsten, 2003; Scoones, 1998). This study uses the framework to demonstrate how three communities collectively use natural resources, their knowledge and their skills through tourism development to achieve commonly shared goals of improved livelihoods in their respective villages.

Assets and resources are inputs to a livelihood system and are the immediate means needed for generating livelihood (Niehof, 2004). Scoones (1998) argues that assets and resources may be seen as the capital base from which different productive streams are derived and from which livelihoods are constructed. Development practitioners use SLFs to identify entry points for understanding root causes of poverty and potential interventions for improving people's lives (Scoones, 1998). The SLF thus brings together the notions of wellbeing, security and capability, through in-depth analysis of existing poverty and/or wealth vulnerability and resilience, as well as natural resource sustainability (Bhandari and Grant, 2007). Bhandari and Grant (2007) note that the concept of livelihood security emerged in response to the question of whether people's lives become better or worse at family and community levels. Livelihood security is the adequate and sustainable access to income and other resources to enable households to meet basic needs (Frankenberger, Luther, and Becht, 2002). Frankenberger et al. (2002) point out that basic needs include adequate access to food, potable water, health facilities, educational opportunities, housing, time for community participation and social integration. In this chapter, the extent to which tourism development at the study communities use natural resources such as wildlife, forest resources, grass species and birds to improve rural livelihoods is analysed using the SLF.

Description of study area

This study was carried out in the Okavango Delta located in north-western Botswana (Figure 2.1). The Okavango Delta is formed by the inflow of the Okavango River, whose two main tributaries (the Cuito and Cubango Rivers) originate in the Angolan Highlands. The Okavango River flows across Namibia's Caprivi Strip and finally drains into north-western Botswana to form a wetland known as the Okavango Delta.

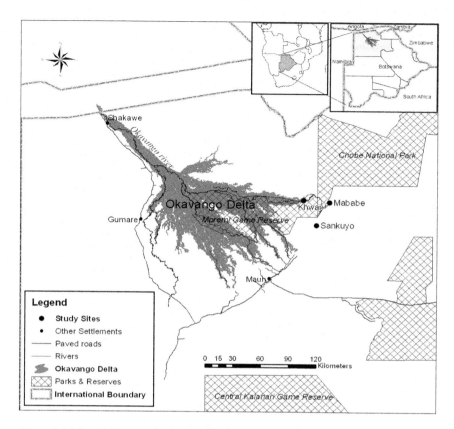

Figure 2.1 Map of Okavango Delta showing Khwai, Mababe and Sankoyo

The Okavango Delta is characterised by a conical and triangular shaped alluvial fan and covers an area of about 16,000 square kilometres (Tlou, 1985). Like the Nile in Egypt, the Okavango River and its Delta sustain life in an otherwise inhospitable environment. An oasis in what would otherwise be semi-desert, the Okavango Delta is characterised by large amounts of open water and grasslands, which sustain human life, and a variety of flora and fauna. For instance, there are 2000 to 3000 plant species, over 162 arachnid species, more than 20 species of large herbivores, over 450 bird species (Monna, 1999) and more than 80 fish species (Kolding, 1996). The Okavango Delta is a major source of livelihoods for the rural communities who have lived in the area for hundreds of years. Due to its rich wildlife diversity, wilderness nature, permanent water resources, rich grasslands and forests, the Delta has become one of the key international tourism destinations in Botswana. The Okavango Delta is, therefore, a suitable site to investigate whether tourism can be used as a tool to achieve conservation and improved livelihoods.

The villages of Sankoyo, Khwai and Mababe were selected as study sites (see Figure 2.1). The village of Sankoyo is located on the north-eastern fringes of the Okavango Delta. It has a population of 372 people (CSO, 2002). In 1996, Sankoyo established the Sankoyo Tshwaragano Management Trust (STMT) to coordinate community-based tourism activities. The government of Botswana allocated land to the people of Sankoyo to be used for photographic and hunting purposes. Khwai village is located on the south-eastern fringes of the Okavango Delta and the Moremi Game Reserve. The Moremi Game Reserve borders the village in the south and Chobe National Park in the north. Most of the people of Khwai are Basarwa or the so-called Bushmen, with a population of 360 people. Mababe with a population of 290 people is also located on the south-eastern fringes of the Okavango Delta between Moremi Game Reserve and Chobe National Park. The people of Mababe are Basarwa who have lived a nomadic life of hunting and gathering until the last two or three decades.

The villages of Khwai, Mababe and Sankoyo were purposively selected because the CBNRM programme has been operational in these villages for over two decades. As such, these villages epitomise some of the best solutions to challenges of livelihoods, tourism development, resource use and conservation in CBNRM areas. For decades, these villages have been the centre of resource conflicts between local communities and tourism companies in the area and conflict between the Department of Wildlife and National Parks and the national government over resource use (Mbaiwa, 2005b).

Data collection methods and analysis

This study made use of longitudinal data on livelihoods available at Khwai, Sankoyo and Mababe since 1998. The availability of this data made it easy to analyse livelihood changes caused by tourism development in the last 10 years. Data were collected between June and December 2007 through ethnographic observation and household interviews. A total of 30 households were randomly sampled in each of the villages. This represents 48.4% of all households in the three villages (Table 2.1).

A household list in each of the villages kept at the Community Trust office was used to randomly pick the first 30 households for interviews. Names were cut out and put in a box, and the first 30 households from repeated draws were eligible for interviews. Male heads of household were interviewed. If absent, the spouse

Table 2.1 Sampled household

Village	Household Sample	Total Households	Total Village Population
Sankoyo	30	76	372
Khwai	30	56	360
Mababe	30	57	290
Totals	90	186	1022

was selected. If neither was available, any household member 18 years or older, considered an adult in Botswana, was interviewed.

In determining livelihood changes, households were asked to provide a list of all the livelihood activities that household members did to earn a living before tourism development in the Okavango Delta. Indicators used to achieve this objective included but were not limited to the following: hunting and gathering, crop and livestock farming, fishing, and rangeland products collection. Households were also asked to make a list of all the tourism-influenced livelihood activities they adopted after tourism development in the area. Indicators that were used to measure the effects of tourism development on livelihoods included but were not limited to household and community income from tourism, employment opportunities for households in tourism enterprises, livelihood diversity within a community, tourism infrastructure development, the provision of social services to community members and reinvestment of tourism revenues.

Household data were supplemented by unstructured interviews with key informants, including biologists, community leaders such as the village chief, Village Development Committee (VDC) chairpersons, board of trustees chairpersons and decision makers in government. In-depth interviews with key informants were essential for gaining long-term knowledge on livelihood changes in each of the villages and how tourism development has made a difference. Interviews progressed in a conversational style.

Focus group discussions were also conducted with the VDC and board of trustees in each village to further understand the livelihood changes. Focus groups were generally composed of three to five people depending on availability at the time of data collection. Discussions in focus groups were unstructured in nature. The open-ended questions focused on livelihoods that communities were engaged in before tourism development, present livelihood options and how they are affected by tourism development. Interview data from households, key informants and group discussions were summarised into specific themes and patterns based on the effects of tourism on livelihoods in their households and community. Themes and patterns were also gleaned on livelihoods before and after tourism development in the study villages.

Results and discussion

CBNRM and rural livelihoods

The results show that the CBNRM programme at Khwai, Mababe and Sankoyo has had both positive and negative effects on rural livelihoods. These communities have joint venture partnerships largely with foreign tourism companies. Joint venture partnerships are assumed by communities to be critical in that they enable them to acquire entrepreneurship and marketing skills in the tourism business. However, results also indicate that much of the management and skilled positions such as accounting, marketing, management and professional guiding were occupied by foreigners or people from outside the three communities. The locals provide unskilled labour. These include cleaning in tourism facilities, security, scullery such as washing dishes in kitchens, laundry, animal tracking and other forms of manual labour. In addition, these jobs are seasonal, particularly in safari hunting.

Foreign ownership and control of the tourism industry in the Okavango Delta suggest revenue leakages from the local economy to developed countries where the relevant companies originate. The reliance of communities on foreign companies particularly through joint venture partnerships can be addressed if skill development in key positions such as marketing, management, accounting and professional guiding are given priority by the three communities. At present, most of the community tourism workers have either no education or lower secondary education.

Analysis of the positive effects of tourism development to livelihoods using the sustainable livelihoods framework indicates that CBNRM has considerably improved livelihoods at all three villages. CBNRM has generated socioeconomic benefits such as the creation of employment opportunities, income generation, provision of social services including water reticulation, availability of game meat, scholarships for hospitality courses, and acquisition of skills in the tourism business, the establishment of facilities such as recreation halls, and sponsorship of local sporting activities in the communities.

Before the introduction of the CBNRM project, local employment opportunities did not exist. Villagers had previously migrated to camps in the Okavango Delta, Maun and other parts of Botswana for that reason. CBNRM has become the main employment sector and income-generating mechanism. Given the small population size of these communities, these changes are significant.

Relying on a single livelihood option is, however, problematic, because tourism in the Okavango Delta is seasonal. As a result, during the months when tourism is either low or temporarily closed, some community members are forced to migrate to urban areas. Rural-urban migration increases pressure on resources in urban centres and often results in unemployment and crime. However, this migratory pattern is reversed during the tourism peak season when employment opportunities become available in CBNRM enterprises. The migration trend indicates, though, that tourism development is failing to form meaningful linkages with the domestic economy and to produce multiplier effects in the form of small-scale enterprises that would otherwise absorb unemployed community members during the tourism low season.

Nonetheless, overall, it is safe to state that even though CBNRM has its problems, it has contributed to improved livelihoods at Khwai, Sankoyo and Mababe. These findings contradict generalistic claims by some scholars such as Brandon (1998), Diamond (2003) and Krech (2007) that community conservation and development projects are failing to achieve rural development.

CBNRM and biodiversity conservation

Results indicate that the CBNRM programme at Khwai, Mababe and Sankoyo has re-introduced trust at a community level in resource use and conservation. As a result, the high level of social capital has led to conservation ethics and practices of resource use almost similar to those used before conventional approaches were introduced in the area. These include observing hunting seasons and harvesting thatching grass only in winter when it is dry. Communities have also returned to selective hunting and using hunting quotas, which contribute to the conservation of these species. Communities shunned the Special Game Licence, which they believed resulted in the over-harvesting of wildlife resources. Community policing of resources through Community Escort Guides was also found to demonstrate commitment by the three villages to conservation.

The commitment of the community to conservation is also shown by the community monitoring of resources through a programme known as the Management Oriented Monitoring System (MOMS). These initiatives not only suggest a restoration of some of the old conservation practices but also indicate the enhanced social capital and community commitment to conservation in their Controlled Hunting Areas (CHAs). In this regard, tourism development has resulted in the community's ability to recognise the value of resources in their area. As a result, illegal hunting in CBNRM areas has decreased. The trust and cooperation on resource use that exists between individual communities in their respective CHAs has been instrumental in achieving conservation goals. Such cooperation also exists with government bodies such as the Department of Wildlife and National Parks and Agricultural Resource Board, which are respectively charged with the responsibility of wildlife and rangeland resources management in Botswana.

Results indicate further that the number of tourists visiting the Okavango Delta has been increasing in the last 10 to 15 years. The increase was reported to be causing environmental problems such as the creation of illegal roads that destroy the aesthetic beauty of the wetland, poor waste management (both liquid and solid) and noise pollution created by tourists and vehicles. Safari hunting tourists in community areas were also reported to be involved in illegal hunting. Community Escort Guides (CEGs) at Khwai blamed the self-drive tourists mainly from South Africa for creating illegal roads and camping illegally in their CHA. They were also unhappy with the government's policy to allow the free movement of self-drive tourists between Chobe National Park and Moremi Game Reserve. The three communities' CHAs form a link between the two protected areas of Chobe National Park and Moremi Game Reserve. CEGs conduct routine patrols, anti-illegal hunting patrols and wildlife resource monitoring patrols in their CHAs. However, the CEGs have been successful in addressing some of the problems, such as the killing of elephants and leopards, in liaison with the Department of Wildlife and National Parks.

Conclusion

The results show that tourism development by local communities through the CBNRM programme can be used as a tool to achieve conservation in the Okavango Delta and in other rich biodiversity areas in developing countries. While the communities of Khwai, Mababe and Sankoyo have met with some challenges,

CBNRM has enhanced trust, an indicator of social capital, between all stakeholders at community level, as well as community trust of the government and the private sector in the joint venture partnerships. Furthermore, CBNRM has brought a wide range of benefits to the community and enhanced livelihoods.

Decentralisation of resources to local people, collective action in resource use and benefits that communities derive from wildlife-based tourism determine the success of the CBNRM programme. If people view wildlife resources as 'theirs' because they realise the benefits of 'owning' wildlife resources and understand that wildlife management needs to be a partnership between them and the government, there is greater potential for them to conserve wildlife species in their areas.

References

Arntzen, J., Molokomme, K., Tshosa, O., Moleele, N., Mazambani, D., and Terry, B. (2003). *Review of CBNRM in Botswana*. Gaborone: Centre for Applied Research.

Bhandari, B. S., and Grant, M. (2007). Analysis of livelihood security: A case study in the Kali-Khola Watershed of Nepal. *Journal of Environmental Management, 85*, 17–26.

Blackie, P. (2006). Is small really beautiful? CBNRM in Malawi and Botswana. *World Development, 34*, 1942–1957.

Boggs, L. P. (2000). Community power, participation, conflict and development choice: Community wildlife conservation in the Okavango region of Northern Botswana. Discussion Paper No. 17, IIED, Maun, Botswana.

Bolaane, M. (2004). The impact of game reserve policy on the river BaSarwa/Bushmen of Botswana. *Social Policy and Administration, 38*(4), 399–417.

Brandon, K. (1998). Perils to parks: The social context of threats. In K. Redford, K. Brandon, and S. Sanderson (Eds.), *Parks in peril: People, politics, and protected areas* (pp. 415–439). Washington DC: The Nature Conservancy and Island Press.

Bromley, D. (1992). *Making the commons work*. San Francisco: Institute for Contemporary Studies.

Central Statistics Office, CSO. (2002). *National population and housing census*. Gaborone: Ministry of Finance and Development Planning.

Central Statistics Office, CSO. (2005). *Wildlife statistics 2004*. Gaborone: Ministry of Finance and Development Planning.

Chambers, R., and Conway, G. (1992). *Sustainable rural Livelihoods: Practical concepts for the 21st century*. Institute of Development Studies (IDS) Discussion Paper 296, Brighton: University of Sussex.

D'Hease, L., and Kirsten, J. (2003). *Rural development: Focusing on small scale agriculture in Southern Africa*. Pretoria: Universities of Ghent and Antwerp and University of Pretoria.

Diamond, J. (2003). *Collapse: How societies choose to succeed or fail*. New York: Viking.

Ellis, F. (2000). *Rural Livelihoods and diversity in developing countries*. Oxford: Oxford University Press.

Fidzani, B., Mlenga, W. S., Atlhopheng, M., and Shatera, M. M. (1999). *Socio-economic effects of CBPP in Ngamiland*. Gaborone: Division of Agricultural Planning and Statistics, Ministry of Agriculture.

Frankenberger, T., Luther, K., and Becht, J. (2002). *Household Livelihoods security assessments: A toolkit for practitioners*. Atlanta, Georgia: CARE USA, PHILS Unit, p. 42.

Gibson, C. C., and Marks, S. A. (1995). Transforming rural hunters into conservationists: An assessment of community-based wildlife management programs in Africa. *World Development, 23*(6), 340–350.

Kgathi, D. L., Ngwenya, B. N., and Wilk, J. (2007). Shocks and rural Livelihoods in the Okavango Delta, Botswana. *Development Southern Africa, 24*(2), 289–308.

Kolding, J. (1996). *Feasibility study and appraisal of fish stock management plan in Okavango.* Bergen, Norway: Department of Fisheries and Marine Biology, University of Bergen, p. 73.

Krech, S. (2007). Afterword. In M. Harkin and D. Lewis (Eds.), *Native Americans and the environment: Perspectives on the ecological Indian.* Lincoln: University of Nebraska Press.

Leach, M., Mearns, R., and Scoones, I. (1999). Environmental entitlements: Dynamics and institutions in community-based natural resources management. *Wildlife Development, 27,* 225–247.

Magole, L. I., and Gojamang, O. (2005). The dynamics of tourist visitation to national parks and game reserves in Botswana. *Botswana Notes and Records, 37,* 80–96.

Mbaiwa, J. E. (1999). *Prospects for sustainable wildlife resource utilization and management in Botswana: A case study of East Ngamiland District* (M.Sc. Thesis), Department of Environmental Science, University of Botswana, Gaborone.

Mbaiwa, J. E. (2003). The socio-economic and environmental impacts of tourism development on the Okavango Delta, North-Western Botswana. *Arid Environments, 54,* 447–467.

Mbaiwa, J. E. (2004). The success and sustainability of CBNRM in the Okavango Delta, Botswana. *South African Geographical Journal, 86*(1), 44–53.

Mbaiwa, J. E. (2005a). The problems and prospects of sustainable tourism development in the Okavango Delta, Botswana. *Journal of Sustainable Tourism, 13*(3), 203–227.

Mbaiwa, J. E. (2005b). Wildlife resource utilization at Moremi game reserve and Khwai community area in the Okavango Delta, Botswana. *Journal of Environmental Management, 77*(2), 144–156.

Mbaiwa, J. E. and Sakuze, L. K. (2009). Cultural tourism and livelihood diversification: The case of Gcwihaba Caves and XaiXai Village in the Okavango Delta, Botswana. *Journal of Tourism and Cultural Change, 7*(1): 61–75.

Mbaiwa, J. E., Toteng, E. N., and Moswete, N. N. (2007). Problems and prospects for the development of Urban tourism in Maun and Gaborone, Botswana. *Development Southern Africa Journal, 24*(5), 725–739.

Moganane, B. O., and Walker, K. P. (1995). *The role of local knowledge in the management of natural resources with emphasis on woodlands, veldt products and wildlife: Botswana case study.* Gaborone: Forestry Association of Botswana.

Monna, S. C. (1999). *A framework for international cooperation for the management of the Okavango Delta and Basin. Ramsar COP7 DOC 205. The Ramsar Convention on Wetlands.* Retrieved from www.ramasar.org/cop7_doc_20.5_etm

Mordi, R. (1991). *Public attitudes towards wildlife in Botswana.* New York: Garland Publishing.

Mubangizi, B. C. (2003). Drawing on social capital for community economic development: Insights from a South African rural community. *Community Development Journal, 38*(2), 140–150.

Niehof, A. (2004). The significance of diversification for rural Livelihoods systems. *Food Policy, 29,* 321–338.

North West District Council, NWDC. (2003). *District development plan six 2003/4–2008/9.* Maun: North West District Council.

Ostrom, E. (1990). *Governing the commons: The evolution of institutions for collective action.* New York: Cambridge University Press.

Perkins, J. S. (1996). Botswana: Fencing out of the equity issue, cattle posts and cattle ranches in the Kalahari Desert. *Journal of Arid Environments, 33,* 503–517.

Scoones, I. (1998). *Sustainable rural Livelihoods: A framework for analysis.* Institute of Development Studies, Discussion Paper 296, Brighton: University of Sussex, United Kingdom.

Swatuk, L. A. (2005). From 'project to context' CBNRM in Botswana. *Global Environmental Politics, 5,* 95–124.

Taylor, M. (2000). *Life, land and power, contesting development in Northern Botswana* (Unpublished Ph.D. Dissertation), University of Edinburgh.

Taylor, M. (2006). *CBNRM and pastoral development in Botswana: Implications for San land rights.* Workshop on Environment, Identity and Community Based Natural Resource Management: Experiences of the San in Southern Africa, Oxford University African Studies Centre and African Environments Programme.

Thakadu, O. T. (2005). Success factors in community-based natural resource management projects' mobilization in Northern Botswana: Lessons from practice. *Natural Resource Forum, 29*(3), 199–212.

Tlou, T. (1985). *History of Ngamiland: 1750–1906: The formation of an African state.* Gaborone: Macmillan Publishing Company.

Tsing, A. L., Brosius, J. P., and Zerner, C. (1999). Assessing community-based natural resource management. *Ambio, 28,* 197–198.

Twyman, C. (2000). Participatory conservation? Community-based natural resource management in Botswana. *The Geographical Journal, 166*(4), 323–335.

Wilshusen, P. R., Brechin, S. R., and West, P. C. (2002). Reinventing a square wheel: Critique of a resurgent 'protection paradigm' in international biodiversity conservation. *Society and Natural Resources, 15,* 17–40.

3 Land reform and the promotion of collaborative community-based ecotourism at Somkhanda Game Reserve, South Africa

Regis Musavengane

Introduction

> *The issue of the land cannot be a campaigning issue. The issue of the land cannot be a rhetoric question. The issue of the land should be the issue of commitment.*
> – (Malema, 2017)

This chapter investigates the contributing factors to the success of collaborative community-based ecotourism schemes in land-reformed communities, using a case study of the Somkhanda Game Reserve (SGR). SGR is a product of the land reform programme in South Africa. The reserve is located in Northern KwaZulu-Natal in the Zululand District Municipality and is owned by the Gumbi community. Focusing on the community's collective efforts, the chapter further examines the role of social capital in promoting successful ecotourism initiatives in land-reformed communities.

In the South African scenario, the issue of land reform is complicated by the diverse expectations on land use options by different actors (Cousins, Sadler, and Evans, 2008; Kamuti, 2018; Musavengane and Simatele, 2016), a situation which emanates from the historical imbalance of land distribution. Having endured a prolonged period of oppression, the perceptions and expectations of land reform beneficiaries tend to be divergent to such an extent that if consensus is not sought, the aim and objectives of the land restitution (or land reform) programme are significantly compromised (see Ngubane and Brooks, 2013). Often, land beneficiaries anticipate owning and accessing their land for personal benefits, such as the opportunity for rearing livestock. Other actors may be planning to use the land for business purposes that will benefit the community as a whole. To complicate the situation even further, the upper echelons of the society may attempt to use their power to gain personal advantages. This scenario can lead to a new form of oppression by people of similar 'skin colour'.

Nonetheless, realising the critical role of communities in managing their own natural resources, it has become a common practice for many states to develop policies that transfer responsibilities for managing natural resources to communities (Cooney, Roe, Dublin and Booker, 2018; Schnegg, 2018). There are two key underpinning theoretical frameworks that inform the policing of such community-based natural resource management (CBNRM) approaches. The first is common-pool resources (CPR) theory which entails the collaborative management of commonly owned resources in the community (Ostrom, 1990); and there is wide evidence of successful management of CPR over long periods of time (see McCabe, 1990; Bromley et al., 1992; Wade, 1994). Secondly, local empowerment theory, which started gaining momentum in the late 1980s and early 1990s, emphasises local economic development (LED) approaches, local participation and ecological sustainability to enhance livelihoods of local people. Agrawal (2001) and Dressler et al. (2010) observed that people seem to care more for their natural resources when they financially benefit directly from them. However, the growing number of CBNRM schemes has increased concerns about their long-term prospects (Büscher, Dressler, and Fletcher, 2014; Blaikie, 2006).

CBNRM failures are commonly attributed to various factors, including (i) the lack of will for people to participate outside capitalistic economies (Pröpper, 2015), (ii) the narrowing of CBNRM to a giving-and-taking scenario while ignoring the relationships (spiritual, moral and emotional) that humans have with their environment, which often has far-reaching consequences on a number of levels (Schnegg, 2018), and (iii) the complicated power relationships (Musavengane, 2019). With respect to power, typically the local elites tend to dominate the social space and benefit disproportionately from CBNRM (Musavengane and Simatele, 2016; Brooks, 2006).

In view of this, the chapter adopts a Social Network Theory (SNT) approach to examine the challenges and contributing factors to the collective success of Somkhanda Game Reserve. The next section defines SNT, followed by an outline of the methodological framework adopted in the study. Thereafter, the nexus between community-based ecotourism and land reform in South Africa is unpacked, followed by the case study analysis.

The Social Network Theory approach to the governance of community-based ecotourism

Social Network Theory is defined as the study of interactions between people and organisations within their networks (Barnes, 1954). SNT views social relationships in terms of nodes and ties, where nodes are the individual actors within the system or network and ties are the relationships between the actors (Liu, Sidhu, Beacom, and Valente, 2017). Diverse kinds of ties tend to form between the nodes being studied.

In the case of the Gumbi community, the main groups with varied interests are community members (diverse cliques), traditional leaders, local authorities and conservation organisations. Lin (1999) notes that SNT can be used to determine the extent to which the social capital of individual actors can influence the success of the network. The premise of SNT is that the effectiveness of individual units and the system as a whole depends on the structure of ties amongst actors and the position of individual actors in the network as they shape the behaviours, perceptions and attitudes of actors (Chung and Crawford, 2016; Knoke and Kulinski, 1992). Thus, SNT produces an alternative view which focuses not on individual attributes but on the relationships and ties within the network.

The essence of SNT in community-based natural resource management, in particular, is that stakeholder identification, analysis and governance or management can be understood at three levels: network level, actor level and tie level. First, at the *network level*, the emphasis is on the importance of the structure of communication networks and its impact on communication flow and performance (Bavelas, 1950). In his study on the network level, Bavelas (*ibid*) concludes that structures that were highly centralised were conducive to solving the problems with minimal errors. Thus, from a stakeholder governance perspective in CBNRM, the extent to which the network is centralised can facilitate or inhibit the flow of information, and this information is valuable for effective stakeholder participation, analysis, governance and management. Communities with a repressive background, as in the case of Somkhanda Game Reserve, thrive on effective communication to avoid speculations which may interfere with the achievement of the community's collective goals.

Second, the *actor level* emphasises the location of actors in relation to others within the network (Chung and Crawford, 2016). A commonly cited social network concept at the actor level is Linton Freeman's 'centrality' idea (Freeman, 1978). He proposed three essential forms of centrality: (i) *degree of centrality*, which indicates communication activities of actors by measuring the number of ties to and from a particular actor; (ii) *closeness centrality*, which indicates the ability of an actor to independently reach all others within the network by measuring the extent to which the actor is close to others; it is also used as a proxy to establish the most cost-effective and efficient communication channel within the network; and (iii) *betweenness centrality*, which measures the shortest possible distance an actor lies relative to all others within the network. The Gumbi community, like other communities established through land reform, needs a tight-knit network to promote unity and minimise the cost and time of distributing important information to all stakeholders/actors.

Third, at the *tie level*, Mark Granovetter's theory on the 'strength of weak ties' is useful (Chung and Crawford, 2016). Granovetter (1973) postulates that the denser the networks become, the lower the rate of diffusion of novel information. New or novel information must therefore come from weak ties (to those or groups outside the closely knit group). This is crucial in terms of innovation and generating new ideas, and hence the 'strength of weak ties' (Chung and Crawford, 2016, p. 376). However, Montjoye, Stopczynski, Shmueli, Pentland, and Lehmann (2014) recently demonstrated that although weak ties are essential for promoting new and novel information transfer, the strong ties appear to be more instrumental in solving complex problems. In natural resource management, these complex problems are sometimes termed 'environmental wicked problems' due to the consequences they cause (see Musavengane and Simatele, 2016). The complexities within land-reformed communities tend to breed environmental problems which require novel strategies to ensure the success of collaborative management of common-pool natural resources.

Study context

After successfully claiming their land in 2005, the Gumbi people decided to keep large portions of it under conservation and create a consolidated game reserve, *Somkhanda Game Reserve*, to drive the economic and social development of the community. The reserve is situated within a Key Biodiversity Area in the Maputaland–Pondoland–Albany Global Biodiversity Hotspot.

The Gumbi community (Figure 3.1) comprises five settlement areas: Hlambinyathi, Zonyama, Cotlands, Bethal and Candover, with an approximate total of 400 households. The game reserve spans 16,418.82 hectares of land, with the settlement and grazing area measuring up to 5209.40 hectares. An area of 11,508.72 hectares is still pending land claim. SGR boasts a large number of species of both fauna and flora, with about 230 bird species. The reserve is home to the big five (rhino, elephant, buffalo, lion and leopard). Although there are no cheetahs, the reserve houses a rich diversity of other wildlife including African wild dogs, spotted and brown hyena, giraffe, zebra, blue wildebeest, kudu, nyala, impala, bushpigs and warthogs, as well as some rarer species such as jackal, aardvark, honey badger, serval and caracal.

The SGR model provides unique experiences for visitors who mainly engage in nature tourism. Mostly, visitors are in groups of at least four persons. Both international and domestic tourists visit the reserve. The majority of visitors are school or college groups, from different parts of the world. The reserve is popular among European college students who seek pristine nature experiences. Visitors can engage in 'science on safari' adventures, an educational ecotourism approach where visitors learn about various aspects of the reserve as they participate in a bush walk or a game drive. Visitors are also provided a free interactive wildlife digital 'app' where they can log their wildlife sightings.

SGR further offers a 10-day theory and practical game ranger course to visitors to enhance their knowledge and appreciation of wildlife, conservation and the African bush. The course is intended to provide participants with skills in various conservation areas including tracking, signs and spoor identification, mammal biology and identification, bird identification, as well as tree and plant identification. In addition, game reserve management training and information are delivered, covering game capture and other population control measures, ecotourism, hunting in conservation veld management, wilderness survival skills, first aid and counter-poaching techniques.

Methods

A case study design was adopted. The Gumbi community was appropriate for the study, given its land reform history and success as a community-based ecotourism project. According to Yin (2003), the case study approach is preferred when 'how', 'what' and 'why' questions are posed in scrutinising a particular phenomenon. To that extent, the case study of the Gumbi community enabled the researcher to understand the issues related to co-management of common natural resources in depth, providing comprehensive socio-ecological scientific analysis,

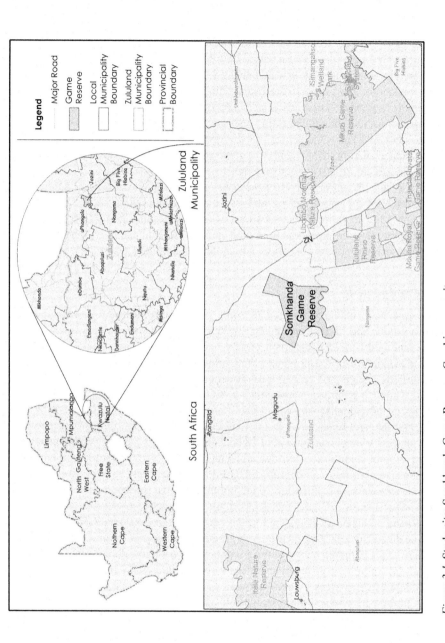

Figure 3.1 Study site: Somkhanda Game Reserve, Gumbi community

particularly of the interplay of social network resource governance and the impact thereof on the community-based ecotourism project (Somkhanda Game Reserve) and on the broader community.

However, although useful in generating useful qualitative data, a number of researchers have criticised case studies because of their lack of generalisability (Easton, McComish, and Greenberg, 2000; Muzeza, 2013; Yin, 2003). To ensure a more rigorous study, the researcher used a number of research techniques or data collection approaches (data triangulation), namely interviews, focus group meetings, personal observations and informal conversations. This enabled the researcher to 'maintain the multiple realities, the different and even the contradictory views of what is happening' (Stake, 1995, p12). Such an approach is critical in spaces that involve wildlife or game ranching, which tend to have diverse actors (see Kamuti, 2018; Ngubane and Brooks, 2013).

It was also essential to collect the data in a flexible and sensitive manner in the context of the sensitivity of land issues in KwaZulu-Natal and South Africa more broadly. In addition, the researcher acknowledges the critical importance of participants' own interpretations of land reform and land use (community-based ecotourism) during data collection, which then inform the interpretivist analysis.

Data and analysis

The data were obtained through personal observation, informal conversations, focus groups and in-depth interviews of key actors and stakeholders involved in the community-based ecotourism project, including community members, Somkhanda Game Reserve employees, SGR project coordinators and managers, local community leaders and chiefs, local government officials and non-governmental conservation organisations operating at SGR. Stakeholders were regarded 'as groups or individual[s] who can affect or are affected by an issue' (Schiller, Winters, Hanson, and Ashe, 2013, p. 1). A systematic random sampling of households was applied, wherein an interval of 18 houses was used to approach 53 households in the Gumbi community. A snowball technique was used to identify and engage with local authorities, community and traditional leaders, and conservation organisation representatives. Interviews were grounded on the appreciation of interviewees' social identity (Crane and Ruebottom, 2011), interests (Orts and Strudler, 2009) and involvement (Carsten, Christensen, and Tarp, 2005) in SGR operations.

The data were analysed qualitatively through a process of coding and theming. In light of the complex nature of the governance of common-pool resources where actors appear to have different and often divergent interests on the use and access to community resources, a social network analysis (SNA) approach was adopted. This framework enabled the researcher to analyse the role of social networks in promoting inclusivity and sustainable management of the community-based game reserve, which in turn promote ecotourism business in the area, and at the same time enhancing community livelihoods.

SNA anchors on SNT and aims to understand a community by mapping the relationships that connect them as a network, and then attempts to draw out key individuals, groups within the network ('components') and/or associations between the individuals. Thus, the mapping of key individuals and groups with an influence (positive or negative) on the operations of the Somkhanda Game Reserve was conducted to illuminate how groups and individuals are critical in establishing strong networks in the Gumbi community (Figure 3.2).

Three key elements of the SNA were analysed: (i) *size of the network*, which shows the number of nodes (the people in the network) and number of links (social connections or relationships between nodes), and number of unique links; (ii) *cohesiveness*, which includes the number of components from distinct groups in the network such as the Emvokweni Community Trust (ECT) which represents the needs of the community, the traditional authorities (TAs), who uphold the cultural values of the community, and the Wildlands Conservation Trust (WCT), whose focus is the promotion of sustainable nature conservation; and (iii) *centrality*, which measures how central nodes in the network are. Cohesiveness of the SGR network was also analysed through 'density', which entails the extent to which nodes (people) are interconnected. This facilitates to determination of the proportion of all links within the Somkhanda Game Reserve and the Gumbi community in general.

To understand the challenges and contributing factors to the collective success of Somkhanda Game Reserve, the analytical approach posed a number of questions: Which individuals are linked together in the group? Who is peripheral to the SGR network and who is not? Why is this? Furthermore, to enable targeting interventions in the governance of the SGR, questions related to the role of individuals in promoting community-based ecotourism were addressed. For example, what role do individuals play in the SGR network? Who is connected to lots of

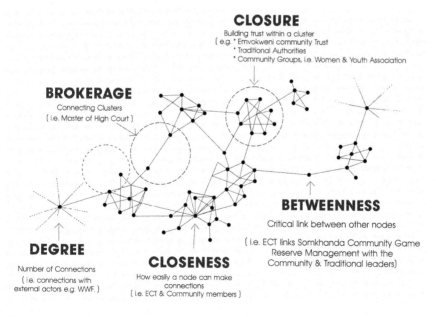

Figure 3.2 Social network analysis of the Somkhanda Game Reserve

others? Who is uniquely connected to lots of others? Who is the gatekeeper of SGR? If an intervention were delivered to individuals, what impact would it have on the network?

Key insights

Collaborative management of Somkhanda Game Reserve

According to SNT, collaborative management promotes the formation of ties between different nodes where there are diverse interests. Liu et al. (2017) note that in SNT, social relationships are viewed in terms of nodes and ties, where nodes are the individual actors within the system or network and ties are the relationships between the actors.

The Gumbi community engaged the Wildlands Conservation Trust (WCT) to manage the reserve on a five-year renewal contract while transferring skills to the local people. The collaborative management arrangement was necessitated by the continual failure of the local people to manage the game reserve on their own in the first five years after establishment.

The Emvokweni Community Trust (ECT – node 1) contracted Wildlands Conservation Trust (WCT – node 2) to manage and transfer skills to local community members (node 3) during the tenure. The ECT is a legally constituted board entrusted with operations of the SGR by the community. Its members are voted in by land beneficiaries. The ECT also leased the tourism section of the game reserve to African Insight to oversee the management of tourism operations that include accommodation and a restaurant, an arrangement that would allow WCT to concentrate on conservation. Both entities are operating on five-year leases.

It can be observed that *weak ties* were an important factor in the success of SGR. By engaging the WCT, the SGR received novel information critical for the establishment and management of the game reserve. Social Network Theory encourages the presence of external actors in building strong networks. The collaborative structure, which includes the WTC, African Insight, Wildlife ACT and the World Wildlife Fund (WWF) in the operation of the SGR, allowed the community to tap into a range of competencies and human resources. For example, WWF supported SGR in its black rhino expansion project, leading to a significant increase in the rhino population. This has attracted many game ranchers and consequently increased revenue to the community game reserve. Wildlife ACT helps in the monitoring of the rhino population to curb poaching. WCT has also been instrumental in the introduction of different species at the SGR including 11 herd of elephants that were transferred from Nambiti Game Reserve (a rural community game reserve in KwaZulu-Natal province). This occurred through a collaboration with the Elephant Rhino and People Project (ERP), who were funded over USD 20,000 by Group Elephant.

Networking at the formation stage of Somkhanda Game Reserve

The foundation of a structure determines its strength and durability. SNT emphasises the importance of 'closeness' in creating critical links between nodes.

Closeness helps to establish how easily a node can make connections to enhance effective communication, which consequently promotes the cohesion of nodes. The Gumbi community's historical background points to the importance of communication to counteract any negative speculation that might compromise the success of the whole system or project.

It is important to note too that individuals' or groups' given socio-historical circumstances often influence their norms, behaviours and perceptions toward new projects (Lee and Scott, 2017). Spierenburg and Brooks (2014) observe that most farms in KZN that were successfully claimed by communities are located close to former 'native reserves', creating an intricate dilemma where community members who witnessed the brutality of Apartheid always associate the term 'reserve' to unfairness. During Apartheid, native reserves were used to quarantine or separate people from their land and associated resources. Thus, community members tend to equate Apartheid reserves to current game reserves, causing reluctance to participate in the ecotourism project (Ngubane and Brooks, 2013).

These attitudes were revealed in interviews, for example, with a founding member and beneficiary of SGR:

> When we successfully claimed the land, the first thing I did was to undertake community consultations, to educate people on the meaning of 'game reserve' as they still have a mind of apartheid reserves. I was blamed by people even my closest relatives who didn't understand what a reserve is. I had to explain to them what the game reserve is and that it belongs to them and is meant to benefit them.

It may be questioned whether the founding member here was using participation as a 'cosmetic label', in order to earn the goodwill of the community (in real terms being a top-down approach), or whether it was an empowering process which enabled local people to undertake their own analysis. In that relation, Chambers (1995) emphasises the need for consultations that seek to empower the majority through bottom-up approaches.

However, in their accounts of the events surrounding formation of the reserve, household participants reported that during the inception stage there was indeed more involvement of community members, and furthermore, the founders and Emvokweni Community Trust (ECT) members were more visible and provided feedback on time. The degree of centrality was high, which promoted an effective social network at the 'actor level' (Freeman, 1978). The vast majority of household participants (90%) reported that they were consulted during the formation stages of the reserve, and that relationships within the community were harmonious.

Collaborative structures and communication processes

The Gumbi people are deeply rooted in their culture and traditions, consistent with the rest of the Zulu clan, generally (see Kamuti, 2018). According to SNT, the 'betweenness centrality' role is crucial for establishing the shortest possible distance between actors to enhance effective communication. In the SGR case, the traditional leaders can be conceived of as playing the *betweenness role* from the perspective of SNT.

The embedment of community members' social life and traditional authorities was reflected in the focus groups held with the community members. Over half of the participants, mainly households (60%), reported having strong ties with traditional leaders. As a further demonstration of the centrality of culture and tradition to the community, a deceased chief was 'appointed' to the operations of the Somkhanda Game Reserve, although not prescribed in the Land Restitution Act. The majority (98%) of the respondents were happy with this symbolic involvement of a traditional institution, as 'he was faithful and resembled the cultural emblem'.

However, WCT representatives and ECT also reported observations of the decay of traditional systems of governance within the community, which in their view had led to corruption and the unfair distribution of benefits from the project. For example, a WCT respondent stated,

> Due to growing squabbles between community members and the ECT which is believed to have been appointed by traditional leaders to divert the money from the community, we have temporarily stopped to remit the money to them till the case is concluded by the Master of Court.

The allegations of corruption and associated conflict between the Gumbi founding family and the traditional leaders had led to litigation at one point, creating an unhealthy socio-political environment. A Gumbi elderly woman lamented this status quo:

> We don't know what the Trust is doing, what we just know is that there is no good relationship between them and the chiefs. You know, the fight of power is not good for us the elderly and our kids are the ones who will lose the jobs if the game reserve is to close. They have to resolve their differences quickly. What is power?

The resultant involvement of the Master of High Court however fulfilled the *brokerage role* – to re-connect the actors within the network, in the event of conflict (see Figure 3.2). In a number of co-management schemes, disagreements have led to violence (see Musavengane and Simatele, 2016; Ngubane and Brooks, 2013; Kamuti, 2014). However, it was reported, when it became clear that the source of conflict could not be addressed fully through the courts, in the interest of restoring harmony among actors, the Gumbi family and the traditional leaders were urged to resolve the differences out of court.

Community livelihoods

The central purpose of SGR is to enhance the livelihoods of community members through effective coordination of complex tasks associated with co-governance of common-pool resources. The project has transformed the lives of the Gumbi people and surrounding communities by providing them with an income stream as well as employment and skills development. At the time of the study, SGR had 55 permanent employees, most of whom (91%) were community members. The community members completed theoretical conservation classes and were then recruited into an 18-month conservation internship program. The majority (74%) of them cited SGR as their first employer.

In addition, income from the community project has been directed towards alleviating the recurrent water shortages resulting from northern KwaZulu-Natal's frequent droughts. The provincial government's provision of water in portable containers had failed to meet the needs of the community. To mitigate the shortages, boreholes were erected, and there are plans to erect more as funds become available.

The reserve also generates revenue for households from the 'Zulu homestays' initiative. The homestays are particularly popular among school groups who are fascinated by the rural set-up. The home owners receive an agreed percentage from the SGR in proportion to the number of visitors accommodated and their duration of stay. The homes are inspected for quality standards by the SGR staff, and the home owners are also provided with additional support (e.g. toiletries for visitors). As a result of the new income streams, community members do not rely solely on farming for their livelihoods income.

Conclusion

The success of the Somkhanda Game Reserve can be attributed to the strong social capital created by the social network of the Gumbi community, through effective information sharing and openness among the various nodes. This has facilitated social cohesion among the varied clusters, which have in turn enhanced the building of trust. Notwithstanding a number of challenges, the community project has improved livelihoods through the creation of employment, skills development and access to water. Thus, land reform can deliver desirable outcomes for communities if strong and effective social networks are developed and nurtured by all actors.

References

Agrawal, A. (2001). Common property institutions and sustainable governance of resources. *World Development, 29,* 1649–1672. doi:10.1016/S0305-750X(01)00063-8

Barnes, J. (1954). Class and committees in a Norwegian Island Parish. *Human Relations, 7,* 39–58.

Bavelas, A. (1950). Communication patterns in task-oriented groups. *Journal of Acoustical Society of America, 22*(6), 725–730.

Blaikie, P. (2006). Is small really beautiful? Community-based natural resource management in Malawi and Botswana. *World Development, 34,* 1942–1957. doi:10.1016/j.world dev.2005.11.023

Bromley, D. W. F., Mckean, D., Peters, M. A., Gilles, P., Oakerson, J. L., Runge, R. J. (1992). *Making the commons: Worktheory, practice and policy.* San Francisco, CA: Institute for Contemporary Studies Press.

Brooks, J. S., Franzen, M. A., Holmes, C. M., Groete, M. N., and Borgerhoff Mulder, M. (2006). Testing hypotheses for the success of different conservation strategies. *Conservation Biology*, *20*, 1528–1538.

Büscher, B., Dressler, W., and Fletcher, R. (2014). *Nature™ Inc.: Environmental conservation in the neoliberal age*. Tucson: University of Arizona Press. doi:10.2307/j.ctt183pdh2

Carsten, N. H., Christensen, S. M., and Tarp, P. (2005). Rapid stakeholder and conflict assessment for natural resource management using cognitive mapping: The case of Damdoi forest enterprises, Vietnam. *Agriculture and Human Values*, *22*, 149–167.

Chambers, R. (1995). Paradigm shifts and the practice of participatory research and development. In N. Nelson and S. Wright (Eds.), *Power and Participatory Development: Theory and Practice*. London: Intermediate Technology Publications, pp. 30–42.

Chung, K. S. K., and Crawford, L. (2016). The role of social networks theory and methodology for project stakeholder management. *Procedia – Social and Behavioral Sciences*, *226*, 372–380.

Cooney, R., Roe, D., Dublin, H., and Booker, F. (2018). *Wildlife, wild Livelihoods: Involving communities in sustainable wildlife management and combatting the illegal wildlife trade*. Nairobi, Kenya: United Nations Environment Programme.

Cousins, J. A., Sadler, J. P., and Evans, J. (2008). Exploring the role of private wildlife ranching as a conservation tool in South Africa: Stakeholder perspectives. *Ecology and Society*, *13*(2), 43. Retrieved July 10, 2018, from www.ecologyandsociety.org/vol13/iss2/art43/

Crane, A., and Ruebottom, T. (2011). Stakeholder theory and social identity: Rethinking stakeholder identification. *Journal of Business Ethics*, *102*, 77–87.

Dressler, W., Büscher, B., Schoon, M., Brockington, D., Hayes, T., Kull, C., McCarthy, J., and Streshta, K. 2010. From hope to crisis and back? A critical history of the global cbnrm narrative. *Environmental Conservation*, *37*(1), 1–11.

Easton, K. L., McComish, J. F., and Greenberg, R. (2000). Avoiding common pitfalls in qualitative data collection and transcription. *Qualitative Health Research*, *10*(5), 703–707.

Freeman, L. C. (1978). Centrality in social networks: Conceptual clarification. *Social Networks*, *1*(3), 215–239.

Granovetter, M. S. (1973). The strength of weak ties. *The American Journal of Sociology*, *78*(6), 1360–1380.

Kamuti, T. (2014). The fractured state in the governance of private game farming: The case of KwaZulu-Natal province, South Africa. *Journal of Contemporary African Studies* *32*(2), 190–206.

Kamuti, T. (2018). Intricacies of game farming and outstanding land restitutions claims in the Gongolo area of KwaZulu-Natal, South Africa. In F. Brandt and G. Mkodzongi (Eds.), *Land reform revisited: Democracy, state making and agrarian transformation in post-apartheid South Africa*. Boston: Brill.

Knoke, S., and Kulinski, J. H. (1992). *Network analysis*. Newbury Park, CA: Sage Publications.

Lee, K. J. J., and Scott, D. (2017). Racial discrimination and African Americans' travel behavior: The utility of habitus and vignette technique. *Journal of Travel Research*, *56*(3), 381–392.

Lin, N. (1999). Building a network theory of social capital. *Connections*, *22*(1), 28–51.

Liu, W., Sidhu, A., Beacom, A. M., and Valente, T. W. (2017). Social network theory. *The International Encyclopedia of Media Effects*. doi:10.1002/9781118783764.wbieme0092

Malema, J. S. (2017, February 28). *Debate in the national assembly on possible amending section 25 of the constitution, Tuesday.* Retrieved July 5, 2018, from www.politicsweb. co.za/documents/malema-and-thesection-25-land-debate-full-transcr

McCabe, J. T. (1990). Turkana pastoralism: A case against the tragedy of the commons. *Human Ecology, 18*(1), 81–103.

Montjoye, Y. A. D., Stopczynski, A., Shmueli, E., Pentland, A., and Lehmann, S. (2014). The strength of the strongest ties in collaborative problem solving. *Scientific Reports (Nature Publishing Group), 4*(5227), 6.

Musavengane, R., and Simatele, M. D. (2016). Community-based natural resource management: The role of social capital in collaborative environmental of tribal resources in Kwa-Zulu Natal, South Africa. *Development Southern Africa, 33*(6), 806–821. doi:10.1 080/0376835X.2016.1231054

Musavengane, R. (2019). Using the systemic-resilience thinking approach to enhance participatory collaborative management of natural resources in tribal communities: Toward inclusive land reform-led outdoor tourism. *Journal of Outdoor Recreation and Tourism,* 25, 45–56.

Muzeza, D. (2013). *The Impact of Institutions of Governance on Communities' Livelihoods and Sustainable Conservation in The Great Limpopo Transfrontier Park (GLTP): The Study of Makuleke and Sengwe Communities.* Retrieved December 14, 2017 from http://etd.cput.ac.za/bitstream/handle/20.500.11838/806/210227028_Muzeza_D_2013. pdf?sequence=1&isAllowed=y

Ngubane, M., and Brooks, S. (2013). Land beneficiaries as game farmers: Conservation, land reform and the invention of the 'community game farm' in KwaZulu-Natal. *Journal of Contemporary African Studies, 31*(3), 399–420.

Orts, E. W., and Strudler, A. (2009). Putting a stake in stakeholder theory. *Journal of Business Ethics, 88*, 605–615.

Ostrom, E. (1990). *Governing the commons: The evolution of institutions for collective action. The Political economy of institutions and decisions.* Cambridge: Cambridge University Press.

Pröpper, M. (2015). Emerging markets for nature and challenges for the ecosystem service approach. *Development and Change, 46*, 247–268. doi.org/10.1111/dech.12153

Schiller, C., Winters, M., Hanson, H. M., and Ashe, M. C. (2013). A framework for stakeholder identification in concept mapping and health research: A novel process and its application to older adult mobility and the built environment. *BMC Public Health, 13*, 428, doi:10.1186/1471-2458-13-428.

Schnegg, M. (2018). Institutional multiplexity: Social networks and community-based natural resource management. *Sustainability Science, 13*(4), 1017–1030.

Spierenburg, M., and Brooks, S. 2014. Private game farming and its social consequences in post-apartheid South Africa: Contestations over wildlife, property and agrarian futures. *Journal of Contemporary African Studies, 32*(2), 151–172.

Stake, R. (1995). *The art of case study research.* Thousand Oaks: Sage Publications.

Wade, R. (1994). *Village republics: Economic conditions for collective action in south India.* Oakland: ICS Press.

Yin, R. K. (2003). *Case research: Design and methods* (3rd ed.). Thousand Oaks: Sage Publications.

4 Understanding the relationships between protected areas, tourism and community livelihoods

A systems thinking approach

Moren T. Stone and Lesego S. Stone

Introduction

In this chapter, we regard a tourism destination as a system made up of many subsystems which are, in turn, dependent on many resources for the entire system to function coherently. These destination resources need to be identifiable and have distinct functionality. Tourism destination resources are defining features that make a destination appealing and give it unique characteristics. Investments and availability of tourism resources provide various tangible and intangible resources such as natural and cultural resources, capital and labour. In the process of tourism development, constituents of the system are coupled and interact with each other on an adaptive basis, producing the systematic spatial, functional and industrial structure of the destination. Such coupling is a dynamic evolutionary process during which agglomerated enterprises engage in related industrial production, and the organisational structure of the system determines the stability and performance of the enterprise (Weng, Lv, and Li, 2016). Within a certain temporal and spatial scope, the relationship among the components achieves dynamic equilibrium or lack thereof.

In the context of protected areas tourism, management of resources entails, among other things, addressing two competing and overlapping goals: conserving biodiversity and improving community livelihoods. Resolving potential conflicts between these two goals is particularly challenging (Karanth and DeFries, 2010). Not only are there competing goals, professionals, including protected-area managers, community development planners, tourism operators and marketing specialists, and paradigms of management often conflict (McCool, 2009). Though protected areas are a popular strategy for managing biodiversity conservation, their contribution to livelihoods improvement and sustainable development remains contested and challenged (Mearns and Lukhele, 2015; Stone and Nyaupane, 2014). In view of this, we argue that understanding protected areas' contribution to conservation and community livelihoods could best be understood via systems thinking rather than mechanical and 'cause-effect' approaches. Traditional methodologies have proven to be ineffective in many tourism studies, as they are often informed by flawed knowledge yielded through poor policies and implementation designs. Such approaches often consider a particular issue in isolation of the whole system in which it resides. The chapter draws on studies carried out at Chobe Enclave Conservation Trust and Khama Rhino Sanctuary Trust.

Protected areas and tourism development

There are 217,155 protected areas throughout the world, covering an area of 34,411,944 km² (UNEP-WCMC and IUCN, 2016). The sites are managed through special rules for conservation objectives (Anderson, 2012). In the developing world, nature-based tourism is dependent on protected areas (PAs) resources, wildlife and wilderness (Ghimire and Pimbert, 1997). In the early 1990s, there was recognition that PAs have prospects to host tourism and improve communities' livelihoods (IUCN, 1994). Today their mandate is to play both conservation and development roles (Janishevski, Noonan-Mooney, Gidda, and Mulongoy, 2008). There has been a global call to link the conservation of PAs and community development through tourism development (IUCN, 1994). As PAs serve different stakeholders, they have been exposed to many transformations and subjected to growing marketisation, multiple competing uses, changing rural economies and technological modernisation (Nyaupane and Poudel, 2011). In view of this, it is important to assess the role PAs play in tourism and community livelihoods improvement by applying a systems thinking approach.

The systems thinking approach

A system is defined as 'a set of connected things, an organised or interrelated group of things, connoting orderliness' (Anon, 1991, p. 1085). According to Forrester (1961), systems thinking seeks to understand system behaviour by examining 'the whole' instead of parts of it. A system is a whole that cannot be divided into independent parts; hence, the essential properties of a system taken as a whole derive from the interaction of its parts, not their actions taken separately (Ackoff, 1981). Ackoff (1981) asserts that a system satisfies the following three conditions:

1   The behaviour of each element has an effect on the behaviour of the whole;
2   The behaviour of the elements and their effects on the whole are interdependent;
3   Subgroups of the elements are formed, each has an effect on the behaviour of the whole and none has an independent effect on it.

(pp. 64–65)

This chapter argues that we should conceptualise PAs, tourism and community livelihoods as a complex system, comprising many interacting components. Literature on systems thinking indicates tourism studies first applied these ideologies during the 1970s (e.g. Holling and Chambers, 1973). The theoretical rationale is that the conservation and development nexus debate cannot empirically be understood in all cases using reductionist thinking and simple unidirectional 'cause and effect' models, particularly if they do not take into account the complex aspects of interaction. The chapter therefore posits that there must be an appraisal of complexity among PAs, tourism and community livelihoods with a framework approach that gives a more vigorous appreciation of complex connections. In doing so, the chapter adopts the community capitals framework (CCF) to examine relevant community linkages.

Community capitals framework through the systems thinking lens

The CCF (Flora, Flora, and Fey, 2004) provides a tool for analysing how communities work. It is an integrative approach to analyse and understand dynamics within rural communities (Emery, Fey, and Flora, 2006). Capital is any type of resource capable of producing additional resources, and when those resources or assets are invested to create new resources, they become capital (Flora et al., 2004). Thus, community capitals represent assets in all aspects of community life. The CCF consists of seven types of capital – natural, cultural, human, social, political, financial and built (Flora, 2005) (see Figure 4.1). Capitals may be tangible or intangible (Emery et al., 2006).

An overview of the seven types of community capital is provided in Table 4.1. The CCF highlights that communities have assets which may be inactive or they may be invested to create more assets (Flora et al., 2004). Using the community capitals framework to assess community development provides concrete evidence of asset development and illuminates interaction among the capitals that can generate an upward spiral of positive community change (Emery et al., 2006). The framework also offers an approach to assess community and development efforts from a systems thinking perspective by identifying assets in each capital (stock), the types of capital invested (flow), the interaction among the types of capital and the consequential impacts on them (Emery et al., 2006). If the assets are sustainably used, the outcomes are healthy ecosystems, vibrant regional economies, social equity and empowerment (Flora et al., 2004), as illustrated in Figure 4.1.

Flora et al. (2004) indicate that while the capitals are separated into seven separate categories, they are connected to each other. To understand the stock and flow among community capitals, we use a case study approach, where two community-based organisations (CBOs) participating in ecotourism projects are analysed.

Methods

Study areas

The Chobe Enclave Conservation Trust (CECT) area is located in northern Botswana's Chobe District and adjacent to the Chobe National Park (see Figure 4.2). The CECT is the first Community-Based Natural Resource Management (CBNRM) project in Botswana. The CECT comprises the five villages of Mabele, Kavimba, Kachikau, Satau and Parakarungu in northern Botswana. The villages

Capitals Explanations

Political Capital
Include: inclusion, leadership, voice, power, etc.

Human Capital
Include: education, skills, self-esteem, knowledge, etc.

Cultural Capital
Include: Cosmo vision, language, rituals, traditional crops, dress, etc.

Natural Capital
Include: Air, soils, water, landscape, biodiversity, etc.

Social Capital
Include: leadership, groups, bridging & bonding, networks, trust, reciprocity

Financial Capital
Include: income, wealth, security, credit, investment

Physical Capital
Include: water systems, sewers, utilities, healthy systems

Figure 4.1 Community capitals framework
Source: Adapted from Flora (2005)

are located outside the Chobe National Park in a buffer zone that is divided into two controlled hunting areas (CHAs), CH1 and CH2. Before the hunting ban in 2014, CH1 was operated as a hunting concession while CH2 was designated for photographic tourism purposes. Since the hunting ban, CH1 is also used

Table 4.1 Summary of community capitals

Capitals	Descriptions
Social	This is the networking account. It includes the close bonds between and among family and friends, communities, groups, organisations, networks and trust in the community, the sense of belonging and bonds between people. It can influence, as well as be influenced by, the stock and flows of other capitals.
Human	This is the human resource 'people' account. It includes leadership capabilities, knowledge, wisdom, information and skills possessed by the people who live in the community.
Natural	This is the environmental account. It includes the resources that exist in the natural world. Some of which may include but are not limited to the soil, lakes, natural resources, nature's beauty, rivers, forests, wildlife and local landscape. Communities work with these resources to meet livelihoods needs.
Financial	This is the financial account. It includes the resources related to money and access to funding, wealth, charitable giving, grants.
Physical/built	This is the building and infrastructure account. It includes houses, schools, businesses, clinics, libraries, water systems, electrical grid, communication systems, roads, transportation systems, etc.
Cultural	This is the account for community cultural resources. The way communities view the world. Culture defines the traditional ways of doing and being – habits and attitudes. It includes dances, stories, heritage, food and traditions and also values and connections to the spirit. Cultural capital is also a resource to attract tourism.
Political	This account represents power and community connections to people who have power. Communities draw upon this resource when they unite to solve a controversial issue. Political capital is built by making connections with political and community leaders both inside and outside the community. It also refers to the ability of people to find their own voice and to engage in actions that contribute to the wellbeing of their community.

Sources: Compiled from Aigner et al. (2002); Emery et al. (2006); Flora et al. (2004)

for photographic tourism. It hosts tourism facilities such as lodges, motels and camping sites. CECT is run by a board of trustees elected from the five member villages. Two individuals are elected from each village, and by virtue of their positions, chiefs are ex-officio members. The CECT board is made up of 15 members, elected for a three-year term. The CECT villages predominantly depend on both pastoral and arable agriculture, supplemented by tourism activities.

The Khama Rhino Sanctuary Trust (KRST) was set up in 1992. It is a community-based organisation involved in tourism to sustainably use natural resources, benefit locals economically and save rhinos (Sebele, 2010). KRST

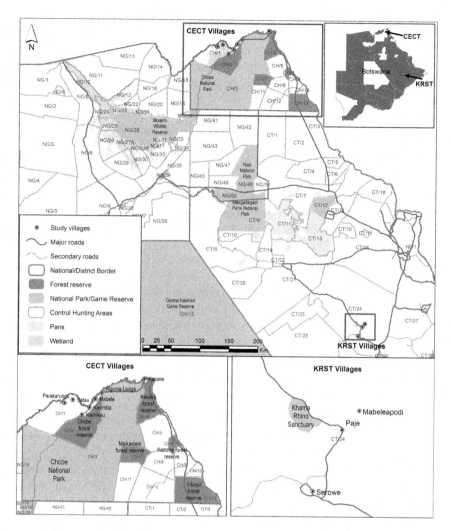

Figure 4.2 Map of study areas

Source: Okavango Research Institute GIS Laboratory, 2018

covers about 4300 hectares and is located 7 km east of Paje, about 11 km north-east of Mabeleapudi and 25 km north of Serowe along the Serowe–Orapa road (Grossman and Associates, n.d.; Sebele, 2006). The sanctuary is in the Central District of Botswana, the largest district in terms of area and population (Sebele, 2005). The three villages of Serowe, Paje and Mabeleapudi make up KRST (Sebele, 2005). In 2011, Mabeleapudi had a population of 2247, Paje had 2507 and Serowe had 50,820 (Statistics Botswana, 2012). A board of trustees administers the sanctuary with members from the three participating villages.

Data collection

Data were collected from various tourism stakeholders in Botswana. These include data collected through interviews with stakeholders from local communities and government officials. The data were collected over a period of 10 years. Fieldwork was carried out at Chobe Enclave Conservation Trust and Khama Rhino Sanctuary Trust.

At the KRST, data were collected through focus group discussions. Two focus group discussions, each comprising 10 participants, were also held in each of the three villages, one with the youth and the other with the elderly. These were held to establish locals' perceptions on KRST and to determine the prospects and challenges of KRST. Formal interviews were also held with relevant stakeholders (KRST board members (10), local farmers, VDC chairpersons (3) and chiefs (3)). In addition, informal interviews were held with the chief warden at KRST to discuss communities' involvement in the management of KRST.

At CECT, data were collected through community asset mapping (CAM). CAM was implemented through 10 focus groups, two held in each village, with the youth and the elders respectively. To ensure that respondents were free to express themselves candidly, groups were separated. Village Development Committee (VDC) chairpersons and village chiefs were instrumental in assisting researchers to identify participants who participated in the CAM exercise. The groups were made up of 10 to 13 members. The 10 focus groups comprised in total 103 respondents.

In addition, data were collected through semi-structured interviews with key informants. These included village leaders, six key governmental officials, lodge manager, CECT board chairperson, VDC chairpersons and chiefs. This made a total of 18 key informants. All interviews at both sites were audio recorded. English and Setswana were used during the interviews, depending on the interviewees' choice.

Published and unpublished secondary data on protected areas, tourism and community livelihoods linkages were also collected. CECT and KRST documents which included land use and management plans, financial and training workshop records, board minutes, constitution and financial and employment records were used to gain more information. Other secondary data sources such as policy documents, journal articles, community-based tourism reports, book chapters and reports on tourism development in Botswana were also consulted.

Data analysis

Thematic analysis was used to glean key patterns in the data. Thematic analysis 'is a method for identifying, analysing, organizing, describing, and reporting themes found within a data set' (Nowell, Norris, White, and Moules, 2017, p. 3). It is valuable for investigating the views of research participants, showing similarities and differences and highlighting unexpected insights (Braun and Clarke, 2006). Thematic analysis allows researchers to identify important themes and patterns in the data that are significant and/or worthy; the themes address or highlight something about the issue at hand (Maguire and Delahunt, 2017). Both primary and secondary qualitative data collected were summarised into themes and patterns. Braun and Clarke's (2006) six-phase framework for conducting a thematic analysis was followed (Maguire and Delahunt, 2017). This involved,

1   Becoming familiar with the data;
2   Generating initial codes;
3   Searching for themes;
4   Reviewing themes;
5   Defining themes; and
6   Write-up.

The researchers familiarised themselves with the data by reading and re-reading it. Next, segments of data that addressed research questions were coded. Throughout the coding process, new codes were generated and others modified. Following this, codes were closely examined and then integrated into themes, based on common patterns or meanings. Next, initial themes identified were reviewed, modified and developed. At this stage, the themes were checked against the data to ensure consistency. After checking and refining the themes, the study was written into a coherent story, integrating the findings within the theoretical framework and other relevant existing literature.

Trustworthiness was enriched through audio-recording interviews, note-taking and triangulation (Stake, 2010). Data triangulation, which involved the collection of data via multiple sources, investigators and methods, further enhanced rigour (Stake, 2010: Anney, 2014). In addition, auditing, which involved the recording of all choices made during data collection, coding and analysis was used. Memos, field notes and methods used were described in detail. To guarantee confidentiality of the data, transcripts, field notes and all research documents were only accessible to the authors (Lincoln and Guba, 1994). Respondents' anonymity was also assured through the use of a coding system for identification purposes.

Results

Employment opportunities

The analysis reveals that tourism development led to changes in the organisation of community capitals and needs due to the availability of cash flows, tourism infrastructure and employment opportunities, conditions that did not exist before. In terms of CECT, the community has partnerships with three private safari companies to run CH1, CH2 and Ngoma Lodge (see Figure 4.2). In CH1 and CH2 (now both photographic areas), a number of locals were employed as hunting assistants during the hunting season while others were employed as community patrol officers. The community also employs drivers for the six tractors they own, as well as office staff who are responsible for the day-to-day running of CECT.

The partnership with Ngoma Lodge has provided employment for 36 community members. The hunting tourism also provided the community with game meat and revenue (Stone and Nyaupane, 2016).

At Khama Rhino Sanctuary Trust, participation in tourism has also created employment opportunities. According to Stone and Stone (2011), by 2009, employment figures had risen to 48, up from 26 in 2004; casual labourers are also employed when the need arose. Although casual wages may be low, they are still beneficial to communities with no alternative options for generating income (Ashley, 2000), and such employment can boost a family's living standard.

Diversified livelihood options

Results indicate that in 1993, after consultations, meetings, workshops and trainings, the five CECT villages elected a CECT board. External assistance from donor agencies such as the African Development Foundation (ADF), African Wildlife Foundation (AWF), Kalahari Conservation Society (KCS) and United States of America International Development (USAID) provided community training that was crucial in organising community social capital as the foundation for community participation in tourism in both communities. At CECT, the community had a choice between hunting for subsistence or selling their hunting quota to professional hunters – they settled on selling the quota. The selling of the wildlife quota generated significant community income, as illustrated in Figure 4.3. Income generated is distributed to CECT households and invested in community projects that are agreed upon during annual general meetings.

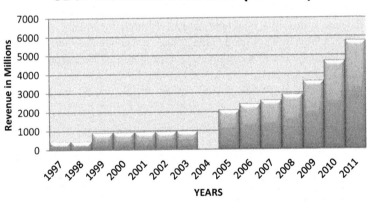

US$1 = BWP 10. 39 as at August 16, 2018

Figure 4.3 Revenue generated by CECT from 1997 to 2011

Source: Authors' data (compiled from CECT's community data baseline (2012) and Revenue records (2011))

Results also show that after the adoption of tourism, the community's culture has become a resource which tourists are interested in and eager to pay for, in the form of staged performances, arts and artefacts. Livelihood options have been diversified and the community's financial capital has improved through advancements in subsistence agriculture, facilitated by benefits from tourism. Results further show that subsistence arable farming has flourished due to the availability of tractors purchased using tourism income. Community members also observed that the over-reliance on tourism was risky; to mitigate the risk, they have reinvested some of the revenue from tourism to buy tractors to help villagers during the ploughing season. The increased revenue generation has also created other livelihood options such as brick moulding workshops, telephone centres and sales from community-owned shops (see Figure 4.4, Plates B, C, D & F).

The new cash economy has led to changing housing structures, from traditional housing to more modern styles; from travelling to Kasane for shopping to shopping in the CECT area; from fencing of crop fields with tree branches to steel wire; from intensive labour to mechanically intensive agriculture; from using artefacts for cultural purposes to selling them to tourists; and the development of a community lodge. Figure 4.4 summarises how participation in tourism has changed community capitals and needs and widened livelihood options. The transition to modern housing is attributed in part to money earned through community-based tourism.

At KRST, community members have an opportunity to sell their commodities at the KRST main entrance. Furthermore, benefits accrue to local house owners in Paje village through the renting of their houses to KRST employees. Thus, tourism at KRST has helped diversify rural livelihoods and has created other income-generating options. In addition, some goods and services are now available for purchase locally. These include food, petrol and diesel from a locally owned filling station, roofing poles, thatching grass and welding. The trust also buys arts and crafts from a San project in a nearby village, thus generating even wider community gains. The use of locally sourced materials creates more economic multiplier effects as most of the income is kept within the local economy.

Empowerment and community participation

To address human capital deficits, four youths from the community were granted scholarships to study tourism at colleges in South Africa. Upon completion of their studies, they are obligated to work for CECT. Furthermore, training workshops for skills and capacity building for the CECT board by government, donors and NGO agencies have been very instrumental. It was also important for the community to hire trained and competent professionals – the CECT manager, programme officer and accountant – to fill in the human capital deficit.

While other forms of community capitals were in short supply, the natural capital was abundant at the CECT community's disposal. For a very long time, this intensified human-wildlife conflicts. However, due to its participation in tourism, the community acquired photography and hunting tourism licences and began

Plate A: Community housing transformation – from mud and reeds to cement bricks and corrugated irons and better sanitation in the

Plate B: CECT community shop was built to cut the distance for community members to travel to the nearby town of Kasane

Plate C: Field crop fencing transformation from tree branches to steel wire fencing. A community member was busy putting the fence during data collection around his field

Plate D: Draught power – six tractors with ploughing implements were bought to help CECT community to till the soil

Plate E: Ngoma Lodge – a community project provides tourists with hospitality services and has employed local

Plate F: cultural capital transformed to serve tourists with souvenir artefacts – generating income for CECT women

Figure 4.4 Physical assets attained from tourism participation

legally harvesting wild resources and developing wildlife management area plans. After satisfying these criteria, they were granted user rights in the form of a wildlife quota for hunting and photographic tourism. Meetings, workshops and training between the community and other stakeholders enhanced community networks, bonding, trust and partnerships with private companies, including hunting and photographic safari companies, donors, NGOs and government. The interactions strengthened social cohesion and fostered better relationships with stakeholders.

External assistance was fundamental in organising the community's social capital as the foundation for community participation in tourism. The formation of tourism planning committees made up of members from the five villages brought the five villages together. Before participation in tourism, there was lack of a community voice, tourism institutions, leadership skills in tourism and devolution of power to manage wildlife, among others. Participation empowered the community to form a board to run CECT, followed by the development of the CECT constitution, land use and management plans, CHAs development and community consultations through annual general meetings.

Natural resource conservation

Participation in tourism has benefited both the CECT community and Chobe National Park (CNP) through, for instance, decreases in occurrences of wild fires and poaching. Police records indicate that poaching incidences recorded are lower than in areas that do not participate in community-based tourism activities (see Table 4.2).

On the other hand, KRST has made significant strides in the reintroduction of rhinos. Starting with four rhinos in 1993, in 2015 KRST had over 50 rhinos; over 20 had also been translocated to other areas in Botswana (Baiphethi, 2015). In addition, KRST offers environmental education to Batswana and tourists. The trust has an Environmental Education Centre (EEC). Operational since 2003, the

Table 4.2 Poaching and related crimes 2001–2012

Type of Crime	Reported & Registered Cases: CECT Area	Reported & Registered Cases: Non-CECT Area
Unlawful possession of government trophy	10	21
Hunting and capturing game	01	09
Hunting protected animals	03	17
Hunting partially protected game	05	18
Hunting without hunting permit	17	34
Hunting outside permitted hunting season	02	23
Total	38	122

Source: Compiled from Kachikau & Kasane Police Stations Case Registries

EEC hosts many tourists, especially school children. It provides them with information on environmental management and conservation. Although the KRST is famous for its rhino breeding, it also has 230 species of birds and more than 30 other animal species (Baiphethi, 2015).

Challenges

The results show that the financial achievements have enabled the acquiring of six tractors, subsequently improving subsistence arable production, which additionally contributes to the CECT community's physical capital attainment. The transition from labour-intensive agriculture to the use of tractors has led to the mechanisation of agriculture. Before, traditional farming was predominantly employed to cultivate the land, resulting in fewer hectares being tilled and low yields.

While there is an overall positive community capitals change, results also indicate an inverse relationship to this new development as increases in the ploughing area have also increased human–wildlife conflicts. The accessibility of draught power has created the need for more agricultural land. Table 4.3 summarises changes in land use, agricultural production and wildlife conservation dynamisms. For instance, from 2005 to 2012 there was a constant increase in areas ploughed, planted and yield harvested as well as in the number of community beneficiaries. At the same time, the area of crops lost to wildlife damage and flooding increased too, an indication that land that may be prone to flooding and wildlife corridors are being colonised by crop production, mainly triggered by the mechanisation of agriculture.

Table 4.3 Crop production and yield outputs from the year 2006 to 2012

Year	2005/ 2006	2006/ 2007	2007/ 2008	2008/ 2009	2009/ 2010	2010/ 2011	2011/ 2012
Area ploughed (ha)	556.90	869.97	990.12	1524.19	1800.69	1873.33	2131.88
Area planted (ha)	556.90	869.97	990.12	1524.19	1795.12	1788.47	2131.88
Yield Harvested (kg/ha)	223.64	272.00	483.13	262.33	593.93	638.98	789.77
Beneficiaries	222	222	503	580	601	654	689
Area (ha) lost to wildlife damage	*	*	*	446.56	472.48	497.19	*
Area (ha) lost to flooding	*	*	*	57.84	136.87	188.22	*

Sources: Compiled from the District Agricultural Office Assistant Field Officer's records

* Missing data

Furthermore, at KRST, although employment has been created, the rate at which it has been created is slow. In addition, the reliance on external donors makes the sustainability of the project questionable. Results also indicate that some community members are passive participants who are not involved in the day-to-day running and decision-making of the business enterprise. Some community members also highlighted a loss of natural resources since the commencement of tourism. These include communal land, access to roofing poles, thatching grass and wild fruits.

Discussion

By adopting the community capitals framework, the chapter provides a holistic assessment in understanding the linkages among protected areas, tourism and community livelihoods. The findings provide insights essential for devising adaptability measures to reconcile conflicts that exist between protected areas, tourism and community livelihoods. The adoption of tourism led to changes of community capitals structure and organisation and in the process brought multiple and multi-scalar drivers of change in community needs at both community and household levels. The community capitals framework is useful as it has multiple indicators, represented by the seven forms of capital that are at interplay to define the degree at which the community is ready to participate or adopt tourism as a new livelihood option.

The use of the CCF revealed that it is crucial to first recognise the essence of organising the social capital, leading to the formation of CECT and KRST through the assistance of other stakeholders such as NGOs, donors and government agencies. The social capital through the CECT and KRST formation linked participating villages together to promote village networks and partnerships. Social capital has indeed been proposed as the 'missing link' in development (Gutierrez-Montes, Emery, and Fernandez-Baca, 2009; Jones, 2005).

The CECT and KRST boards provide the political capital and will to lead: they consult with the general membership, take decisions, outsource services and account for the welfare of the community, creating a political sphere to lead the tourism project. The CECT and KRST boards sought external funding from NGOs and donor agencies to bridge the community's financial capital gap, in line with Aigner, Flora, and Hernandez's (2001) observation that political capital represents power and community connections to people who have power. In view of this systems interdependence of community capitals, we can argue that the improved social, political and financial capitals' connections provided the basis to influence the community's use of the natural capital. The engagement in tourism development consequentially yielded the financial capital from tourism, which was then invested further in acquiring human capital (hiring professionals – managers and accountants) and physical capital (EEC, restaurant, safari cars, tractors, lodge, shops, better houses). The mechanisation and intensification of agriculture benefitting from finances accrued from tourism resulted in more demand for land for cropping, leading to colonisation of land that is prone to flooding as well as blocking wildlife pathways or corridors to the river waters.

The heightened human-wildlife conflicts may not be linked to the increase in wildlife numbers, but could alternatively be explained by the attainment of more physical assets due to the availability of draught power in the form of tractors, consequentially blocking animals' access to the river. In view of these combinations of positive and negative feedback loops, while tourism development is credited for improved community livelihoods at CECT and KRST, it is also accountable for accelerating changes in community needs. In this respect, the sustainability of PAs, tourism and community livelihoods in the long term becomes debatable.

The biggest challenge to PAs managers, tourism developers and community development planners is to develop mitigation measures that can reconcile these unintended outcomes. As Weaver (2002) argues, the challenge for PA tourism is not the absence of any resulting negative impacts, but rather the ongoing intent by managers to pursue sustainability outcomes in line with the best available knowledge and to quickly and effectively address any negative impacts that inadvertently arise from tourism core activities. Stone and Nyaupane (2017) caution that we must be vigilant in remembering the dangers that arise from a tendency to engage in short-term, geographically bounded thinking. Applying the systems thinking approach could be a good policy communication device for all stakeholders involved in community tourism projects. We cannot think of tourism development without accounting for the physical, cultural, social, political, economic and ecological contexts for rural development processes.

Conclusion

Before tourism development, the CNP and KRST were not linked to other community capitals. Rather, they were treated as sovereign systems that had nothing to do with each other. This perceived relationship inhibited the linkages between CNP, KRST and the CECT community. Regardless of the community's endowment with natural capital, the 'asset flow' was technically 'locked' and could not be converted to benefit other forms of community capitals. To harness the natural capital, other capitals systematically needed to be enhanced first to create a foundation on which the CECT community could build blocks and adopt tourism to complement their livelihood opportunities. Sustainable tourism development calls for the involvement of local communities at destination areas as the custodians of the resources that attract tourists.

From a methodological perspective, this study makes an important contribution to the literature by demonstrating the importance of more holistic analyses of tourism's performance and contribution to both conservation and community development. The same holistic approach as demonstrated by the use of the CCF is informed by the adoption of systems thinking management regimes to reconcile the unintended consequences emanating from the interaction between protected areas, tourism and community livelihoods. As the upsurge of accommodating tourism by PAs moves forward, it will be of importance to closely monitor and evaluate not only its advancement, but also how PAs and communities incorporate change, as communities and natural resources are dynamic and change is inevitable.

References

Ackoff, R. (1981). *Creating the corporate future.* New York: John Wiley and Sons.

Aigner, S., Flora, C., and Hernandez, J. M. (2001). The premise and promise of citizenship and civil society for renewing democracies and empowering sustainable communities. *Sociological Inquiry, 71,* 493–507.

Aigner, S., Raymond, V., and Smidt, L. (2002). "Whole community organizing" for the 21st century. *Community Development, 33*(1), 86–106.

Anderson, K. (2012). Local governance of forests and the role of external organizations: Some ties matter more than others. *World Development, 43,* 226–237.

Anney, V. N. (2014). Ensuring the quality of the findings of qualitative research: Looking at trustworthiness criteria. *Journal of Emerging Trends in Educational Research and Policy Studies (JETERAPS), 5*(2), 272–281.

Anon. (1991). *Chambers concise English dictionary.* Edinburgh: W. and R. Chambers.

Ashley, C. (2000). *Pro-poor tourism: Putting poverty at the heart of the tourism agenda.* London: Department for International Development.

Baiphethi, T. (2015). *Khama Rhino Sanctuary, Botswana.* Retrieved August 12, 2018, from http://safaritalk.net/topic/15053-thapelo-t-baiphethi-khama-rhino-sanctuary-botswana/

Braun, V., and Clarke, V. (2006). Using thematic analysis in psychology. *Qualitative Research in Psychology, 3*(2), 77–101.

CECT. (2011). *CECT revenue generated record from 1997–2011: Financial Report.* Kasane, Botswana.

Emery, M., Fey, S., and Flora, C. (2006). *Using community capitals to develop assets for positive community change Practice.* Retrieved August 13, 2018, from www.commdev. org/index.php?option=com_content&view=article&i

Flora, C. (2005). Social aspects of small water systems. *Journal of Contemporary Water Research, 126,* 6–12.

Flora, C., Flora, J., and Fey, S. (2004). *Rural communities: Legacy and change* (2nd ed.). Boulder, CO: Westview Press.

CECT. (2012). *Community data base: community baseline information inventory report 2010–2012.* Kasane, Botswana.

Forrester, J. W. (1961). *Industrial dynamics.* Cambridge, MA: MIT Press.

Ghimire, K., and Pimbert, M. (1997). Social change and conservation: An overview of issues and concepts. In K. Ghimire and M. Pimbert (Eds.), *Social change and conservation environmental politics and impacts of national parks and protected areas* (pp. 1–45). London: Earthscan.

Grossman, and Associates. (n.d.). *Management and development plan for the Khama Rhino Sanctuary Trust.* Publisher Unknown.

Gutierrez-Montes, I., Emery, M., and Fernandez-Baca, E. (2009). The sustainable livelihoods approach and the community capitals framework: The importance of system-level approaches to community change efforts. *Community Development, 40*(2), 106–113.

Holling, C., and Chambers, A. (1973). Resource science: The nurture of an infant. *BioScience, 23*(1), 13–20.

IUCN. (1994). *Guidelines for protected area management categories.* Gland: Author.

Janishevski, L., Noonan-Mooney, K., Gidda, S. B., and Mulongoy, K. J. (2008). *Protected areas in today's world: Their values and benefits for the welfare of the planet* (CBD Technical Series (36). Montreal: UNEP.

Jones, S. (2005). Community-based ecotourism: The significance of social capital. *Annals of Tourism Research, 32*(2), 303–324.

Karanth, K., and DeFries, R. (2010). Nature-based tourism in Indian protected areas: New challenges for park management. *Conservation Letters, 11*, 1–13.

Lincoln, Y. S., and Guba, E. G. (1994). Competing paradigms in qualitative research. *Handbook of Qualitative Research*, 105–117.

Maguire, M., and Delahunt, B. (2017). Doing a thematic analysis: A practical, step-by-step guide for learning and teaching scholars. *AISHE-J: The All Ireland Journal of Teaching and Learning in Higher Education, 9*(3).

McCool, S. F. (2009). Constructing partnerships for protected area tourism planning in an era of change and messiness. *Journal of Sustainable Tourism, 17*(2), 133–148.

Mearns, K., and Lukhele, S. (2015). Addressing the operational challenges of community-based tourism in Swaziland. *African Journal of Hospitality, Tourism and Leisure, 4*(1), 1–13.

Nowell, L., Norris, J., White, D., and Moules, N. (2017). Thematic analysis: Striving to meet the trustworthiness criteria, *International Journal of Qualitative Methods, 16*, 1–13.

Nyaupane, G., and Poudel, S. (2011). Linkages among biodiversity, livelihood, and tourism. *Annals of Tourism Research, 38*(4), 1344–1366.

Sebele, L. (2010). Community-based tourism ventures, benefits and challenges: Khama rhino sanctuary trust, central district, Botswana. *Tourism Management, 31*, 136–146.

Sebele, L. S. (2006). *The social impacts of community-based tourism: A case study of Khama Rhino Sanctuary Trust in the Central District of Botswana* (M.A. Dissertation), University of the Witwatersrand, Johannesburg.

Stake, R. E. (2010). *Qualitative research: Studying how things work*. New York: Guilford Press.

Statistics Botswana. (2012). *2011 Botswana population and housing census*. Gaborone: Statistics Botswana.

Stone, L., and Stone, M. (2011). Community-based tourism enterprises: Challenges and prospects for community participation: Khama rhino sanctuary trust, Botswana. *Journal of Sustainable Tourism, 19*, 97–114.

Stone, M., and Nyaupane, G. (2014). Rethinking community in community-based natural resource management. *Community Development, 45*(1), 17–31.

Stone, M., and Nyaupane, G. (2016). Protected areas, tourism and community livelihoods linkages: A comprehensive analysis approach. *Journal of Sustainable Tourism, 24*(5), 673–693.

Stone, M., and Nyaupane, G. (2017). Ecotourism influence on community needs and the functions of protected areas: A systems thinking approach. *Journal of Ecotourism, 16*(3), 222–246.

UNEP-WCMC and IUCN. (2016). *Protected planet report 2016*. Cambridge, UK and Gland, Switzerland: UNEP-WCMC and IUCN.

Weaver, D. (2002). *Ecotourism*. Brisbane: Wiley.

Weng, X., Lv, X., and Li, X. (2016). Study on the implementation mechanism of symbiosis theory used in economic field. *Economics, 5*(4), 56–63.

5 How community-based tourism can survive in turbulent environments

The Mahenye CAMPFIRE project, Zimbabwe

Takaruza Munyanyiwa, Shepherd Nyaruwata and Cleopas Njerekai

Introduction

Governments across most of Southern Africa have embraced the concept of community-based tourism (CBT) in their tourism development agendas as a way of ensuring that rural communities benefit from local resources. This chapter highlights the challenges and conditions for survival for CBT operating in turbulent environments, using the case of the Mahenye community project in Chiredzi, Zimbabwe. The Mahenye CBT project's resilience is particularly notable and interesting in the face of Zimbabwe's volatile economic and political climate.

The CBT approach emerged through a combination of progressive actions by governments, donors, non-governmental organisations, tourism companies and communities themselves (Miller, 2004). CBT may be defined as a form of tourism where the local community has substantial control over and involvement in its development and management and where a major proportion of the benefits remain within the community (Denman, 2001). The World Tourism Organization (2014) argues that in order for CBT to be sustainable, it should give full and fair participation to local people throughout the tourism planning and development process.

CBT has, along with other integrated conservation and development schemes, gained popularity over the last three decades. It has emerged as one of the most promising methods of integrating natural resource conservation, local income generation and cultural conservation, particularly in the developing world (Miller, 2004). The CBT approach takes economic, environmental and socio-cultural sustainability into account. This means that, ideally, projects must be managed and owned by the community. However, in practice, different types of tourism projects will assume different forms and functions for various reasons, and how they are developed and managed will influence the degree to which they can contribute to the development of the community.

CBT can contribute towards protecting local cultures from the influence of globalisation through creating cultural awareness and pride within the community. In addition, CBT provides, expands and improves sources of livelihood and opportunities to earn income, which in developing economies is typically used to fund basic living needs, education, healthcare, sanitation and accommodation facilities. As such, CBT is considered a viable form of tourism for improving the living standards of underprivileged communities in remote, rural, impoverished, marginalised, economically depressed, undeveloped, poor, indigenous and ethnic minority areas and of people in small towns (Tasci, Semrad, and Yilmaz, 2013). Table 5.1 shows different kinds of CBT products.

Literature review

Overview of CBT

CBT is fast becoming a popular experience for travellers seeking unique interactions with local communities at the destination. However, the level and nature of community involvement in tourism development varies dramatically, from degrees of tokenism to full community control (Arnstein, 1969; Connor, 1988; Tosun, 2006). Firello and Bo (2012) posit that counteractions to conventional/mass tourism and the 'expectations of the new tourists' facilitate and enable the development of alternative forms of tourism such as pro-poor tourism, volunteer tourism, ecotourism and community-based ecotourism.

In the past few decades, tourism has not only been recognised for its financial benefits but also for increasing the involvement of communities in planning and management of resources. The following countries have been identified as leading in CBT: Bolivia, Brazil, Cuba, Ecuador, Laos, Guatemala, Indonesia, Peru, Morocco, South Africa, Tanzania and Thailand (Tasci et al., 2013). Across these countries, the CBT participatory development has, to varying degrees, empowered local community members by building the skills, knowledge and confidence needed to take control over their land and resources (Tasci et al., 2013). When CBT is conducted effectively, the results bear minimal costs and maximum benefits of tourism. Successful CBT may bring to a community healthy economic development, cultural and environmental awareness, cross-cultural understanding and

Table 5.1 CBT products

Accommodation	Activities	Attractions
• bed and breakfast • family home stay • traditional homes/huts • open air tents • tree houses • rest camps • compound family lodges	• boat trips • cycling • cooking workshops • traditional dancing • handcraft workshops • nature trails hiking • village tours • tea and coffee/wine tours • volunteering	• archaeological sites • cultural centres • cultural gastronomic heritage and route trails farms • folk groups • landscape sceneries • local markets • museums • plantations • wildlife sanctuaries

peace and sustainable destination development. Rural communities will then have their own sources of income to complement often volatile agriculture income, rather than depending on government handouts (Sebele, 2010; Tasci et al., 2013).

According to Giampiccoli and Saayman (2017), CBT is not inferior to conventional tourism and neither are other alternative forms such as pro-poor tourism (PPT), CBT and ecotourism. Properly managed CBT projects can appeal to diverse tourism markets. Studies have shown that the CBT market profile consists generally of travellers who are well-educated, have a relatively high income and are relatively experienced (CBI, 2016). CBT travellers may be categorised into 'hard' and 'soft' segments. Soft CBT travellers desire some comfort and form the majority of the market (Nowaczek and Smale, 2010). They are generally interested in culture, adventure and interaction with locals. Hard travellers, on the other hand, are interested in deeper interactions with locals and stay longer at the destination.

Studies show that the older generation is the largest group of CBT travellers. Europe, a key source market, has a relatively large generation of people between 50 and 70 years old, a time- and money-rich segment. Often their children have moved out, or they are entering retirement. They are less tied to summer holidays and travel more in the low season. The segment is mainly interested in soft adventure activities, combined with luxury (CBI, 2016).

Critical success factors of CBT

A number of critical success factors for CBT operations have been identified in various studies (Tasci et al., 2013; Denman, 2001):

1   Full participation by community stakeholders members in decision-making;
2   Community attachment that encourages strong member relationship at all levels;
3   Equitable and transparent sharing of benefits of dividends;
4   Members must have equal opportunity to input and share resources;
5   Joint conservation programme responsibility including management;
6   Collaboration among stakeholders working towards sustainable programs;
7   Local ownership and buy-in from the community; and
8   Local leadership form the core of implementation of programme and high visitor satisfaction.

Southern African Development Community (SADC)
trends and challenges

Southern African countries have adopted policies that promote sustainable tourism development. South Africa, Botswana, Zimbabwe, Tanzania and Zambia have made significant strides in promoting CBT. Community-Based Natural Resource Management (CBNRM) programmes in these countries are now being implemented across different resources, including veld products initiatives in Botswana, artisanal fisheries in Zambia/Zimbabwe/Malawi and forestry resources in Mozambique. South Africa has a number of notable cases. For example, Sunder, its Fair Trade Tourism South Africa (FTSA) scheme, has awarded certification to CBT businesses such as the Masakala Traditional Guest House, owned by Mehloding Community Tourism Trust. The Trust represents 25 villages including Masakala, which accommodates up to 12 guests in traditional accommodation. The accommodation features indigenous designs and was built using a government grant to create temporary jobs in the village. Village residents are employed as field guides for tourists. The guest house is a base for hiking, horse riding, rock art viewing, birding and cultural excursions (Miller, 2004).

The drive for the adoption of pragmatic programs and policies across the Southern African region is driven by recognition of the importance of CBT as a stimulant of employment, infrastructure development partnerships, increased NGO presence, experiment products, financial benefits from the income realised, new knowledge and skills development. However, the implementation of various pro-CBT policies into actions faces a plethora of challenges, including conflicts over resource ownership, limited project managerial and operational skills, lack of interest in participation among community members, incompatibility of policies and legislation, low quality and standard of products and services and weak cooperation among stakeholders (Mathiseon and Wall, 1982; Meseret, 2015). Cooper (2004) identified infrastructural challenges as a major challenge in the sustainable development of CBT.

The Zimbabwe CAMPFIRE programme

Zimbabwe's Communal Areas Management Programme for Indigenous Resources (CAMPFIRE) was borne out of the Zimbabwean government's drive to involve rural communities in natural resources conservation. This was achieved through the devolving of user rights of natural resources including wildlife to rural communities (Taylor and Murphree, 2007). Through the department of National Parks and Wildlife Management (DNPWLM), now the Parks and Wildlife Management Authority (PWMA), the government instituted a policy of devolving Appropriate Authority (AA) to the rural communities through the Rural District Councils (RDCs). This was accomplished through the amendment of the 1975 Parks and Wildlife Act in 1982 (Taylor, 2007). The amendment gave rural communities the legal right of utilising wildlife resources through RDCs. The programme aimed at promoting rural development and sustainable land use based on wildlife in agriculturally marginal rural areas.

The programme was initially introduced in a few rural districts such as Mahenye in Manicaland and Nyaminyami in Mashonaland West. However, it is now being implemented in 58 rural district councils covering a total area of 50,000 square kilometres of the country's land mass (CAMPFIRE Association, 2015). The operational models entail a variety of joint venture partnership and local community owned and managed business entities.

The majority of rural communities concentrated initially on the exploitation of wildlife through consumptive tourism mainly because hunting brought quick financial benefits, which the whole community could easily appreciate. The policy gave clear guidelines on how income from wildlife resources was to be shared between the three parties involved, namely the RDCs, the communities and the CAMPFIRE Association. The rural district councils were to retain 41% of the income, the communities were entitled to receive 55%, and the remaining 4% was allocated to the Association (Taylor, 2009)

The policy assumption was that rural communities would value wildlife more because of the financial and the social benefits they were receiving and therefore meaningfully participate in the conservation of the resource. However, the programme has not been without its challenges. In particular, the involvement of Rural District Councils has given rise to conflicts as rural communities have consequently been left relatively disempowered. For example, in big game hunting CBT, RDCs are reported to stall the process of disbursing funds after collecting hunting fees. These practices have in many instances soured the relationships between the rural councils and the communities, and in turn diminished rural communities' interests in participating in wildlife conservation (Taylor, *ibid*).

Nonetheless, project revenues have been used for a range of community development projects, including drilling boreholes, building school classrooms and teachers' housing, and upgrading road infrastructure (CAMFIRE Association annual report, 2016). As a result, the CAMPFIRE programme has had a significant overall impact in changing the ambivalent attitude of rural communities towards biodiversity conservation. Table 5.2 shows the incomes that have collected from consumptive tourism in 14 districts in 2014.

The success of the CAMPFIRE programme has encouraged other countries in the region to implement similar programmes. For example, in 1996 the government of Namibia amended the 1975 Nature Conservancy Ordinance and introduced a new act which established conservancies in the country. The act gave

Table 5.2 Zimbabwe income from consumptive tourism in 2014

District	*Income($)*
Beitbridge	118055
Bubi	21270
Binga	91770
Bulilima	68995
Hwange	89170
Chipinge	106605
Chiredzi	287856
Gokwe North	32718
Matobo	28981
Nyaminyami	283695
Tsholotsho	420500
Umuguza	32500

Source: CA 2015 internal reports: 2015

rights on wildlife and tourism to rural communities that formed themselves into conservancies (Government of Namibia, 1996). In 1998, the Namibian government authorised the establishment of four conservancies which included, for example, the Torra Conservancy in the Kunene province in northern Namibia. By 2008, the number had grown to 50, and in 2017 they stood at 84 (Namibia Association of CBNRM Support Organizations- NACSO, 2018). Some conservancies are involved in consumptive tourism; others are involved in photographic safaris and the provision of accommodation facilities (Jones and Weaver, 2009). The majority of the communities owning conservancies operate their businesses through different types of joint venture arrangements with the private sector (*ibid*). The programme has helped communities to use proceeds from the businesses to invest in social amenities like schools and clinics. There is also evidence that the participation of rural communities in the conservancies has led to a decrease in poaching and an increase in endangered wildlife populations in provinces such as Kunene (*ibid*, 227).

The Mahenye Project

The Mahenye ward is located in the Chipinge District in Manicaland province, covering an area of 210 square kilometres (Zunza, 2012). The Mahenye community is made up of the Shangaani people who have managed to retain their traditional culture despite a range of modern influences. They were removed from their original homesteads in the 1980s by the government to make way for the creation of the Gonarezhou National Park. The community resented the government's action because it robbed them of one of their traditional livelihood sources, namely wildlife hunting, which supplemented subsistence farming. The community responded by resorting to wildlife poaching as an act of defiance towards the government.

When the Zimbabwean government adopted the policy of devolution of natural resources to rural communities in 1982, Mahenye was chosen as one of the first few areas targeted for the new CBT concept. Accordingly, the Chipinge RDC was granted Appropriate Authority status in 1991 (Zunza, 2012). The Mahenye community was assisted by the CAMPFIRE Association in creating an appropriate institutional framework and a constitution that governed the operations of the community venture.

The project has gone through a phase of growth, decline and recovery. During the period from 1991 to 1999, the project experienced consistent growth, receiving a wide range of benefits at both household and community levels (Zunza, 2012). The project then faced a crisis during the period 2000 to 2008 because of the economic and political challenges Zimbabwe as a whole was experiencing. Since 2009, there has been marked improvement in income and in recent years the community has embarked on further diversification of the project (*ibid*).

The geographical location of the Mahenye CAMPFIRE project has given it some leverage in terms of its resilience. CAMPFIRE projects particularly thrive in close proximity to national parks. The Mahenye Ward is located 47 km from the edge of Gonarezhou National Park (Sithole, 2006), one of Zimbabwe's biggest national parks and tourist magnets. Wildlife is therefore abundant in the ward, as the locale serves as a wildlife dispersal area. The abundant wildlife has helped the project to withstand the negative impacts of climate change and its associated dry spells. The revenue streams from wildlife-related activities have therefore continued to flow to the local community (CAMPFIRE Association, 2015).

The Mahenye conceptual model

From the onset, the project was operated as a joint venture partnership driven through a Public Sector–NGO–Private Sector–Community model, that is, Chipinge RDC–CAMPFIRE Association–Private Contractor–Mahenye Community (Figure 5.1). Over the course of its existence, new stakeholders have been brought into the project. However, this has not changed the core principles of the model adopted at its inception in 1991.

The community income initially came from consumptive tourism (mainly trophy hunting), which was shared with the Chipinge Rural District Council and

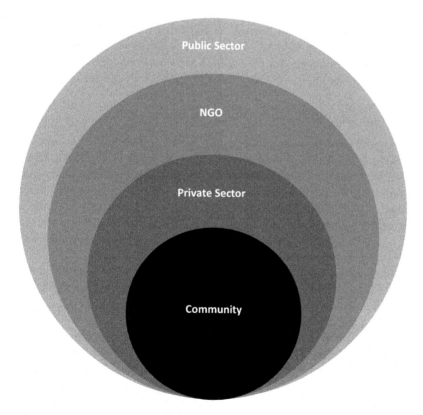

Figure 5.1 Mahenye Project conceptual model

CAMPFIRE Association as stipulated by the 1982 Act. However, in 1990 the community through the Chipinge RDC entered into a contractual arrangement with one of the country's major hotel groups, African Sun, whereby the company took a 10-year land lease agreement to construct Chilo and Mahenye lodges. The agreement entailed the company paying 8% of its gross revenue to the RDC, which then passed on 80% of the revenue to the Mahenye community (Zunza, 2012).

However, the decline of the tourism industry, which began in 2000 following the infamous land redistribution programme in Zimbabwe, saw the hotel group disinvesting from the Mahenye area. The properties were taken over by River Lodges Holdings, whose major shareholder is a local entrepreneur, Clive Stockil, who has had a long relationship with the Mahenye community (*ibid*).

The Mahenye CBT is currently expanding its activities through the development of integrated wildlife conservation and agriculture. The integrated project will create opportunities for the community to diversify its product base through undertaking photographic safaris, sale of live wildlife for breeding purposes and processing of game meat products, value addition and niche products distribution (WILD, 2016).

The Mahenye CAMPFIRE project has demonstrated tremendous resilience in its 30 years of existence and, notwithstanding internal challenges, the project has survived several major external shocks, in the form of recurrent droughts, withdrawal of donor funding and the political and economic crisis the country has experienced in the last two decades, as mentioned already (Zunza, 2012).

Community benefits

The benefits brought by the projects can be assessed at both community level and at the individual household level. At the community level, income from the project was used to undertake further income-generating activities that included the following: the purchase of two grinding mills which bring an average monthly income of USD 1200 since 2010 (Zunza, 2012); the construction of a grocery shop, where members of the community are able to access a number of their basic needs; and the purchase of a 35-tonne truck which is hired out to the members of the community and other organisations within the area.

Households earn small cash dividends, proportional to the total income generated. The project has also invested in a number of social projects, including the construction of classroom blocks and teachers' houses at the local primary school, construction of a clinic, access to electricity and piped water, and the grading of the road connecting the community and joining the Chiredzi-Mutare highway. In addition, the project has generated employment for villagers. Of the 28 workers employed by the Chilo lodge in 2012, only one was from outside the Mahenye community (*ibid*). The project further employs a number of people in its income-generating projects as well as security guards who monitor potential wildlife poachers. This has seen poaching drop by over 90%.

Key survival factors of the project

The resilience of the Mahenye project can be attributed to a number of factors:

A cohesive community with a strong culture and ethos that are centred on traditional leadership

The strong bonding of the community centred on its Shangaani culture has helped to maintain community cohesion in the face of many internal and external challenges.

An institutional framework that allowed open dialogue between the different stakeholders

The participatory framework empowered communities to become highly involved in determining their developmental trajectory. The model has ensured broad community and other stakeholder participation through the involvement of two ministries and their executive arms and several cascading committees at district, ward and village levels. Regular re-election of committee members, auditing of financial records and annual general meetings are also conducted to fortify the levels of community participation.

The presence of a local entrepreneur who understood and shared the common values of the Shangaani people

Clive Stockil, who grew up with the Shangaani people, is trusted by the community as one of their own. He has helped the community to navigate the government bureaucracy, the often ambiguous agendas of NGOs and private sector contractual details. His role helped to shield the community from predatory practices, which can often arise in these types of ventures, and at the same time helped to increase the confidence of the community in the project.

The presence of abundant wildlife and a pristine ecosystem

The large numbers of wildlife in the area ensured that the community was allocated viable annual hunts which brought meaningful income to the community. Furthermore, the new integrated project the community is currently embarking on is likely to further entrench community ownership of their natural resources because it is planned to directly involve more members of the community in agricultural and other activities.

Diversified sources of income

Since its inception, the Mahenye CAMPFIRE project has consistently been judged as a model project because of its diversified sources of income. Today, the project still generates its income from various wildlife and tourism activities including sport hunting whose concessions contribute about 70% of the income, game-viewing and photographic safaris, revenue from accommodation facilities such as Chilo Gorge and Mahenye Lodges, cultural tourism and other ecotourism activities. Other revenue streams include donor funds from NGOs such as the UK-based Mahenye Charitable Trust and several others.

Challenges

The main challenges encountered by the CAMPFIRE programme in various contexts include:

1   Internal institutional framework challenges which hamper the effective operation of the programme;
2   Lack of effective marketing strategies;
3   Limited skilled labour and business acumen/exposure;
4   Accessibility challenges because of remote locations;
5   Low-quality product perception in the market;
6   The banning of elephant and ivory-related products;
7   Donor-driven enterprises, where community involvement is superficial, making the projects unsustainable in the long term, if sufficient capacity building does not occur to allow the community to take over; and
8   The community has also faced challenges with hunters who fail to meet their contractual obligations. For example, in the Gaerezi fishing CAMPFIRE project, the communities have complained about the lack of transparency and participation on the part of their marketing partner, Nyanga Downs Fly Fishing Club, who unilaterally set prices for trout fishing without consultations with community members (CAMPFIRE Association, 2007).

Conclusion

The CAMPFIRE programme was introduced as an antidote to the colonial legacy's autocratic approach to natural resource management, which undermined people's control of their resources and criminalised the use of their game. The programme has withstood the test of time and has demonstrated that community tourism development founded and anchored on the CAMPFIRE philosophy and its institutional framework can be resilient even in the face of the toughest external shocks and internal challenges. The programme has been a role model in community tourism development in marginalised rural areas of the country and should be recognised for its innovative way of promoting both tourism and local control of natural resources.

The Mahenye CAMPFIRE project has registered successes on a number of fronts. Poaching has been drastically reduced by over 90%; employment has been generated; roads have been upgraded; and schools, clinics, police stations and grinding mills have been built. In the words of the local leadership, 'CAMPFIRE has turned conflict into cooperation and everyone has benefitted. The community is happy, the parks are happy and the animals are happy. Everyone wins'.

The project confronts a number of challenges into the future, including recurrent droughts, the reduction in donor funding after the land reform programme in 2000 and the banning of elephant and ivory-related products. However, charitable organisations, a diversified revenue base, the abundant wildlife and a highly stable and participatory institutional structure and framework have all ensured that the benefits of this project continue to flow to the local communities. In a more stable macro-political and macro-economic climate, the project could achieve even greater success.

References

Arnstein, S. R. (1969). A ladder of citizen participation. *Journal of the American Institute of Planners, 35*(4), 216–224.

CAMPFIRE Association. (2015). Hunting incomes and distribution Report.

CAMPFIRE Association Report. (2007). Retrieved from www.campfirezimbabwe.org

CBI. (2016). What are the opportunities for community-based tourism from Europe? Ministry of Foreign Affairs of the Netherlands CBI – Centre for the promotion of imports from developing countries.

Connor, D. (1988). A new ladder of citizen participation. *National Civic Review, 77*(3), 1–2. https://doi.org/101002/ncr.4100770309

Cooper, G. (2004). *Community based tourism experiences in the Caribbean: Lessons and key consideration.* Paper presented at the Caribbean tourism organization sixth annual Caribbean conference on sustainable tourism development: 'Keeping the right balance – land and sea encounters.' Havana, Cuba.

Denman, R. (2001). *Guidelines for community based ecotourism development.* Gland: WWF International.

Firello, A., and Bo, D. (2012, October). Community-based ecotourism to meet the new tourist's expectations: An exploratory study. *Journal of Hospitality Marketing and Management, 21*(7). doi:10.1080/19368623.2012.624293

Giampiccoli, A., and Saayman, M. (2017). Community-based tourism, responsible tourism, and infrastructure development and poverty. *African Journal of Hospitality, Tourism and Leisure, 6*(2), 1–28.

Government of Namibia Report. (1996). Retrieved from https:// www.gov.na.org

Jones, B., and Weaver, C. (2009). *CBNRM in Namibia: Growth, Trends Lessons and Constraints: Evolution and Innovation in Wildlife Conservation.* London: Earthscan.

Mathiseon, A., and Wall, G. (1982). *Tourism: Economic, Physical, and Social impacts.* London: Longman.

Meseret, T. (2015). Challenges and opportunities of community based tourism development United Nations World Tourism Organisation (UNWTO in Awi Zone: A case study in Guagusa and Banja Woredas, Ethiopia. *Journal of Tourism, Hospitality and Sports, 11*(1), 50–78.

Miller, K. L. (2004). *Evaluating the design and management of community based ecotourism projects in Guatemala* (Unpublished MSc Thesis), B.S. Montana University, Montana.

Namibia Association of CBNRM Support Organizations. (2018). Retrieved from www.nasco.org/conservancies

Nowaczek, A., and Smale, B. (2010). Exploring the predisposition of travellers to qualify as ecotourists: The Ecotourist Predisposition Scale. *Journal of Ecotourism, 9*(1), 45–61.

Sebele, L. S. (2010). Community-based tourism ventures, benefits and challenges: Khama Rhino Sanctuary Trust, Central District, Botswana. *Tourism Management, 31*(1), 36–146.

Sithole, E. (2006). Trans-boundary environmental actors: The Zambezi society's campaign for sustainable tourism development in the Zambezi Bioregion. *Journal of Sustainable Tourism, 13*(5), 486–503.

Tasci, A. D. S., Semrad, K. J., and Yilmaz, S. S. (2013). *Community based tourism finding the equilibrium in COMCEC context: Setting the Pathway for the Future*. Ankara: COMCEC Coordination Office.

Taylor, M. (2007). *CBNCM for whose benefits? A case study of subsistence hunting on the boundaries of Botswana's Northern Protected Areas* (Occassional paper No.5). Botswana: CBNRM support programme.

Taylor, R. D. (2009). Community based natural resource management in Zimbabwe: The experience of CAMPFIRE. *Biodiversity Conservation, 18*(10), 2563–2583.

Taylor, R. D., and Murphree, M. W. (2007). *Case studies on successful southern African NRM initiatives and their impacts on poverty and governance*. Zimbabwe. IUCN/USAID FRAME.

Tosun, C. (2006). Expected nature of community participation in tourism development. *Tourism Management, 27*(3), 493–504.

WILD. (2016). Retrieved from www.wild.org

World Tourism Organization. (2014). *Tourism highlights report*. Retrieved from www.unwto.org

Zunza, E. (2012). *Local level benefits of CBRM: The case of Mahenye ward campfire*. (Master's Dissertation), Harare, Zimbabwe: University of Zimbabwe.

Part II

Positive Afro-identities and indigenous cultural resources

6 The 'Afro-positive turn'

Undermining Afro-pessimism through Afro-positive digital counter-narratives

Mucha Mkono

Introduction

Positive stories on Africa are scarce across most fields of study, whereas poverty, for instance, is a popular theme. The result is a rather bleak representation that comes to be accepted as the complete reality. It simplifies Africa and African countries as a homogeneous block of hopelessness in need of saving by the West – it reproduces hegemonic, colonial discourses. For tourism, this means that Africa's hosts and guests are cast repeatedly as the hopeless and the saviours, respectively. However, in view of the critical turn in tourism studies and in the social sciences more broadly (Ateljevic, Harris, Wilson, and Collins, 2005; Hollinshead, 2006; Tribe, 2008), more balanced images of Africa are overdue. As Grant, Djomo, and Krause (2016, p. 326) urge, a new kind of scholarship is needed, united by 'the pursuit of an Afro-optimist approach to scholarship on Africa – an approach that seeks to counterbalance Afro-pessimism while acknowledging the challenges and the range of realities faced by actors across all African societies'.

However, in the digital era, an Afro-positive counter-narrative is emerging in various social media, renegotiating the image of the destination and its diverse peoples. Social media narratives are especially important, given their role in shaping perceptions of place in the technology-driven age (Dwivedi, 2009; Hays, Page, and Buhalis, 2013; Tham, Croy, and Mair, 2013). Engaging with these narratives provides the opportunity to redress representational biases in tourism studies, intentional or inadvertent. Thus, in this chapter, essentialist characterisations of Africa are problematised, and assumptions are illuminated. More complex, plural images of Africa are produced, signalling a move towards a more inclusive and nuanced body of knowledge. As Harding (2003) and Wall (2009) put it, new media formats and genres are transforming how Africa is seen in the West – as new technologies have become more widely available in Africa, Africans themselves are creating and distributing their own representations, in the process undermining Afro-pessimism.

Defining Afro-pessimism

The term *Afro-pessimism* was coined by former United States Assistant Secretary of State for African Affairs Chester Crocker, describing African countries' challenges following their independence (Grant et al., 2016). In its most extreme form, Afro-pessimism is an unremittingly bleak view of Africa; the belief that Africa is irredeemably doomed to backwardness and chaos (De Beer, 2010; Gordon and Wolpe, 1998; Momoh, 2003). For Momoh (2003), put simply, Afro-pessimism is a continuation of the 'dark continent' thesis and the view that nothing good can ever come out of Africa. However, Afro-pessimism need not always be extreme or overt.

Momoh (2003, p. 32) further argues that Africa has been constructed and reconstructed as a representation of the West's negative image, 'a discourse that, simultaneously, valorises and affirms Western superiority and absolves it from existential and epistemological violence against Africa'. The resulting Western representations of the continent and its peoples have produced dehumanising stereotypes and racist discourses (Nothias, 2016). Satirising this critique of Western representations, Wainaina (2005) wrote an essay 'How to Write about Africa' in which he derides the way Westerners write about Africa:

> Always use the word 'Africa' or 'Darkness' or 'Safari' in your title . . . Also useful are words such as 'Guerillas', 'Timeless', 'Primordial' and 'Tribal'. . . . In your text, treat Africa as if it were one country. It is hot and dusty with rolling grasslands and . . . tall, thin people who are starving.

Engaging with postcolonial theory

A postcolonial framework is appealing because it creates intellectual spaces for subaltern peoples to speak for themselves, in their own voices, and thus produce cultural discourses in various areas of thought (Aitchison, 2001; Byrd and Rothberg, 2011; Caton and Santos, 2009; Spivak, 1988). This voicing of the subaltern is a key concern of the present study.

The postcolonial critique analyses and problematises discourses of neocolonialism and its over-inclusive terms, questioning the factual and cultural accuracy of homogeneous concepts, such as 'the Third World' and 'the First World'. Furthermore, a postcolonial framework accommodates a more complex rendering of poverty, one that recognises that poverty is not just as an economic measurable phenomenon, but also a moral issue involving moral imperatives and judgments, as well as a personal question relating to individual identity or status, as Dean (1992) puts it. Postcolonial theory illuminates the focus on negative stories and asserts that a 'crisis-driven' representation of Africa, relying on a specific set of vocabulary, creates a peculiar image of Africa, grounded in a colonial repertoire (Nothias, 2016).

A further objective of postcolonial theory is to expose *essentialism*, a term which denotes the dangers inherent to representing subaltern voices in ways that might oversimplify the cultural identity of heterogeneous social groups, and, in the process, create and recreate stereotyped representations of them (Escárcega, 2010; Narayan, 1998; Pande, 2017; Paradies, 2006). In other words, 'postcolonial' is used to describe an attitude of critical engagement with colonialism's consequences and its constructions of knowledge (Yeoh, 2001).

Theorisations of Africa have been communicated via metaphors of darkness, innocence, emptiness, crisis, a basket case in need of imperial saving (Grant et al., 2016). In postcolonial, lexical terms, this has been described as the 'overlexicalisation' of Africa; its effect is to create a form of overpersuasion (Nothias, 2016). Thus postcolonial theory engages with language, discourse, power, ideology, stereotyping and Othering differences (Nothias, 2016). In this relation, for Spivak, postcolonialism also plays the role of identifying and redressing *epistemic violence* – the destruction of non-Western ways of perceiving the world, and the resultant dominance of Western ontologies. Postcolonial theory thus sees the decolonised world as an intellectual space of contradictions, of half-finished processes, of confusions, of hybridity and of liminalities (Lee and Lam, 1998). It argues that resisting the process of Othering is critical for forming constructive debate on Africa (Grant et al., 2016). To do this, postcolonialist scholars must question why Africa is routinely portrayed as a country; a homogenous block of violence, helplessness, human rights abuses and lack of democracy (Nothias, 2016).

Postcolonial theory's particular concern is that the subaltern is not given the opportunity to speak; that African hosts' lived realities are articulated and evaluated by someone else. Analysis of tourism studies in this space, such as pro-poor tourism, volunteer tourism, slum tourism and community-based tourism, reveals indeed that instances where the African subaltern does actually speak are scanty (Alexander, 2012; Burgold and Rolfes, 2013; Gustav, 2004; Meschkank, 2011, 2012). In addition, with only a few exceptions (for example, Ferreira, 2006; Spenceley and Goodwin, 2007; Strickland-Munro, Moore, and Freitag-Ronaldson, 2010), marginalised communities who are directly affected by tourism are rarely voiced in tourism impact studies (for example, Mbaiwa, 2005). These factors contribute to an Afro-pessimistic epistemology that reduces the agency of local communities in relating their own lived experiences.

Excepting a few cases (for example, Sin, 2010), in analyses of volunteer tourism, in particular, there is a preoccupation with the experiences of volunteers (Alexander, 2012; Benson and Seibert, 2009; Stoddart and Rogerson, 2004). For example, Zahra and McIntosh's (2007, p. 116) study analysed

> the nature of the experiences the volunteers had gained; events, experiences, cultural differences that had had an impact on them; things they found the most difficult and also the most personally rewarding. Participants were asked . . . to explain what the lasting impact has been, if at all.

Similarly, Alexander (2012) studied ' the impact of a volunteer tourism experience on international volunteers'. There are a number of other such studies, where the volunteer's personal development and *perceived* contributions to the 'poor community' are measured. All the while, the poor community's experiences with the volunteers, and whether they actually found benefit in it, do not appear to interest researchers. The narratives of the volunteers typically paint a doom and gloom picture of the recipient communities. For example, Benson and Seibert (2009, p. 309) quote German volunteer tourists extensively: 'To see how bad the standards of the rural schools are, the children in the rural areas cannot expect much from their future with an education like this; to see how many orphans there are because of HIV/Aids and TB. (Female 23)'; 'I got robbed and three guys in Capetown pushed me against a wall and wanted to have my money . . . as well to see that children take glue before they go to school and are on drugs and you can't do anything. (Female 24)'. Reading through these tourist experiences, without broader knowledge of the context, with their emphasis on the AIDS scourge and the helpless children, the consequence is that an image of Africa is produced that is morally one of an undifferentiated, helpless Other; a place that is depraved and economically barren, whose future is, mostly assuredly, also hopeless (Fair, 1993). It creates a pitiful victim whose fate, if it is to be good, must be helped from outside. Alternative narratives of diverse individual experiences are overshadowed. Thus, the specificity of African experiences and actions is lost (Fair, 1993).

A notable exception within the vast Afro-pessimistic scholarly landscape is Chuhan-Pole, and Angwafo's (2011) book titled *Yes, Africa Can: Success Stories from a Dynamic Continent*, which includes Nielsen and Spenceley's (2011) chapter, 'The success of tourism in Rwanda: Gorillas and more'. The title *Yes, Africa Can* is explicit in its optimistic thrust on Africa. The book notes, among other encouraging trends in Africa, a more fair and effective leadership, improving business climate, increasing innovation, a more involved citizenry, and growing relevance on home-grown solutions. Consistent with the Africa-can-do thrust of the book, in their chapter on gorilla tourism in Rwanda, Nielsen and Spenceley (2011) note that although Rwanda is known for its violent past, in the last decade, its image has shifted and it is now considered one of the safest destinations in East Africa. Its gorilla tourism industry continues to be a resounding success, demonstrating that, with the right strategy, a post-conflict country can successfully develop high-end tourism and achieve conservation and poverty alleviation goals at the same time.

However, changing the narrative on Africa 'requires not only sustained economic progress in the continent, but also a collaborative platform for telling the story in a compelling way' (Chuhan-Pole and Angwafo, 2011). Furthermore, it is important for academics, and other constructors of knowledge, to 'seek out and tell more of Africa's many success stories; to help put Africa's achievements on the map' (Chuhan-Pole and Angwafo, 2011). Thus, the present study may be viewed as a direct response to the quest for alternative narratives on Africa. In the next sections, I outline the online study method and findings.

Method and data

Counter-narratives were sought from various online platforms, including YouTube TEDx talks, Twitter hashtag posts, blogs, Instagram posts, as well as TripAdvisor forums and reviews. The counter-narratives were identified through a Google search as well as specific online platform searches using trial-and-error keyword combinations of 'Africa', 'real Africa', 'stereotypes of Africa', 'misrepresentation of Africa', and 'dark continent'. The various searches produced a total of 124 pages of broadly relevant results. Through a process of elimination, the results were narrowed down to 13 diverse URLs, ensuring both breadth and depth of data for addressing the research intent.

The analysis proceeded in five steps. First, relevant video content (that is, the seven YouTube/TEDx videos) was transcribed manually. Next, the rest of the textual pages were then printed and collated with the transcripts. This was followed by reading through all the data twice, to gain a sense of its content. Next, the data were coded, highlighting sections that advanced an Afro-positive view and/ or responded to Afro-pessimism, and making interpretive notes beside them. The next step involved identifying patterns in the data, by grouping related categories from the coding. This process produced three counter-narrative themes. The emergent themes were then refined and labelled to capture their essence, and illustrative quotes were marked for reference in the presentation of findings. The quotes provided in this instance are longer than usual, because the context and nuances therein are particularly important for the arguments that are advanced. Quotes are also provided verbatim, to preserve their raw authenticity.

The 13 URLs were:

1 www.youtube.com/watch?v=GVKlWINwf54, TEDx talk 'A new narrative for Africa' by Mark Eddo, uploaded February 13, 2015, with 37, 3801 views.

2 www.youtube.com/watch?v=Nerg-Nx0f3c&t=129s TEDx talk 'The phenomenal mindset of Africa's future leaders' by Nkosana Mafico, uploaded September 2, 2016, with 16,631 views.

3 www.youtube.com/watch?v=D9Ihs241zeg TEDx talk 'The danger of a single story' by Chimamanda Ngozi Adichie, uploaded October 7, 2009, with 3,105,396 views.

4 www.youtube.com/watch?v=hemD116ipcg&t=234s TEDx talk 'A new self-identity for Africans' by Panashe Chigumadzi, uploaded September 17, 2013, with 50,580 views.

5 www.youtube.com/watch?v=0-1msPDY0_U&t=691s TEDx talk 'Africa's bright future' by Guy Lundy, uploaded September 22, 2014, with 3700 views.

6 www.youtube.com/watch?v=D70ZybuB-rE&t=612s TEDx talk 'Africans can save Africa' by Arnold Ekpe, uploaded April 10, 2012, with 42,471 views.

7 www.youtube.com/watch?v=wQYK8XSCwEQ TEDx talk 'Where are the contemporary Pan-African intellectuals' by Tutu Agyare, uploaded February 2, 2015, with 15,905 views.

8 www.instagram.com/everydayafrica/ Instagram account, everydayafrica' with 4067 posts, 367,000 followers.

9 https://twitter.com/hashtag/theafricathemedianevershowsyou?vertical=defa ult Twitter hashtag #theafricathemedianevershowsyou

10 www.facebook.com/everydayafrica/ Facebook page 'Everyday Africa' with 71,251 followers.

11 www.facebook.com/TheAfricaTheMediaNeverShowsYou/ Facebook page 'TheAfricaTheMediaNeverShowsYou' with 195 followers.

12   http://voicesofafrica.co.za/about-voa/ Blog 'Voices of Africa'
13   www.facebook.com/seeafricadifferently Blog and Facebook page 'See Africa differently', with 8936 followers.

Ethics

From an ethics perspective, it is important to stress that all online data were sourced from publicly accessible URLs. It was therefore not necessary to seek individual consent for their use in this analysis. However, individual names are not provided unless where they are public or material to the arguments being made. Also important to note, participants were not probed for further information; only texts that were already available were used in the analysis.

Digital transitions: countering Afro-pessimism through online counter-narratives

Focusing on 'everyday Africa'

The analysis revealed that a growing number of digital platforms are producing counter-narratives that undermine Afro-pessimism in various ways. The majority of counter-narratives were produced by Africans living in Africa and in the diaspora, as well as by tourists who had visited Africa. Most prominently, these platforms foreground 'everyday' Africa, thus capturing ordinary but positive 'human moments': moments of joy, play, celebration, love and human interaction. For example, the blog 'Voices of Africa' aims to

> tell the stories the world doesn't hear often enough. We believe the everyday accounts of Africans getting on with life deserve more attention. From the fashion-crazy women in Dakar to the eligible bachelors in Somalia; from the extravagant weddings in Tanzania to the nightlife in Nairobi, we want to showcase life in Africa by those who live it.
>
> (blog post)

With article titles such as 'Gorillas not guerrillas: Tourism hope in troubled Congo', the blog seeks to reconstruct and redirect the stories emerging from Africa. Such a lens for viewing the continent reclaims agency for those living in Africa, by giving them the platform to choose and present how they want to be seen. They reject stories built on the outsider's gaze and create their own emic stories.

Similarly, the blog and Facebook page 'See Africa differently' describes itself as 'a new way of seeing Africa and talks about the continent in a positive way through culture, entertainment, development, politics, sports and business'., with a mission to 'celebrate Africa'. An explicit celebratory theming serves to preclude any negative associations with Africa. The Instagram account, 'everydayafrica', likewise shows an array of images of clean children laughing, playing, on their way to school or engaged otherwise, but always in an everyday, happy sort of way; it shows men at work, plants thriving, busy produce markets and other such ordinary depictions. The point is that this un-remarkableness is remarkable in its symbolic distancing from the stereotypical, pessimistic portrayal of Africa.

Correcting misconceptions

A particularly notable narrative emerges from tourists who have visited Africa. When their experience did not fit the stereotype they had entertained about the destination, they admit as such, for instance:

> Yesterday myself and 5 other girls went into Nairobi city . . . while we stood waiting for around 20 minutes, four different people came to check on us, asked if we needed directions, and were generally just making sure we were okay. This goes against all the misconceptions you so often hear.
> (British tourist, Facebook post)

> Having recently returned, it is now apparent that there is a lot of misinformation about safety/danger etc around. We were in numerous places and never once felt unsafe etc. We just took all the usual precautions of travelling in a city.
> (TripAdvisor South Africa forum, Australian tourist)

In the first post, the British tourist addresses 'misconceptions' of Nairobi, detailing how her experience in Nairobi demonstrates the friendliness of the people she encountered there. In the second narrative, the Australian tourist contradicts safety concerns about South Africa. Such experiences serve to demonstrate that Nairobi and South Africa are not homogeneous blocks of danger for the tourist. Similarly, a Russian tourist writes in a TripAdvisor review, 'I am in Africa for the first time. There are many negative stereotypes about Africa. In reality, I feel safe walking around the city. People are sociable and friendly'.

Real-life experiences such as these have added credibility to them, compared to mere claims that a particular characterisation of Africa is unfair. This is what makes tourist narratives particularly powerful, if not for altering the image of Africa, then for complexifying it.

Exposing one-sidedness

Through YouTube videos, a growing number of Afro-positive speakers are seeking to undermine what they see as the one-sidedness of representations of destination Africa. For example, one TEDx speaker advocates 'a new narrative' for Africa, explaining:

> The BBC did a story called 'Welcome to Lagos'. . . . They went to a beach where prostitutes and drug addicts hang out. They went to a dump where people were living on the dump and surviving. These are stories that should be told, but they are told again and again and again.
> (TEDx talk, YouTube)

The speaker takes issue with media organisations who choose the worst of Lagos (prostitutes, drugs, rubbish dumps) to paint a picture of the city. The impact on the desirability of Lagos as a tourist destination, he reckons, is predictable: anyone who watches the resulting story would never want to visit Lagos. He therefore argues in favour of more nuanced stories of the city.

Similarly, in TEDx talk titled 'The danger of a single story', the speaker urges, drawing on her Nigerian upbringing, that multiple stories are important for forming a complete image of any country or place:

> Every time I'm home I'm confronted with the usual sources of irritation for most Nigerians . . . but also by the incredible resilience of people who thrive despite the government, rather than because of it. . . . Stories can break the dignity of a people, but stories can also repair that broken dignity.
>
> (TEDx talk, YouTube)

This talk is particularly notable due to the international profile and visibility of the speaker, Chimamanda Ngozi Adichie, a public intellectual and recipient of the prestigious MacArthur Fellowship. She adds, 'Show a people as one thing, as only one thing, over and over again and that is what they become'. Ngozi further asserts that stories which have been written about Africa, through their singular focus on negativity, have broken the dignity of African peoples, and that new stories can be written to restore that dignity. Commenters on YouTube acknowledge how her arguments have led them to reconsider assumptions they have held about Africa; as one commenter writes, 'This is why I want to travel. I want to discover countries and their people for myself, not the single stories I hear in Western media. I may not engage with all of them, but at least, more than a single one'.

On other online platforms, various posters also seek to showcase 'the Africa they don't show you on tv'. For example, under the Twitter hashtag #TheAfricaTheMediaNeverShowsYou, posters point to the facets of Africa that the media rarely reports on: 'I'm exploring Kigali streets. Clear why it's named cleanest African city, even plastics are banned! The Africa they don't show us on tv'. Another poster describes Kampala as a city 'full of hope and promise'. The posters counteract the Afro-pessimism 'code book' (De Beer, 2010), with its use of famine, civil conflict and disputed elections as quintessential African-ness.

It is legitimate to conceive of the various social media voices as engaged in a discursive struggle to contest the legitimacy of cultural codes and taken-for-granted points of view (Carroll and Hackett, 2006). It is also interesting to note, in engaging with this struggle, how many of the Afro-positive posters and speakers blame the media for the misrepresentation of Africa. For example, a young African speaker argues in a TEDx talk posted on YouTube:

> For they, the media . . . the story that will shock and get more attention, is the story that portrays Africa as a place of death, disease and despair. This focus on negativity results in a negative perception of the continent, which in turn has negative implications for Africa and its people.

However, as has been explained in previous sections, the issue of skewed representation extends beyond the media. Academics may also have a role to play in restoring balance and exposing the implicit postcolonial implications of those representations.

Conclusion

Counter-narratives about Africa are already growing in volume and influence in the cyber-sphere. Through various platforms, advocates of a new, more nuanced narrative of Africa respond to the (perceived) vilification of African experiences by pointing out inaccuracies, generalisations and lack of balance. Over-inclusive terms of cultural representation are abrogated. These African advocates argue portrayals of Africa are stuck in the colonial mindset where Africa is still the dark continent needing Western salvation, where in fact the continent is seeing new opportunities emerging. They draw attention to everyday African images to destabilise the Us-and-Them basis of differentiation by writing a new narrative that claims: we are just like you, we shop, laugh, go to school, dress up, cycle, play, and so on. Thus everydayness portrayed in the social media images is about reclaiming normalcy and stability of everyday African existence. Everydayness presents African experiences as being not-different, in the sense of rejecting Otherness. This narrative positionality challenges the assumption that Africa is so different from the West, that fathoming it escapes the bounds of Western rationality (Nothias, 2016). It is in this respect that social media has an important role to play. Indeed, as Nothias (2016) notes, through social media, African voices are increasingly contributing to a sustained public critique of Western representations of the continent and its people.

The counter-narratives conscientise various audiences to be aware that it is often difficult to see past the stereotypes to the far more complex and sometimes promising African reality (Gordon and Wolpe, 1998). The Afro-positive speakers reject the label of poverty, because, as a moral discourse, poverty carries with it an implication that something must be done about it; it conjures images of victims and villains; it minimises their agency as people living full lives (Dean, 1992).

However, Afro-positivism is not about whitewashing Africa either, as the TEDx speaker explains, but about challenging the simplistic neo-colonial nature of Afro-pessimism, through introducing multiple, complex images of Africa (Grant et al., 2016). Indeed a worthwhile Afro-optimist approach does not ignore or deny the still real challenges that Africa faces (Grant et al., 2016). There is, however, an increasing rate of publications by African tourism academics.

The postcolonial lens, through engagement with, and contestation of, colonialism's discourses, power structures and social hierarchies (Glynn and Tyson, 2007) unravels stereotypes and problematises the 'single story', as Ngozie expresses it, that is told of Africa. Tourism scholars can mobilise postcolonialism to destabilise dominant discourses and to critique hegemonic discursive legacies of colonialism. Postcolonial theory facilitates the interrogation of representations that are racialised, essentialised, selective or ethnocentric (Scott, 2017). It helps us dislodge the us-and-them binary implicit in some Western characterisations of Africa.

By tapping into postcolonial theory, instances of the 'epistemic violence' covert in tourism study as a body of knowledge can be interrogated. Alternative ways of ways of seeing Africa are not only missing, they are thwarted when the same, single story is told, again and again. As Gordon and Wolpe (1998) argue, deep-seated stereotypes have the consequence of filtering out stories of African reform and renewal, reinforcing a distinctly negative image of Africa – simplistic representations cheat Africa of its complex landscapes (Grant et al., 2016). It is hoped that these insights will animate the currently stagnant discussion on African representations within tourism studies and beyond.

References

Aitchison, C. (2001). Theorizing other discourses of tourism, gender and culture. *Tourist Studies*, *1*(2), 133–147. doi:10.1177/146879760100100202

Alexander, Z. (2012). International volunteer tourism experience in South Africa: An investigation into the impact on the tourist. *Journal of Hospitality Marketing and Management*, *21*(7), 779–799.

Ateljevic, I., Harris, C., Wilson, E., and Collins, F. L. (2005). Getting 'entangled': Reflexivity and the 'critical turn' in tourism studies. *Tourism Recreation Research*, *30*(2), 9–21.

Benson, A., and Seibert, N. (2009). Volunteer tourism: Motivations of German participants in South Africa. *Annals of Leisure Research*, *12*(3–4), 295–314.

Burgold, J., and Rolfes, M. (2013). Of voyeuristic safari tours and responsible tourism with educational value: Observing moral communication in slum and township tourism in Cape Town and Mumbai. *DIE ERDE – Journal of the Geographical Society of Berlin*, *144*(2), 161–174.

Byrd, J. A., and Rothberg, M. (2011). Between subalternity and indigeneity: Critical categories for postcolonial studies. *Interventions*, *13*(1), 1–12.

Carroll, W. K., and Hackett, R. A. (2006). Democratic media activism through the lens of social movement theory. *Media, Culture and Society*, *28*(1), 83–104.

Caton, K., and Santos, C. A. (2009). Images of the other. *Journal of Travel Research*, *48*(2), 191–204. doi:10.1177/0047287509332309

Chuhan-Pole, P., and Angwafo, M. (2011) (eds). *Yes, Africa can: Success stories from a dynamic continent*. Washington, DC: World Bank Publications.

De Beer, A. S. (2010). News from and in the 'dark continent' afro-pessimism, news flows, global journalism and media regimes. *Journalism Studies*, *11*(4), 596–609.

Dean, H. (1992). Poverty discourse and the disempowerment of the poor. *Critical Social Policy*, *12*(35), 79–88.

Dwivedi, M. (2009). Online destination image of India: A consumer based perspective. *International Journal of Contemporary Hospitality Management*, *21*(2), 226–232.

Escárcega, S. (2010). Authenticating strategic essentialisms: The politics of indigenousness at the united nations. *Cultural Dynamics*, *22*(1), 3–28. doi:10.1177/0921374010366780

Fair, J. E. (1993). War, famine, and poverty: Race in the construction of Africa's media image. *Journal of Communication Inquiry*, *17*(2), 5–22.

Ferreira, S. L. A. (2006). Communities and transfrontier parks in the Southern African development community: The case of Limpopo National Park, Mozambique. *South African Geographical Journal*, *88*, 166–176.

Glynn, K., and Tyson, A. F. (2007). Indigeneity, media and cultural globalization. *International Journal of Cultural Studies*, *10*(2), 205–224. doi:10.1177/1367877907076788

Gordon, D. F., and Wolpe, H. (1998). The other Africa: An end to Afro-pessimism. *World Policy Journal*, *15*(1), 49–59.

Grant, J. A., Djomo, A. N., and Krause, M. G. (2016). Afro-optimism reinvigorated? Reflections on the glocal networks of sexual identity, health, and natural resources in Africa. *Global Change, Peace and Security*, *28*(3), 317–328.

Gustav, V. (2004). The developmental impacts of backpacker tourism in South Africa. *GeoJournal*, *60*, 283–299.

Harding, F. (2003). Africa and the moving image: Television, film and video. *Journal of African Cultural Studies*, *16*(1), 69–84.

Hays, S., Page, S. J., and Buhalis, D. (2013). Social media as a destination marketing tool: Its use by national tourism organisations. *Current Issues in Tourism*, *16*(3), 211–239.

Hollinshead, K. (2006). The Shift to Constructivism in Social Inquiry: Some Pointers for Tourism Studies. *Tourism Recreation Research*, *31*(2), 43–58.

Lee, G. B., and Lam, S. S. (1998). Wicked cities: Cyberculture and the reimagining of identity in the 'non-Western' metropolis. *Futures*, *30*(10), 967–979.

Mbaiwa, J. E. (2005). Enclave tourism and its socio-economic impacts in the Okavango Delta, Botswana. *Tourism Management*, *26*(2), 157–172.

Meschkank, J. (2011). Investigations into slum tourism in Mumbai: Poverty tourism and the tensions between different constructions of reality. *GeoJournal*, *76*(1), 47–62.

Meschkank, J. (2012). Negotiating Poverty. The interplay between Dharavi's production and consumption of Dharavi as a tourist destination. In F. Frenzel, K. Koens, and M. Steinbrink (Eds.), *Slum tourism: Poverty, power and ethics*. London: Routledge.

Momoh, A. (2003). Does pan-Africanism have a future in Africa? In search of the ideational basis of Afro-pessimism. *African Journal of Political Science*, *8*(1), 31–57.

Narayan, U. (1998). Essence of culture and a sense of history: A feminist critique of cultural essentialism. *Hypatia*, *13*(2), 86–106.

Nielsen, H., and Spenceley, A. (2011). The success of tourism in Rwanda: Gorillas and more. In P. Chuhan-Pole and M. Angwafo (Eds.), *Yes Africa can: Success stories from a dynamic continent* (pp. 231–249). Washington, DC: The World Bank.

Nothias, T. (2016). How Western journalists actually write about Africa: Re-assessing the myth of representations of Africa. *Journalism Studies*, 1–22.

Paradies, Y. C. (2006). Beyond black and white. *Journal of Sociology*, *42*(4), 355–367. doi:10.1177/1440783306069993

Scott, M. (2017). The myth of representations of Africa: A comprehensive scoping review of the literature. *Journalism Studies*, *18*(2), 191–210.

Sin, H. L. (2010). Who are we responsible to? Locals' tales of volunteer tourism. *Geoforum*, *41*(6), 983–992.

Spenceley, A., and Goodwin, H. (2007). Nature-based tourism and poverty alleviation: Impacts of private sector and parastatal enterprises in and around Kruger National Park, South Africa. *Current Issues in Tourism*, *10*(2–3), 255–277.

Spivak, G. (1988). Can the subaltern speak? In C. Nelson and L. Grossberg (Eds.), *Marxism and the interpretation of culture* (pp. 271–313). Urbana: University of Illinois Press.

Stoddart, H., and Rogerson, C. M. (2004). Volunteer tourism: The case of habitat for humanity South Africa. *GeoJournal*, *60*(3), 311–318.

Strickland-Munro, J. K., Moore, S. A., and Freitag-Ronaldson, S. (2010). The impacts of tourism on two communities adjacent to the Kruger National Park, South Africa. *Development Southern Africa*, *27*, 663–678.

Tham, A., Croy, G., and Mair, J. (2013). Social media in destination choice: Distinctive electronic word-of-mouth dimensions. *Journal of Travel and Tourism Marketing, 30*(1–2), 144–155.

Tribe, J. (2008). Tourism: A critical business. *Journal of Travel Research, 46*(3), 245–255. doi:10.1177/0047287507304051

Wainaina, B. (2005). How to write about Africa. *Granta, 92*(1), 4.

Wall, M. (2009). Africa on YouTube: Musicians, tourists, missionaries and aid workers. *International Communication Gazette, 71*(5), 393–407.

Yeoh, B. S. A. (2001). Postcolonial cities. *Progress in Human Geography, 25*(3), 456–468. doi:10.1191/030913201680191781

Zahra, A., and McIntosh, A. J. (2007). Volunteer tourism: Evidence of cathartic tourist experiences. *Tourism Recreation Research, 32*(1), 115–119.

7 Broadening Uganda's tourism product base through indigenous cultural resource utilisation

Jim Ayorekire, Joseph Obua and Michael Bruce Byaruhanga

Background to tourism in Uganda

Tourism is one of the key drivers of Uganda's economy because it generates foreign exchange, creates jobs and enhances livelihoods. The government of Uganda has prioritised tourism in the national development frameworks such as Vision 2040 and National Development Plan II (2015–2019), which emphasises product diversification and conservation, investments, infrastructure development, capacity building, increased marketing and promotion of the country as a destination. To further guide sustainable development of the tourism sector, various planning, policy, regulatory and legislative frameworks have been established over the years. These include the Uganda Tourism Development Master Plan 2014–2024, the Tourism Policy 2015, the Wildlife Policy 2014, the Uganda Tourism Act 2008 and the Tourism Sector Development Plan (2015–2020), among others. Over the last 10 years, the tourism sector has experienced drastic development; for instance, international tourist arrivals doubled from 642,000 in 2007 (generated USD 449 million) to 1.3 million in 2016 (generated USD 1.35 million). The sector accounts for approximately 9% of the GDP and 23.5% of the foreign exchange earnings (Uganda Bureau of Statistics, 2009, 2017; Ministry of Tourism, Wildlife and Antiquities, 2016).

For a long time, Uganda's tourism has relied heavily on nature-based tourism, especially on wildlife in national parks and tropical forest reserves. Such areas have supported ecotourism, one of the fastest growing tourism segments, based on key flagship products such as mountain gorilla tracking and chimpanzee viewing. However, reliance on nature-based tourism has limited the country's product range, competitiveness and exploitation of cultural, historical and aesthetic resources for tourism. Given the intricacy of climate change and the unpredictable environmental consequences, and the fact that Uganda's neighbours offer the same tourism products, it is no longer tenable for Uganda to continue relying on nature-based tourism. Uganda's tourism industry should instead diversify and promote cultural tourism.

Uganda has diverse and unique cultures and traditions across the different ethnic communities that form a huge pool of potential tourism resources. In spite of the high cultural tourism potential, cultural resources in Uganda have not been mapped, documented, packaged and marketed for tourism. In addition, there has been limited awareness of the need to protect, conserve and promote cultural heritage resources. Consequently, cultural norms and practices have been gradually eroded and a number of cultural heritage sites neglected, degraded and damaged.

The Uganda Tourism Development Master Plan 2014–2024 and Tourism Policy 2015 recognise the above challenges and the need to conserve and harness cultural heritage resources for tourism. Several strategies have been put in place to support cultural institutions and private enterprises to develop cultural attractions, enforce laws and regulations, increase public awareness and harness and package cultural tourism products. This chapter makes a significant contribution towards that agenda by unpacking some of Uganda's cultural tourism resources and analysing research and policy gaps in that regard. Prospects for promoting cultural tourism in Uganda in an 'Afro-positive' manner – capturing the positive African narrative (Mkono, 2018) – are illustrated with two case studies. The first case study examines traditional healing practices that can be harnessed for cultural tourism in central Uganda in the absence of wildlife resources. This is a unique cultural practice that has hitherto not been studied despite its potential for promoting cultural tourism. The second case study focuses on cultural festivals and sites of the Baganda, one of the largest ethnic Bantu groups in central Uganda, which has huge potential for supporting cultural tourism.

Uganda's cultural heritage resources

Uganda is endowed with rich cultural heritage resources that can be exploited for tourism. Exploitation of such resources would create a unique and competitive tourism product and reduce competition with neighbouring countries, such as Kenya and Tanzania, that have comparative advantage over Uganda in the nature-based tourism market. Tourists' changing tastes, lifestyles and the desire to experience the cultures of destinations combine to create an opportunity for promoting cultural tourism as part of the mainstream tourism experience in Uganda. Smith (2011) defines culture as a holistic way of life which includes common meanings, learning, arts, discovery and creativity of a society. This definition affirms the uniqueness of culture between and within societies which can be exploited for tourism. According to Ismail, Masron, and Ahmad (2014) and Ahebwa, Aporu, and Nyakaana (2016), cultural tourism involves experiencing the lifestyle and history of people in various geographical settings – the art, architecture, religion and other elements that shape their way of life. Culture encompasses materials and symbolic resources that can be harnessed for tourism and for the benefit of the local people and tourists (Smith and Robinson, 2006). In Uganda, cultural tourism entails the consumption of culture through experiencing cultural heritage resources such as sites, monuments, arts, crafts, values, traditions, beliefs and lifestyles (Ministry of Tourism, Wildlife, and Antiquities, 2014).

Cultural diversity in Uganda is documented in the Constitution of 1995 (amended in 2005) which recognises 56 tribes and nine indigenous communities in the country. In addition, there are 650 cultural heritage sites and monuments and a variety of cultural practices (Ministry of Gender, Labour and Social Development, 2006). These cultural heritage resources define the identity, social respect and dignity of Ugandans which can be harnessed for cultural tourism (Government of Uganda, 2007; Ministry of Tourism, Wildlife and Antiquities, 2014).

According to The Cross Cultural Foundation of Uganda (2008), Uganda is a multicultural society each with unique traditional values, beliefs, principles, knowledge, skills, governance systems, language and practices. The ethnic groups are traditionally governed by kings, chiefs, clan heads or a council of elders. Almost all ethnic groups in Uganda are organised in clans, which are social units comprising a number of families of the same lineage or joined together by common traditional occupations. In some ethnic groups, a totem symbolises cultural identity, in the form of an animal, a plant or an object. In some instances, a clan may have more than one totem but several clans can also subscribe to the same totem. Clan members are taught from early childhood to identify and respect their totem – which they must not hunt, eat, harass or kill. Clan leaders are responsible for transmitting information about the clan and its totem, along with the associated taboos, sanctions and penalties which they enforce. Many of the totemic animals are found in protected forest reserves or national parks, which limits local communities' access to them.

Uganda has 10 kingdoms and chiefdoms that have attempted to harness cultural heritage resources such as songs, dances, festivals, ritual and totems for tourism (Ahebwa et al., 2016). In Buganda kingdom, found in the central region on the northern shores of Lake Victoria, the resources include the Kabaka's (king's) palaces, Kabaka's trail, Namugongo martyrs shrine, Kasubi tombs (a UNESCO World Heritage Site), Wamala tombs (kings' burial sites), Kabaka's coronation site in Naggalabi (Buddo), Sezibwa Falls and Katereke ditch (where royal prisoners were allegedly starved to death during the upheavals that characterised the reign of Kabaka Kalema, 1888–89), among others. All the above cultural heritage resources are rich in indigenous knowledge that has been used over the years to promote nature conservation and social cohesion (Nuwagaba and Kiwere, 2014).

Traditional healing practices and cultural tourism: a case study of PROMETRA in central Uganda

Traditional healing is as age-old and diverse as humanity itself. The diversity of healing traditions is linked to evolutionary cultural processes in which the application of indigenous knowledge and beliefs can be exploited for tourism (Pesek et al., 2006). Diversity is the attribute that renders traditional healing a unique cultural heritage resource. Traditional healing involves the application of indigenous knowledge and skills that are consistent with the cultural values of the local people. Whereas it is a cultural practice that complements modern medicine and healthcare, it can be exploited for cultural tourism.

According to Segen's Medical Dictionary (2011), a traditional healer is a person who uses traditional knowledge to alleviate human suffering. However, the surge in interest for traditional healing has attracted a number of practitioners whose activities need to be regulated. PROMETRA (Promotion of Traditional Medicine) in Uganda is one of the 27 chapters worldwide that builds the capacity of traditional healers, instils ethics in the practice and promotes knowledge sharing. It is located in Buyijja village, Buwama sub-county, Mpigi district (N 0°32'–39' and E 32°5'–47'). PROMETRA's activities include training workshops on African spiritual health and conferences on traditional medicine and traditional healing.

In order to determine the characteristics of traditional healing practices that can be exploited for cultural tourism, a case study of PROMETRA was undertaken. The objectives were to (i) examine traditional healing practices that can be packaged for cultural tourism and (ii) assess traditional healers' views on harnessing their practices for tourism. A questionnaire was administered to collect information on traditional healing practices from 60 respondents consisting of staff of PROMETRA (10), traditional healers (30) and local people (20) living around the centre. The respondents were selected based on their involvement, position in the community and knowledge of traditional healing practices. Data were entered in SPSS to generate statistical summary (frequency and percentage) and subjected to a chi-square test to show whether women were more involved in traditional healing than men.

Results indicated that two-thirds (66.7%) of the respondents were female and the same percentage was aged between 45 and 64 years. Slightly less than half (46.6%) were married, 30% divorced and 16.7% were single. Thirty percent had attained primary, 40% secondary and 16.7% tertiary education levels while 13.3% had no formal education. The chi-square test showed that there was no significant relationship between sex and involvement in traditional healing ($\chi^2 = 1.493$, $p = 0.22$). Therefore, there is no evidence that women are more involved than men in traditional healing.

Sources of traditional medicines and categories of healers are presented in Table 7.1. The traditional healers obtained herbal medicines from wild plants in the forest, cultivated medicinal plants and dealers in the market. As indicated above, most of the healers are mature people aged 45 or older, and considered to be experienced in the practice, while the younger healers are mainly trainees expected to perpetuate the practice. Some of the traditional healers had no formal education, and this was unsurprising because the practice utilises indigenous knowledge (Malehu, Egan, Du Plessi, and Pottinger, 2015). Discussions with the respondents revealed that PROMETRA receives tourists although the centre lacked tourist facilities. The tourists visit the natural forest and medicinal plant

Table 7.1 Sources of traditional medicines and categories of healers ($n = 60$)

Source of medicine	%	Category of healer	%
Cultivated plants	33.3	Women	33.3
Natural forest	26.6	Young (trainees)	30.0
Spirit guided	23.3	Advanced age (> 50 years old)	26.7
Markets	16.7	Uneducated	10.0

gardens, are exposed to treatments of patients with herbal medicines and incantations, and are entertained with traditional songs and dances. Visits to the forest suggest that in future, trails can be established for forest nature walks.

The traditional healers reported over-harvesting of medicinal plants and increased number of charlatans in the practice. There was concern that this might create a negative impression about traditional healing, leading to clients' loss of trust and perceptions of duping of tourists. In spite of these challenges, traditional healers and local residents supported harnessing traditional healing for cultural tourism and development of tourism facilities at PROMETRA. The introduction of cultural tourism at the centre would preserve traditional healing and make the practice an authentic attraction. According to Besculides, Martha, Lee, and McCormick (2002), cultural attractions promote tolerance, respect and understanding of other cultures. Traditional healing offers a learning opportunity sought after by tourists and would create a distinctive cultural Afro-positive identity rooted in a rich indigenous knowledge base.

Harnessing cultural festivals and sites for tourism: a case study of the Baganda

The Buganda Kingdom, with a population of approximately 9.5 million (Uganda Bureau of Statistics, 2017), is mainly occupied by the *Baganda*, and the major language spoken is *Luganda*. The *Ganda* culture is centred on the kingdom (*Obwa'kabaka*), kingship and cultural sites and traditions (*Ebyo'buwangwa nenono*). The *Kabaka* (king) is the cultural leader of Buganda assisted by county (*Saaza*) chiefs and clan heads. Buganda's cultural sites have been used for preservation of customs and traditions.

The Baganda settled and occupied large parts of the present-day Buganda Kingdom as part of the Bantu migration in the 13th century. The kingdom came into existence during the reign of Kabaka Kato Kintu between 1200 and 1230 (Nuwagaba and Kiwere, 2014; Buganda Tourism Board, 2018). With the support of the clan heads, Kato Kintu fought and defeated Bemba, the then ruler, and declared himself the king of Buganda. At that time, Buganda had only five clans, but over the years the number has increased to 56 (BUCADEF, 2018). For centuries, the Baganda have practiced cultural traditions that have shaped their lifestyle and behaviour, which can be packaged for tourism.

In order to assess the prospects of developing tourism based on the cultural resources in Buganda, a study was conducted at Bamunanika Palace and Walusi hill in Luwero district in central Uganda. Bamunanika Palace was built in 1948 by Kabaka Sir Edward Muteesa II. The current king, Kabaka Ronald Muwenda Mutebi II, uses it as a country home. Walusi hill is located about 25 kilometres from Luwero town and is named after the chief spirit, '*Silusinsi*'. 'Walusi' in the Ganda tradition means the foundation that holds the earth including all living things. The hill, which consists of 102 rock outcrops, harbours shrines for traditional worship and thanks giving (Michael, 2012).

The study sought local communities' views on introducing cultural tourism based on the Kabaka's palace and Walusi hill and the expected benefits. A structured questionnaire was administered to collect data from 50 respondents comprising district local government staff (10), palace employees (10), shrine attendants (5) and local communities (25) in Luwero district. The socio-demographic characteristics of the respondents revealed that the majority (60%) of the respondents was male and 60% were aged between 26 and 45 years. Thirty-six percent had primary education, 34% secondary and 28% tertiary while 2% had no formal education.

Bamunanika Palace and Walusi hill are visited by tourists even without a formal cultural tourism framework. Clearly, there is latent demand for cultural tourism based on the cultural heritage resources. To harness the opportunities created, local music, dance and drama groups have been formed to entertain visitors. Some tourists camp at the hill overnight. One of the rock outcrops is a prayer point frequented by women in search of spiritual powers to conceive (Figure 7.1). In the vicinity is another rock outcrop used for appeasing the gods (Figure 7.2).

The local residents supported promotion of cultural tourism based on the Kabaka's Bamunanika Palace and Walusi hill and indicated the expected benefits presented in Table 7.2. Other cultural resources across Buganda Kingdom that can be utilised for tourism development are discussed next.

Kabaka's coronation and commemoration festivals

Succession in the Buganda Kingdom leadership system is patrilineal. When the Kabaka dies, the crown prince is enthroned as the new king. The coronation ceremony lasts nine days and is performed at Naggalabi on Buddo hill where the first

Figure 7.1 Rock outcrop where barren women worship gods to conceive

Figure 7.2 Rock outcrop where thanks are given to the gods

Table 7.2 Benefits expected by the local communities from cultural tourism

Benefit	% response
Market for local produce	63.3
Business opportunities	51.0
Employment	69.4
Social services (roads, health centres, schools)	79.6
Social cohesion	77.6

king of Buganda was enthroned in the 13th century. Rituals are carried out, such as when bundles of sticks cut from Nansove sacred forest are laid in the compound of 'Buganda House', bathing the new king by one of the aunties, jumping over a virgin girl (*naaku*) and engaging in a mock fight with young men to commemorate the enthronement of the first king, Kabaka Kato Kintu. It is considered a taboo for a new king to revisit Naggalabi site after his coronation, as it is believed that he would lose the throne and die.

Kabaka's burial sites and related rituals

In the beginning, the kings of Buganda were buried in their palaces. This changed later and Kabaka Suuna II (1832–1856), the 29th king, was the last king to be buried in the palace now known as Wamala tombs. Since then Kabaka Mutesa I (1837–1884), Mwanga II (1884–1897), Daudi Chwa II (1897–1939) and Sir

Figure 7.3 Wamala tombs where Kabaka Suuna II was buried

Edward Walugembe Mutesa II (1942–1966) have been buried in Kasubi tombs (*amasiro ga ba Ssekabaka*), which became a UNESCO World Heritage Site in 2001. According to Buganda customs, the Kabaka does not die but disappears into a 'forest', and his title changes from *Ssabbasajja* (reigning king) to *Sseka-baka* (deceased king). In the mausoleum, a bark cloth curtain is placed between the burial place and where the royal regalia are kept as a symbol of movement from the tomb to the 'forest', and it is a taboo to look beyond the curtain. For a long time, the royal regalia have been kept at Wamala (Figure 7.3) and Kasubi tombs, which are visited by tourists and local people. The tradition also prohibits the reigning king from attending burial ceremonies because he is not supposed to shed tears in public.

Research and policy gaps

Uganda has experienced increased growth in the tourism sector, which in turn has given rise to economic and social development. This growth has attracted investments in the sector which requires empirical research data for policy formulation, review, monitoring and projection of tourism trends. However, tourism research faces methodical challenges globally as documented by Mathieson and Wall (1982) and Jamieson, Godwin, and Edmund (2004). The most commonly cited constraint is lack of consensus on methodology and depth of analysis (Simpson,

2009). Traditionally, tourism research has been qualitative, and a number of studies in Uganda have mainly focused on natural resources and short-term academic projects involving small sample sizes and generating indicative results. Harnessing cultural heritage resources for tourism in Uganda should ideally be informed by research that details the resources and generates empirical evidence to guide planning and investments. There has been no robust national research programme in tourism partly due to the emphasis on science, technology and innovation which are prioritised in Uganda's National Development Plan II.

Notably, traditional healing has received inadequate recognition and legal and policy backing even though it is widely practiced in Uganda. There is currently no law to guide, regulate and control the relevant practices, partly due to the colonial legacy that negatively branded indigenous knowledge and culture as primitive (The Cross Cultural Foundation of Uganda, 2008). For instance, the Witchcraft Act of 1957 outlawed traditional medicine and is still in the statute books. The Indigenous and Complimentary Medicine Bill drafted in 2015 has not been passed into law because of controversies surrounding the interpretation of traditional medicine and certification of practitioners. Although there are statutory instruments that refer to different aspects of traditional healing, e.g. the Public Health Act 1935 (cap 281), Uganda Mental Treatment Act 1938 (cap 279), the Medical and Dental Practitioners Act 1998 (cap 272), National Drug Policy and Authority Statute 1993, National Health Policy 1999, the Allied Health Professionals Act 2000 (cap 268) and others, the information is scattered, and some are outdated and out of tune with current national and international realities about indigenous knowledge and its contribution to tourism development.

The Public Private Partnership (PPP) Policy in Health is the only official document that provides a framework for the regulation of traditional and complementary medicine (Ministry of Health, 2011). This implies that if traditional healing practices were exploited for cultural tourism, they would lack legal backing from the health sector. However, the lack of legal support does not mean that the opportunity for mainstreaming traditional healing into cultural tourism should be discarded. The practices can be harnessed under the Tourism Policy 2015 and Uganda Tourism Development Master Plan 2014–2024.

Although these policies emphasise the need to develop cultural tourism, the specific aspects and strategic directions are not defined. At the same time, the Uganda National Culture Policy 2006 highlights the need to promote cultural tourism. The policy outlines interventions including the conservation of cultures, promotion of cultural sites and preservation of indigenous knowledge. However, specific guidelines and methodologies for harnessing cultural sites and traditions for tourism are lacking, thereby hindering strategic development of Afro-positive cultural tourism.

Conclusion

This chapter has documented the rich and diverse cultural heritage resources that can be harnessed for cultural tourism in Uganda. The resources bring to the fore the need for an Afro-positive discourse that enhances the prospects for development of unique and authentic cultural tourism products. A formal account of Uganda's history reinforces this point. The history indicates that Uganda attracted the interest of the Arabs and Europeans as far back as the mid-19th century, and Buganda kingdom became the centre of events that led to the colonisation in 1894 (Mukasa-Mutibwa, 2016). Although the information presented in this chapter focuses on Buganda only, it underlines the opportunity for promotion of cultural tourism in other parts of the country with equally rich and diverse cultural heritage resources.

Culture and tourism have backward and forward linkages in which tourism enhances culture and generates income, which in turn supports and strengthens cultural heritage, creativity and economic development (OECD, 2009). These synergies and linkages can be harnessed to make Uganda an attractive and competitive destination in the region and globally. To be optimally harnessed, traditional practices, ceremonies and customs should be mainstreamed in the planning, implementation and monitoring programme of the tourism sector for three main reasons: firstly, to enforce compliance with a code of ethics, in accordance with moral and societal norms; secondly, to instil professionalism in the practice based on the principles and strategies of tourism development; and thirdly, to remove the negative undertone about culture and traditional practices that are viewed as primitive so that an Afro-positive image is fostered, societal pride enhanced and tourists made to appreciate the cultural practices as tourism products.

There is need to increase Uganda's comparative advantage by adding cultural tourism to the existing attractions, to minimise over-reliance on nature-based tourism. A clear policy framework and structure should be put in place for harnessing and promoting cultural heritage resources for domestic and international tourists. Cultural institutions, government and the private sector should collaborate to promote cultural tourism with well-defined roles and benefits. A strategy should be put in place by the Ministry of Tourism, Wildlife and Antiquities in conjunction with the Uganda Tourism Board to market genuine Afro-positive cultural tourism products locally and internationally. Tourism marketing should tap into social media, which has demonstrated to be a good medium through which the Afro-positive narrative can effectively be conveyed (Mkono, 2018).

Lastly, a comprehensive national tourism research programme coordinated by the Ministry of Tourism, Wildlife and Antiquities in conjunction with research institutions and other stakeholders should be developed with a focus on cultural tourism and other priority areas. This can be achieved with core funding from government and complementary funding from the private sector and development partners. In this way, the development and growth of Uganda's cultural tourism will be structured, systematic and monitored regularly using empirical data. In addition, Uganda will be positioned as a competitive and sustainable cultural tourism destination in the world.

References

Ahebwa, W. M., Aporu, P. J., and Nyakaana, J. B. (2016). Bridging community livelihoods and cultural conservation through tourism: Case study of Kabaka's heritage trail in Uganda. *Tourism and Hospitality Research*, *16*(2), 103–115.

Besculides, A., Martha, E., Lee, P., and McCormick, D. (2002). Residents' perceptions of the cultural benefits of tourism. *Annals of Tourism Research, 29*(2), 303–319.

BUCADEF (Buganda Cultural and Development Foundation) (anon). *Origin of Buganda.* Retrieved July 15, 2018, from https://bungandafriend.wordpress.com/origin-of-buganda

Buganda Tourism Board. (2018). Retrieved July 15, 2018, 20.00pm from www.buganda. or.ug/index.php/our-history/the-past/cultural-setup.

Government of Uganda. (2007). *Uganda vision 2040 – A transformed Ugandan society from a peasant to a modern and prosperous Country within 30 years.* Retrieved from https://npa.ug/wp-content/themes/npatheme/documents/vision2040.pdf

Ismail, N., Masron, T., and Ahmad, A. (214). *Cultural heritage tourism in Malaysia: Issues and Challenges.* SHS web of Conferences 12, 01059. Retrieved from https://doi. org/10.1051/shsconf/20141201059

Jamieson, W., Godwin, H., and Edmund, C. (2004). *Contribution of tourism to poverty alleviation: Pro-poor tourism and the challenge of measuring impacts.* Suva, Fiji: Transport Policy and Tourism Section, Transport and Tourism Division, United Nations Economic and Social Commission for Asia and the Pacific (UN ESCAP). Retrieved July 9, 2018, from www.researchgate.net/publications/26600851

Malehu, K. M., Egan, B. A., Du Plessi, H. J., and Pottinger, M. J. (2015). Socio-cultural profile of Bapedi traditional healers as indigenous knowledge custodians and conservation partners in Blouberg area, Limpopo Province, South Africa. *Journal of Ethnobiology and Ethnomedicine, 11*, 49. doi:10.1186/s13002-015-0025-3.

Mathieson, A., and Wall, G. (1982). *Tourism physical and social impacts.* Harlow, Essex: Longman.

Michael, C. (2012). *The districts of Uganda information handbook.* Kampala, Uganda: Kampala Press.

Ministry of Gender, Labour and Social Development. (2006). *The Uganda national culture policy.* Kampala, Uganda: Government of Uganda.

Ministry of Health. (2011). *The public private partnership policy in health.* Entebbe, Uganda: Government Printers and Publishers.

Ministry of Tourism, Wildlife and Antiquities. (2014). *Uganda tourism development master plan.* Kampala, Uganda: Government of Uganda.

Ministry of Tourism, Wildlife and Antiquities. (2016). *Ministry of tourism, wildlife and antiquities statistical bulletin* (Vol. 1). Kampala, Uganda: Government of Uganda.

Mkono, M. (2018). *Changing the African narrative through social media platforms.* Retrieved August 24, 2018, from https://theconversation.com/changing-the-african-narrative-through-social-media-platforms-97097

Mukasa-Mutibwa, P. (2016). *A history of Uganda: The first 100 years 1894–1995.* Kampala, Uganda: Fountain Publishers.

Nuwagaba, T. F., and Kiwere, N. (2014). *Totems of Uganda – Buganda Edition: Culture embracing nature.* Kampala, Uganda: Taga Nuwagaba and Nathan Kiwere Publishing.

OECD. (2009). *The impact of culture on tourism.* Paris, France: OECD Publishing.

Pesek, T., Helton, L., and Nair, M. (2006). Healing across cultures: Learning from traditions. *Economic Health, 3*(2), 114–118.

Segen's Medical Dictionary. (2011). Retrieved July 9, 2018, from https://medical-dictionary.thefreedictionary.com/traditional + healer

Simpson, M. C. (2009). An integrated approach to assess the impacts of tourism on community development and sustainable livelihoods. *Community Development Journal, 44*(2). doi:10.1093/CDJ/BSM048. Retrieved July 9, 2018, from www.researchgate.net/ publications/31363957

Smith, M. K. (2011). *Issues in cultural tourism studies: Current issues in tourism* (1st ed., Vol. 14). London, UK: Routledge.

Smith, M., and Robinson, M. (2006). *Cultural tourism in a changing world: Politics, participation and representation.* New York, USA: Channel View Publications.The Cross Cultural Foundation of Uganda. (2008). *Promoting Herbal Medicine in Uganda. Culture in Development Series.* Kampala, Uganda: CCFU.

Uganda Bureau of Statistics. (2009). *Uganda statistical bulletin.* Kampala, Uganda: Government of Uganda.

Uganda Bureau of Statistics. (2017). *National population and housing census 2014.* Kampala, Uganda: Government of Uganda Report.

8 Insight into Africa

Wildlife tourism as educational transformation

Chloe Rooks, Garry Marvin, Caroline Ross and Jonathan Skinner

Wildlife tourism and the stereotyping of Africa

Around the world, wildlife conservation and tourism are intimately connected. Newsome and Rodger (2013) suggest that wildlife tourism has grown to become a vital niche within the global tourism industry, accounting for at least $45 billion/year. Moorhouse, Dahlsjö, Baker, D'Cruze, and Macdonald (2015) estimate that visits to wildlife tourist attractions (WTAs) account for 20%–40% of global tourism, resulting in significant negative impact upon wildlife. Governments and other institutions and organisations establish zones of protection and conservation and people pay to visit them, to see and experience what is deemed worthy of such conservation, from dingo spotting in Australia (Burns and Howard, 2003), to a 'Big Five' safari in Tanzania (Stone and Stone, 2018; Salazar, 2006), to whale spotting off Argentina (Tapper, 2006, p. 58). In South Africa, it is estimated that 80% of the 9 million annual overseas visitors will spend some of their visit in wildlife-related activities (South African National Parks Annual Report, 2016/2017). SANParks (South Africa National Parks) recorded 6,750,083 visitors to its 19 operational parks in 2017, who generated, for the organisation, just over $24 million in revenue (South African National Parks Annual Report, 2016/2017). These figures do not capture the full extent of wildlife tourism: in South Africa, as in addition to the national parks, there are also regional wildlife parks, community wildlife parks, private parks and reserves, and thousands of wildlife game ranches, all which contribute to the tourism industry in South Africa.

The vast majority of visitors to these enclosed, protected areas pay to see wildlife in wild environments. As such, they are non-consumptive wildlife tourists viewing non-domesticated, semi-free-ranging animals (Higginbottom, 2004a). They are interested in what they can see and experience; most do not engage with the complexities of conservation history, philosophies, management plans and policies, politics, economics, social and cultural impacts or benefits that underlie and underpin the surfaces of the wildlife on show. For these tourists, the places are simply there, as is the wildlife within them. How they have been brought about and how they are sustained are not issues that concern them as visitors. This chapter will focus on a wildlife tourism organisation which ensures that tourists do engage with the complexities listed above. The company educates its visitors on the history of the South African land it uses and informs them of the politics, goals, management and social exchanges which surround what they do.

African land and resources were previously seized and exploited by Europeans wishing to profit from the continent's assets (Anderson and Grove, 1987). Both colonial and apartheid systems actively inhibited the ability of rural Africans to control their resources (Adams and McShane, 1996), creating huge problems for South Africa and its people. Post these eras, there are now many initiatives emerging which aim to restore rights and responsibilities to a local level (Nelson, 2010) and to prevent neo-colonial wildlife tourism across Africa (Akama, 2004). These initiatives are mostly led by conservation and tourism bodies, companies seeking to develop strategies that accommodate, include and centralise local communities and their livelihoods in their goals (Nelson, 2010). As previously stated, most tourists take little interest in these aspects of conservation and wildlife tourism; however, this chapter offers a case study of a tourism enterprise that seeks to engage university students, and other tourists, with the contexts and complexities of conservation. The study illustrates how tourism companies acknowledge that African wildlife is intimately tied to the future of African rural communities (Anderson and Grove, 1987) and how conservation is not just simply the protection of species and habitats, it is now also connected to rural development and the survival of agrarian societies (Nelson, 2010). Provision of this evidence that tourists are being taught more about the context of what they are observing, instead of merely seeing and photographing, offers an optimistic portrayal of tourism prospects and development in South Africa.

African insight and Afro-positivism

The case study focuses on African Insight, an educational wildlife tourism company based in northern KwaZulu-Natal (KZN). The company was founded in 1996 by Andrew Anderson with goals to instruct tourists in wildlife, conservation and its management. In recent years, one focus of its activities has been the Somkhanda Game Reserve – a 12,000-hectare area that was formerly a group of cattle and game farms and now owned by a Community Trust of the Gumbi people. The land was returned to the Gumbi in 2005 through the Restitution of Land Rights Act, 22, 1994 (see Somkhanda Fact Sheet 2). African Insight started as a tourism partner responsible for the development and management of tourism in Somkhanda. This is evident in the company logo and keywords 'Inspire – Educate – Empower' (see Figure 8.1) that reflect its innovative direction in experiential education. It is not just nature that is being 'dynamically empowered' (Crouch, 2003, p. 23), but also the student learner and the emancipated hosts in a postcolonial environment.

The company develops visitors' personalised experiences of South Africa, tailoring packages to suit the tourist group's desires and expectations (conservation, community outreach, education, youth development, cross-curricular programmes). From an academic perspective, the African Insight Academy educational dimension offers 'experiential outdoor education, driven by curriculum

Figure 8.1 African Insight Academy logo

objectives' (AIA, 2018a, p. 4). Students, interns, visitors and tourists experience the wildlife and get involved in the reserve's baseline data collection – real-world research into conservation and biodiversity management in the reserve. They inter-act with the place, people and wildlife, respectfully approaching Somkhanda as 'an enormous wildlife laboratory' where they can undertake 'Science on Safari', as visits are advertised on the company website (AIA, 2018b). The empowerment theme of the engagement is important for all actors – host, guest, community. It resonates with a postcolonial self-determination from the bottom-up independ-ence for the people, but also for the scholarly visitor. When cultural geographer David Crouch (2003, p. 23) writes that 'Nature is dynamically empowered', he is suggesting that we cultivate a relationship with nature, setting up conditions to encounter it, 'naturing' spaces. African Insight is one of these naturing providers.

The University of Roehampton, in south-west London, has had a decade-long partnership with African Insight, with the two institutions working together to deliver the module *Conservation, People, and Wildlife: South Africa Field Course* to final year undergraduate students of anthropology, biology and zoology. The module is experience-rich, being delivered entirely in South Africa, outside the confines of a classroom, where students are completely immersed in issues of conservation on the ground. During their stay, the students spend time at Som-khanda where they learn about the reasons for and the practicalities of re-wilding compared with attempting to farm the land. The key issues here are what benefits the local community might gain by having wildlife tourists visiting the reserve and what issues arise in terms of conflicts over competing claims of management and ownership relating to wildlife and livestock. Coupled with the stay on the reserve, the students spend time in a local community where, in groups of two or three, they stay for two nights with families who volunteer, and are paid, to host them. With their local facilitators to help them, the students attempt to find out as much as possible about what it is like to live close to a wildlife reserve and the local people's experience of wildlife tourism and the importance of conservation.

In addition to the talks, presentations, guided wildlife drives and immediate experience, all the students are given a work package of academic articles related to conservation issues. These are read and then discussed in informal seminar settings during the field trip.

These experiences highlight to students what it means to take a community-based approach to wildlife tourism. Students can see that community members have a voice in matters of land use and management. They also observe the opportunities there are for employment, education, growth (e.g., some staff start as kitchen workers and within a few years have become trained wildlife guides) and revenue for local people. These features of the company are befitting and progressive, given that the owner of African Insight's goal is to improve rural livelihood and provide opportunities for local people, alongside offering educational wildlife experiences (Hulme and Murphree, 2001). However, students are also encouraged to evaluate and question the company's practices and are given the opportunity to discuss their queries with both guides and local people.

The module and the company are providing optimistic insight into the innovations that South African tourism bodies are taking. Although the students do go on game drives and bush walks while they are there, and these are no different from those offered in other parks, they learn about the environment and the wildlife it contains from the rangers and they participate in their activities. This is a more involved educational pedagogy and immersive experience for the visitor. They learn by doing (setting a camera trap, using a tracking device, operating the GPS). They do see wild animals, as close as possible, to secure their souvenir photographs, and in this sense they are tourists. However, they are also being given an awareness and an appreciation of the complex contexts in which they are seeing these animals in these spaces. African Insight uses wildlife conservation, adventure and cultural immersion as tools to generate knowledge and to encourage more responsible global citizens who have respect for other cultures and the environment. With their field school approach, they have been characterised as 'university in the bush' (Carnie, 2018). They are inclusive of communities, they are teaching future generations and they are showcasing wildlife conservation efforts in a sustainable touristic way – an exemplary model of Afro-positive tourism.

On the field trip, we observed an additional unique feature that the company provides in terms of wildlife tourism. It is not just students who are being offered growth opportunities through tourism but also the staff, and the community are encouraged to learn. Prior to the village stay, the hosts from the village visited Somkhanda to spend an afternoon and overnight visit with the students and to go on a game drive with them. Speaking with the hosts, the students learnt that they had never done this before and that they felt it was an exciting opportunity for them. They were tourists in their own environment, meeting new people from a different culture and venturing out in game vehicles to see large animals they hadn't before encountered. The university students were not the only tourists; African Insight provides local people with wildlife tourism opportunities they might otherwise never experience. Community members themselves through this can gain an understanding of the appeal of tourists who come just to 'see' the wildlife, but they are also made aware of how university students are being taught about more than just the wildlife, but also local and national history, Zulu culture and conservation as practice.

In addition to this, tourism is being made available to local people in another way – the company facilitates community members to access tourism as a career. Speaking with one of our local guides, students learnt that he had started working for African Insight as a kitchen porter, but after expressing his interest in wildlife and his desire to progress in the company, he has developed to become a successful wildlife guide. This illustrates how African Insight is not only instructing tourists in the complexities and contexts of conservation, but also educating local people and recruiting them to share this knowledge with tourists. Wildlife tourism is then a way for all involved bodies and institutions to benefit and develop (Higginbottom, 2004b), and African Insight are achieving this effectively.

Safari in the curriculum: Roehampton's educational experience

Other elements of the field course include a visit to a commercial game ranch where students are introduced to issues such as the breeding, ranching and economics of wildlife compared with ranching systems of domesticated livestock; a few days at Tembe Elephant Park, partly for the traditional tourist experience of seeing wildlife from game-viewing vehicles but also to explore issues of the management of wildlife, particularly elephants, in this fragile sand forest environment; a few days at Kosi Bay to learn about marine conservation and, in particular, something of the importance of traditional fish traps and trapping to the local Tsonga family economies and Tsonga identities.

The focus of the module is the suggestion that issues of conservation can only be fully appreciated by understanding that people and wildlife are intimately connected in such ventures and that the relationships between them are paramount. Here, all the staff and students explore the Africa-facing elements of issues related to conservation. This includes questions such as: How are local people included or excluded in the conservation projects they live alongside? The protection or conservation of biodiversity in all its forms is perceived by many to be a pressing global issue, but how can the particularities be best worked out at local levels? Vibrant, sustainable and diverse wildlife populations might be seen as a universal good, but are some of them also a local burden? Overall, what are the different values espoused within conservation, what are the different claims of and for conservation, how are the practicalities of conservation projects and how can they best be managed? The claim of the module is that through engaging with the particular complexities of the contexts of conservation on the ground, all those who participate in it develop a richer, more sensitive and more nuanced appreciation of how conservation involves multi-faceted issues of particular people, with particular wildlife and all in particular South African landscapes and environments.

Field course assessment: student assessments, transformations and testimony

For the students of Roehampton, prior to any consideration of the educational value of the trip it was obvious that for many, the experience would be life changing. One student had never been on a flight before, many others had never left the country without their parents; the group were embarking on personal journeys, gaining invaluable life experiences, not just academically, but also individually. Lonergan and Andresen (1988) describe how field-based learning can stimulate attitudes of appreciation and value for the subject of study, especially in natural settings. Comments from several students supported this view: two said they wished to return to Somkhanda to do internships, another student said the trip had solidified her desire to work with animals and wildlife, and an anthropology student said the trip had invigorated him to seek work and further experiences with local communities in agricultural areas. It is evident that the mode of tourism education the University of Roehampton and African Insight are providing is contributing to the shaping of students' interests and career paths.

The educational components of the trip were described by one individual upon return as a 'perfect balance of academic and practical learning'. He expressed that reading an article in 'the bush' about something you have encountered that day is very different from reading something of which you have no experience. Other students agreed that being in the actual environment provides insights that they could not access from reading a book or an article or in classroom learning. This kind of transformative learning, being in the field and having first-hand experience catalyses a shift in the students' basic premises of thought; it alters their understanding of themselves, other people and the world we live in (O'Sullivan, Morrell, and O'Connor, 2002).

Prior to the trip, most students expressed that their enthusiasm for visiting South Africa was mainly either to see the wild animals, 'I just wanna see animals, man', or to meet the local people in the village. However, on our return, students spent more time conversing about the ethics of the game hunting park we visited, the opportunities staff were given, the knowledge and personalities of the guides, the lives, practices and involvement of the villagers, the sustainability of the company and the ethics surrounding animal management. They had evidently learnt, grown and vastly enhanced their knowledge and understanding of South Africa, its conservation, its communities and the country's prospects in tourism. On the flight to South Africa, one student described the trip as a 'once in a life time experience'. She felt that a trip such as this would be very difficult to organise outside the structure provided by the university and African Insight; tourists could not get the same educational insight and knowledge from traditional touristic activities. When asked a month after the trip if she still felt the same way, she responded, 'Even more so, you couldn't put a price on it'.

Bibliography

Adams, J. S., and McShane, T. O. (1996). *The myth of wild Africa: Conservation without illusion*. London: University of California Press.

AIA. (2018a). *African insight academy story*. Retrieved November 3, 2018, from www.africaninsightacademy.co.za/

AIA. (2018b). *Somkhanda Game Reserve*. Retrieved November 3, 2018, from www.africaninsightacademy.co.za/somkhanda-game-reserve/

Akama, J. (2004). Neocolonialism, dependency and external control of Africa's tourism industry: A case of wildlife safari tourism in Kenya. In C. Hall and H. Tucker (Eds.), *Tourism and post-colonialism: Contested discourses, identities and representations* (pp. 140–152). London: Routledge.

Anderson, D., and Grove, R. (Eds.). (1987). *Conservation in Africa: People, policies and practice*. Cambridge: Cambridge University Press.

Burns, G., and Howard, P. (2003). When wildlife tourism goes wrong: A case study of stakeholder and management issues regarding Dingoes on Fraser Island, Australia. *Tourism Management, 24*, 699–712.

Carnie, T. (2018). From the classroom to Somkhanda Game Reserve. *The Independent*, January 14, 2018. Retrieved November 3, 2018, from www.independent.co.uk/news/long_reads/from-roehampton-to-somkhanda-game-reserve-south-africa-kwazulu-nata-a8148516.html

Crouch, D. (2003). Performances and constitutions of natures: A consideration of the performance of lay geographies. In B. Szerszynski, W. Heim, and C. Waterton (Eds.), *Nature performed: Environment, culture and performance* (pp. 17–31). Oxford: Blackwell Publishing.

Higginbottom, K. (2004a). Wildlife tourism: An introduction. In K. Higginbottom (Ed.), *Wildlife tourism: Impacts, management and planning* (pp. 1–14). Victoria: Common Ground Publishing Pty Ltd.

Higginbottom, K. (2004b). *Wildlife tourism: Impacts, management, and planning*. Victoria: Common Ground Publishing Pty Ltd.

Homewood, K. (1993). Economics for the wilds: Wildlife, wildlands, diversity and development T. M. Swanson E. B. Barbier. *Africa: Journal of the International African Institute, 63*(2) 292–293.

Hulme, D., and Murphree, M. (Ed.). (2001). *African wildlife and Livelihoods: The promise and performance of community conservation*. Oxford: James Currey Ltd.

Lonergan, N., and Andresen, L. W. (1988). Field- based education: Some theoretical considerations. *Higher Education Research and Development, 7*(1) 63–77.

Moorhouse, T., Dahlsjö, C., Baker, S., D'Cruze, N., and Macdonald, D. (2015). The customer isn't always right: Conservation and animal welfare implications of the increasing demand for wildlife tourism. *PLoS One, 10*(10), 1–15.

Nelson, F. (Ed.). (2010). *Community rights, conservation and contested land: The politics of natural resource governance in Africa*. London: Earthscan.

Newsome, D., and Rodger, K. (2013). Wildlife tourism. In A. Holden and D. Fennell (Eds.), *The Routledge handbook of tourism and the environment* (pp. 345–358). New York: Routledge.

O'Sullivan, E., Morrell, A., and O'Connor, M. A. (2002). *Expanding the boundaries of transformative learning: Essays on theory and praxis*. New York: Palgrave Macmillan.

Salazar, N. (2006). Touristifying Tanzania – local guides, global discourse. *Annals of Tourism Research, 33*(3), 833–852.

Somkhanda Fact Sheet 2 (No date). Retrieved November 2, 2018, from www.environment. gov.za/sites/default/files/docs/fact_sheet2_somkhandaV1.pdf Last

South African National Parks Annual Report 2016/2017. Retrieved November 2, 2018, from www.sanparks.org/assets/docs/general/annual-report-2017.pdf

Stone, L., and Stone, M. (2018). Safari tourism. In J. Jafari and H. Xiao (Eds.), *Encyclopedia of tourism – living edition*. Cham: Springer. doi:10.1007/978-3-319-01669-6_387-1, Retrieved November 4, 2018, from http://avayezenderood.com/wp-content/uploads/2017/12/Encyclopedia-of-Tourism.pdf.

Tapper, R. (2006). *Wildlife watching and tourism: A study on the benefits and risks of a fast growing tourism activity and its impacts on species.* Bonn: UNEP/CMS Secretariat.

9 Building cultural resilience in community-based tourism

The case of Goo-Moremi, Eastern Botswana

Joseph E. Mbaiwa, Gladys Siphambe and Tsholofelo Mbaiwa

Introduction

Cultural tourism accounts for 37% of global tourism and grows at a rate of 15% per year (McKercher, 2002). Thus, in many places cultural tourism can present an ideal vehicle for local and regional development, bringing income and promoting national identity and the preservation of cultural heritage (Richards, 2007). In Botswana, however, cultural tourism has been given little attention, as the tourism branding has focused primarily on wildlife attractions in northern Botswana (Mbaiwa, 2017). In the last decade, though, the history, heritage attractions and lifestyles of Botswana peoples have increasingly become the object of interest for tourists. This case study in brief explores in summary how a rural community in Botswana, Goo-Moremi, has resisted the commoditising and globalising forces of tourism development and maintained its cultural integrity and unique place identity.

Study context: the Goo-Moremi cultural landscape

The Goo-Moremi cultural landscape includes two components, namely, the Goo-Moremi Village and the Goo-Moremi Gorge (Figure 9.1).

a   *Goo-Moremi Village* – The Goo-Moremi village is located 76 kilometres east of Palapye Township in eastern Botswana. The Goo-Moremi people migrated from South Africa to Botswana around the 1800s (White, 2001), led by Chief Mapulane. Approximately 600 people live in the village (Statistics Botswana, 2012). Agriculture is the dominant source of livelihood (Mbaiwa, 2011). From 1999, the community became involved in tourism development through the Community-Based Natural Resource Management programme.

b   *Goo-Moremi Gorge* – The Goo-Moremi Gorge occupies a fenced area of about 1797.3880 hectares. It is located about 342 km from Botswana's capital city of Gaborone, 4 km from Goo-Moremi village and 76 km east of Palapye (Maruping, 2017). The Gorge is considered by the residents as the spiritual seat of their ancestors (White, 2001; Dichaba, 2009). The Gorge

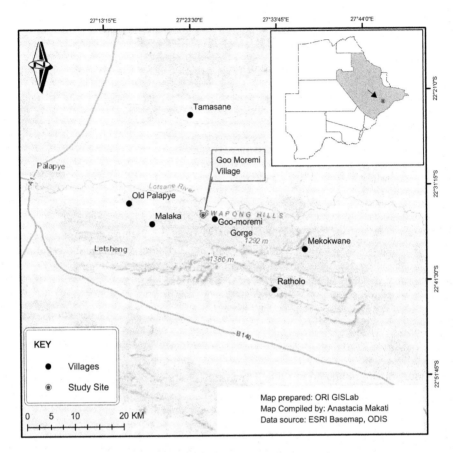

Figure 9.1 The location of Goo-Moremi Cultural Landscape, Botswana

area also boasts historical and archaeological attractions (for example, the graves of Chief Mapulane and his sons), rich biological diversity, spectacular perennial streams and water ponds. The ancestors are believed to watch over the area's socioeconomic, socio-cultural and political development (White, 2001; Dichaba, 2009).

Both the village and Gorge have become key cultural tourism sites in Botswana. Notably, in spite of the significant tourism development at Goo-Moremi, which includes chalets, a campsite and gate house, walking trails, interpretation signs and road networks, the community has maintained a strong sense of cultural identity and integrity, resisting the commoditising and bastardising impacts of tourism reported in comparable contexts. This study sought to explore the sources of cultural resilience in this regard.

Methods

Primary and secondary data were collected and analysed qualitatively. Secondary data included policy documents and journal articles on cultural heritage and tourism development, annual reports of Goo-Moremi culture, as well as historical data about the area's cultural heritage and tourism development. Primary data were collected through face-to-face interviews with household representatives, through focus group discussions and from key informants, who included village leaders and decision makers.

Household interviews were conducted using a structured guide which included both closed and open-ended questions. Open-ended questions were used to solicit the views of participants on tourism development and how it has impacted local traditional values. Questions also covered how residents interact with the Goo-Moremi Gorge and their sense of place, identity and attachment to their culture. For the focus group discussions (FGDs), 100 household representatives were randomly sampled from a total of 165 households at Goo-Moremi Village. This sample represented 61% of the village households. A total of three FGDs were conducted, using a pre-determined interview guide. The first group included young people of ages between 18 and 35. The second group included older participants of ages 36 to 92 years. The third group was a combination of both young and older participants.

Key informants included representatives from the Department of National Museum and Monuments, Department of Lands, Department of Tourism, Department of Wildlife and National Parks, District Environmental Health, Ngwato Land Board, Tribal Administration at Goo-Moremi Village, the Botswana Tourism Organisation, the chief of Goo-Moremi Village and the spiritual mediators in the village. The sampling of key informants took into consideration their positions of influence, knowledge of the ancestral culture and long-term knowledge of the cultural and historical characteristics of the landscape and the tourism development processes at the Goo-Moremi. Content analysis was then used to summarise the data into themes and patterns.

Findings: the sources of cultural resilience

A strong sense of place and cultural identity

The Goo-Moremi Gorge and its immediate environs have sentimental value and are held in great respect by residents. Residents regard the Gorge as a 'seat of the Gods' (Mbaiwa, 2011, p. 294). During FGDs, a village elder noted that 'the gods have told us that they drink water at the Gorge and they should not be disturbed'. When asked what they considered to be the main use of the Gorge, it was interesting to observe that none of the community residents viewed the Gorge's purpose in tourism terms, instead foregrounding its cultural significance.

It was found further that the Gorge is not considered sacred by the people of Goo-Moremi alone, but by the entire surrounding Tswapong Hills communities who live in 13 villages.

At the centre of ancestral worship at the village are spiritual mediators composed of a male group known as *Bazina*, and their ancestral spirit council where they take decisions known as the *Komana*. The *Bazina* hold regular spiritual council meetings or *Komana* to direct the affairs of the village. The *Komana* is headed by a spiritual leader who directly communicates with ancestors or gods. The *Bazina* interpret the wishes and concerns of the ancestral spirits to the people of Goo-Moremi and vice versa (Mbaiwa, 2011). The *Bazina* are responsible for organising ceremonies and sacrifices to ancestors. They also perform intermediary roles between the community and the ancestral spirits.

By maintaining consistent observance of the traditional practices tied to the physical and cultural landscape, the village maintains a unique sense of place attachment and identity (Hashemnezhad, Heidari, and Hoseini, 2013; Cighi, 2008; Smith, 2015; Steele, 1981). Sense of place is associated with sentiments of attachment that people have about a physical place or environment (Casey, 1996; Kahn, 1996; Najafi and Shariff, 2011; Stedman, Beckley, Wallace, and Ambard, 2004; Um and Crompton, 1987). Furthermore, the villagers' implicit faith in the ancestors' providence also creates a strong spiritual connection among residents that makes them resilient in the face of outside influences and the potential corrupting impacts of tourism involvement.

Cultural sovereignty in tourism development

Participants reported that it was important for all tourism developments to be approved by ancestors. For example, when there are plans for village electrification, water reticulation, school development and road construction, consultations with the ancestors must be initiated through *Bazina*, who then perform a traditional ceremony known as *Mophaso*, involving libations, singing and dancing. The *Bazina* approach the ancestors and present them with the proposed developments. The ancestors, in turn, communicate with *Bazina* and offer their responses. During interviews, the chief spiritual mediator of *Bazina* noted, 'we need developments in our village, but all development projects should be requested from ancestors'.

Participants also reported that projects which were undertaken without observing the appropriate cultural-spiritual protocols were destined to fail, citing a number of instances as proof. For example, they reported, the Tshekedi road linking Moeng College to Palapye was initiated by Chief Tshekedi Khama but later abandoned because the ancestors were not happy with it (Lesotlho, 1983; Dichaba, 2009). Moeng College was the first secondary school in pre-independence Botswana that most of the country's first leaders attended. Key informants claimed that workers on the road project would spend all day clearing the bushes, but in the morning would be stunned to find the trees had re-grown overnight. It was widely believed that this was an act of sabotage by the ancestors. According to reports, Chief Khama finally abandoned the project and sought an alternative route to reach the college.

In another example cited by participants, when in the 1990s the Department of Water Affairs sought to fence and secure a water spring at the Gorge known as *Motlhodi*, without seeking the blessing of the ancestors, the fence would repeatedly unravel. When the Department persisted, the ancestors were angered and responded with a mosquito infestation as punishment.

Thus, even in modern Botswana, occurrences at Goo-Moremi Gorge which modern science could interpret as caused by physical natural conditions such as exfoliation and erosion are interpreted as acts of the ancestors and the gods. These traditional beliefs were also evident in the interpretive signage around the Gorge. For example, a framed poster placed on a rock on site reads,

> On the morning of the 13th of July 1980 between 2am and 5am, a loud rumbling was heard by the villagers of Goo-Moremi as this stone fell from the Gorge above. The stone falling is said to be a sign that someone of great importance had passed away. Later that morning, it was formally reported to the village that Sir Seretse Khama had passed away.

Tourism planners and developers were also cautious not to undermine the traditions and belief system of the place. When the rules and protocols are violated, it was believed, there are consequences. White (2001, p. 16) notes that violations of the 'rules are not subject to sanctions by human authority but by the ancestors' who may bring bad luck to people who contravene the rules. The ancestors must then be propitiated by sacrificing either a black ox or a goat, whose portions will then be cooked and placed at the *Kgotla* as an offering to the ancestors for someone to escape bad luck. Reports of disobedience of the cultural codes of behaviour are relayed through the *Komana* to alert the whole community. The offenders are then summoned to the *Kgotla* for flogging or other appropriate punishment. The ancestors may forgive the offender if he or she shows remorse. Thus in every aspect of behaviour, including tourism-related actions, the cultural rules must be followed without exception. The meanings that are held about the place – the sense of place – are therefore given precedence over economic imperatives.

Taboos and norms governing tourists' behaviour

Findings revealed that tourists are also expected to observe strict codes of behaviour when visiting Goo-Moremi. These include:

- Swimming in the pools is not allowed. There are six deep pools receiving water from a permanent waterfall and a stream running across the Gorge. The pools are viewed as bathing places for their ancestors' spirits.
- All tourists, whether married or unmarried, should avoid sexual activity the night before visiting Goo-Moremi Gorge and during the course of their stay.
- Female tourists should refrain from visiting the Gorge during their menstrual period.
- All campfires should be extinguished at night.
- No noise is permitted at the Gorge at night.
- The use of offensive language is not allowed at the Gorge, as this will be tantamount to insulting the ancestors at their abode.
- Visitors may not remove anything from the area.

The system of rules and taboos governing behaviour serve to reinforce the cultural integrity of Goo-Moremi and its significance to the local people. In doing so, the community maintains its cultural identity and resists the commoditising influences of tourism which would otherwise corrupt the sacred landscape, both physical and symbolical. In contrast with other commoditised cultural tourism attractions around the world, the Goo-Moremi people have remained resolute about not bending their sacred cultural norms and codes of behaviour to accommodate tourism.

Conclusion

This brief case study sought to examine the sources of cultural resilience at Goo-Moremi: how has the community maintained its cultural identity in spite of its significant involvement in tourism? The findings suggests that the community's cultural resilience is largely due to the strong resolve not to bend longstanding cultural norms and codes of behaviour to accommodate tourism. Instead, tourism is expected to adhere to the Goo-Moremi people's prescriptions – not the other way around. Three key themes were discussed, namely the strong sense of place, cultural sovereignty over all tourism development and a system of taboos and norms that govern both residents and tourists. Viewed through a Western lens, the spiritual beliefs of the people of Goo-Moremi may be dismissed as baseless myths and fantasy, but their symbolic role may be the reason behind cultural resilience. From that perspective, the 'unscientific' beliefs may indeed be effective safeguards that have saved Goo-Moremi from the fate which has befallen many cultural attractions around the world. In addition to cultural preservation, the people of Goo-Moremi have maintained a strong sense of pride and identity rooted in cultural symbols.

References

Casey, E. S. (1996). How to get from space to place in a fairly short stretch of time: Phenomenological prolegomena. In S. Feld and K. Basso (Eds.), *Senses of place*, p. 27. Santa Fe: School of American Research Press.

Cighi, C. I. (2008). *Senses of place* (Unpublished Master's Theses), Department of Hospitality and Tourism Management, University of Massachusetts Amherst.

Dichaba, T. S. (2009). *From monuments to cultural landscapes: Rethinking heritage management in Botswana* (MA Thesis), Rice University.

Hashemnezhad, H. Heidari, A. A., and Hoseini, P. M. (2013). Sense of place' and 'place attachment':. *International Journal of Architecture and Urban Development, 3*(1), 5–12.

Kahn, K. B. (1996). Interdepartmental integration: A definition with implications for product development performance. *Journal of Product Innovation Management, 13,* 137–151.

Lesotlho, John. (1983). Badimo in the Tswapong Hills. *Botswana Notes and Records, 15,* 7–8.

Maruping, M. (2017). *The adventurous and inspiring Goo-Moremi Gorge memoir.* BotswanaUnplugged Magazine, Gaborone, Botswana.

Mbaiwa, J. E. (2011). Cultural commodification and tourism: The Goo-Moremi community, central Botswana. *Tijdschrift voor Economische en Sociale Geografie, 102*(3), 290–301.

Mbaiwa, J. E. (2017). Poverty or riches: Who benefits from the booming tourism industry in Botswana? *Journal of Contemporary African Studies, 35*(1), 93–112.

McKercher, B. (2002). Towards a classification of cultural tourists. *International Journal of Tourism Research, 4*(1), 29–38.

Najafi, M., and Shariff, M. K. B. M. (2011). The concept of place and sense of place in architectural studies. *International Journal of Human and Social Sciences, 6*(3), 187–193.

Richards, G. (2007). *Cultural tourism: Global and local perspectives.* New York: Haworth Press.

Smith, S. (2015). A sense of place: Place, culture and tourism. *Tourism Recreation Research, 40*(2), 220–233.

Statistics Botswana (CSB). (2012). *National population and housing census 2011.* Gaborone: Ministry of Finance and Development Planning.

Stedman, R. C., Beckley, T., Wallace, S., and Ambard, M. (2004). A picture and 1000 words: Using resident-employed photography to understand attachment to high amenity places. *Journal of Leisure Research, 36*(4), 580–606.

Steele, F. (1981). *The sense of place.* Boston, MA: CBI Publishing Company, Inc.

Um, S., and Crompton, J. L. (1987). Measuring resident's attachment levels in a host Community. *Journal of Travel Research, 26*, 27–29.

White, R. (2001). *Integrated development and management plan for Moremi gorge.* Gaborone: Moremi Manonnye Conservation Trust.

10 Leveraging tourism in Kenya through indigenous knowledge

Tom Kwanya

Introduction

Tourism is a crucial sector in the global economy. The World Travel and Tourism Council (2015) reports that tourism contributed 10% of the global GDP in 2014. The report further states that the tourism sector grew faster than other economic sectors, including financial, transport and manufacturing, in the same period. It generated 277 million jobs, translating to one in every 11 jobs globally. Moutinho (2011) observes that tourism contributes significantly to the economy of developing countries. According to Njoya and Seetaram (2018), tourism is also one of the fastest growing sectors in Kenya's economy and contributes directly and indirectly to national development. Statistics from the World Travel and Tourism Council (2017) reveal that in 2016, tourism directly contributed 257.4 billion Kenya shillings (about USD 2.547 billion), 3.7%, to the country's GDP and 399,000 (3.4%) jobs. Consequently, Njoya and Seetaram (2018) conclude that tourism directly and indirectly leads to socioeconomic growth amongst rural and urban poor by increasing income and demand for labour. This ultimately leads to a fall in the poverty headcount as well as the poverty gap and severity in these communities.

Development of the tourism sector in Kenya began soon after independence in 1963. Indeed, Smart (2018) reports that Kenya spent at least two million sterling pounds to market its tourism industry during the 1960s and 1970s. This promotion was conducted in conjunction with projects aimed at facilitating a good experience for tourists. Some of these included the expansion and advancement of transportation infrastructure and hospitality facilities. The government of Kenya also prioritised strengthening technical and institutional capacity of tourism service providers through professional courses in tourism and travel management, catering and accommodation management, events and convention management as well as foreign languages. The government also streamlined visa requirements, application and processing to make it easy for tourists to obtain visas expeditiously. Further, the government embarked on preserving the country's flora and fauna to increase their appeal to tourists. In addition, there were programmes to mainstream the tourism ethos such as courtesy and hospitality amongst the citizenry. Smart (2018) argues that these efforts were largely successful and tourism grew by 20% per year in the 1960s and earned higher revenues than coffee, which was then the top cash crop. Mayaka and Prasad (2012) opine that the growth in the tourism sector in Kenya during this period was boosted by the desire for adventure, sightseeing and big-game hunting by international tourists. This growth rate was maintained into the 1970s.

The pace of growth of the tourism sector slackened in the late 1970s and early 1980s. According to Sindiga (2000), the use of the package tours model lowered tourism prices and diminished the return on investment on related infrastructure and accommodation facilities. Similarly, Smart (2018) observes that tourists to Kenya were mobilised by firms in their countries of origin. This approach ensured that a significant portion of the revenues was retained in the countries of departure resulting in a leakage, rendering the sector unprofitable. In spite of these challenges, the government of Kenya has used diverse strategies to buttress tourism as a top socioeconomic activity in the country. Some of the strategies include increasing the volume of communication on tourism amongst the potential tourists in Europe and North America, for instance, through opening more liaison offices in these regions; increasing the budgetary allocation to and investment in tourism infrastructure and promotion; diversifying tourist attractions to include unique cultural heritage, activities and cuisine; projecting a positive image of the country through international media; as well as repackaging Kenya as the preferred destination for international tourists seeking an exquisite and unique African experience. According to Akama (2002), in the 1980s, tourism accounted for more than 12% of Kenya's GDP, employed about 140,000 people directly and provided indirect income for another 350,000 people. In the same period, tourism surpassed tea and coffee and became Kenya's top foreign exchange earner.

However, Ikiara (2001) describes the status of the tourism sector in Kenya in the 1990s as being erratic and lacklustre. Akama (2002) explains that the growth momentum in the tourism sector witnessed in the 1960s to 1980s was lost in the 1990s due to increased competition from other destinations in the region, particularly southern and northern Africa; loss of marketing networks in traditional tourist-generating countries in Europe and North America; as well as growing insecurity in the region exacerbated by political violence and terrorist attacks resulting in unfavourable travel advisories. Mayaka and Prasad (2012) attribute this decline to poor planning and preoccupation with mere tourist numbers and bed capacity rather than investing in wholesome sector development and sustainable growth. Ng'ang'a (2018) concurs and explains that the growth in the sector was intermittent, depending on the prevailing government policies and external shocks such as insecurity. Smart (2018) adds that the decline in the tourism revenues in Kenya continued throughout the 2000s, resulting in a reduction of employment in the sector by 25% in 2015. This led the government to take myriad actions to redeem the sector. The actions included extensive rebranding as well as marketing and promotion of Kenya as 'a land of contrasts', offering diverse experiences to tourists. These efforts, championed by President Uhuru Kenyatta, resulted in an increase of earnings in the sector by 17.8% in 2016. One key component of these strategies was mainstreaming of indigenous knowledge in the tourism packages.

Indigenous knowledge

Warren (1991) defines indigenous knowledge as the local knowledge or knowledge that is unique to a given culture or society. Johnson (1992) defines it as a body of knowledge developed by a group of people through generations of living in close contact with nature. Onyancha and Ocholla (2005) define indigenous knowledge as a dynamic archive of the sum total of knowledge, skills and attitudes belonging to a community over generations and expressed in the form of action, object and language. Ocholla (2007) states that indigenous knowledge is a complex set of knowledge and technologies existing and developed around specific conditions of populations and communities indigenous to a particular geographic area. According to Kwanya (2015), indigenous knowledge can also be perceived as the knowledge and practices invented by indigenous communities as a means of enhancing their capacity to survive in a given context. Such knowledge relates to, among other things, the cultivation of crops, management of natural resources, art and crafts, and indigenous medicine. Kwanya and Kiplang'at (2016) explain that indigenous knowledge is passed down orally from generation to generation and reflects thousands of years of experimentation and innovation in all aspects of life in a particular indigenous context.

It can be deduced from the foregoing that indigenous knowledge is local since it is engrained in a specific indigenous community; is established within the boundaries of broader cultural traditions and developed by a specific community; is intangible and consequently not easily codified; is conveyed orally; is experimental rather than theoretical; is learnt through repetition; and changes continuously with conditions around and within the concerned community. According to the World Bank (2004), indigenous knowledge is constantly created and recreated, discovered and lost, even though outsiders may perceive it to be static. This view concurs with Johnson (1992), who asserts that indigenous knowledge evolves in the local environment so that it is specifically adapted to the needs and conditions of the local people. So, it is not old-fashioned, backward or static. Langill (1999) explains that indigenous knowledge is creative and experimental, constantly incorporating outside influences and internal innovations to meet emerging needs. Semali and Kincheloe (1999) hold the view that indigenous knowledge reflects the dynamic ways in which the residents of an area have come to understand themselves in relation to their environment and how they organise that folk knowledge of flora and fauna, cultural beliefs and history to enhance their lives. A similar view is expressed by Flavier, de Jesus, Navarro, and Warren (1995) who state that indigenous knowledge systems are dynamic and are continually influenced by internal creativity and experimentation as well as by contact with external systems.

Fleer (1999) explains the distinction between indigenous knowledge and scientific knowledge using the concept of worldviews. She points out that while indigenous knowledge is founded on traditional worldviews and produced for specific purposes to maintain particular societies, scientific knowledge is founded on the 'civilised' worldview and produced for the sake of it. She argues that while scientific knowledge seeks power over nature and people, indigenous knowledge seeks to coexist with the same. On the one hand she describes scientific knowledge as being materialistic, reductionist, rational, de-contextualised, individual and competitive, while on the other hand she extols indigenous knowledge as being spiritual, holistic, intuitive, contextualised, communal and cooperative. Table 10.1 contrasts scientific and indigenous worldviews as applied in this chapter.

According to Agrawal (1995), indigenous knowledge has often been perceived by some as being inefficient, inferior and anti-development. However, he reports that it is gaining prominence and has become a new area of attraction in development. Semali and Kincheloe (2002) concur and assert that indigenous knowledge is gaining prominence in the search for solutions to challenges relating to socioeconomic development and prosperity of societies, not just in indigenous communities but also in the global community as a whole. This increased focus on indigenous knowledge represents a shift from the preoccupation with scientific knowledge, which has failed to alter the lives of the majority of the poor over the decades.

A study sponsored by the United Nations Environment Programme (UNEP) in Kenya, Tanzania, Swaziland and South Africa conducted between 2004 and 2006 concluded that the value of indigenous knowledge for socioeconomic development lies in its ability to deliver social and economic goods. The study also concluded that certain traditional practices, if popularised and integrated with modern knowledge systems, can help to alleviate poverty (Steiner, 2008). It was also evident from the study that the rural poor depend on indigenous knowledge for specific skills essential for their survival. Kwanya (2015) argues that indigenous knowledge improves the livelihoods of indigenous communities and other stakeholders, provides the basis for solving their problems and promotes a global knowledge on development issues. According to Chepchirchir, Kwanya, and Kamau (2018), indigenous knowledge contributes to socioeconomic development by generating income through activities such as tourist attraction as well as sale of cultural artefacts and music. Similarly, indigenous knowledge creates a physical environment supportive of forests and herbal plants which support socioeconomic activities. They also argue that protection of cultural expressions enriches the national heritage and promotes tourism as a socioeconomic activity.

Table 10.1 Contrasting scientific and indigenous worldviews

Scientific Worldview	Indigenous Worldview
Distant	Immediate
Abstract	Need-based
Materialistic	Spiritual
Reductionist	Holistic
Rational	Intuitive
De-contextualised	Contextualised
Power over nature	Co-existing with nature
Individual	Communal
Competitive	Cooperative
Explains mystery	Celebrates mystery

Indigenous tourism

Tourism is one of the socioeconomic activities in which indigenous knowledge can be gainfully applied. Through the concept of indigenous tourism, indigenous communities are able to generate economic value from their traditional practices. Also a form of cultural tourism, indigenous tourism can be defined as a tourism activity in which the indigenous people are directly involved either through control and/or by having their culture serve as the essence of the attraction (Hinch and Butler, 1996; Zeppel, 2006). Smith (1996) states that habitat, heritage, history and handicrafts are the four 'Hs' which underpin indigenous tourism. Kwanya (2015) explains that indigenous tourism can be provided, for instance, by restaurants which serve indigenous foods; hotels and accommodation facilities owned and managed by indigenous people or constructed using indigenous architecture; indigenous games and cultural events; lifestyles of indigenous communities; indigenous art exhibitions, music, dances and stories around campfires; cultural ceremonies, festivals and special events; visits to cultural sites and shrines; cultural, environmental and spiritual beliefs and practices of indigenous people; and museums holding indigenous artefacts. Besides creating jobs for local people, indigenous tourism also gives indigenous communities an opportunity to tell their story to the world. For tourists, indigenous tourism offers an authentic experience with the indigenous communities as well as their culture and environment.

Control, identity and authenticity distinguish indigenous tourism from the other forms of tourism. Cohen (1988) explains that one of the factors influencing the growth of indigenous tourism is the pursuit of authenticity. He explains that authenticity is a modern value that leads the tourist to seek the pristine, natural experience, untouched by modernity. Wang (1999) explains that authenticity is a saleable attribute which enhances the uniqueness of tourist attractions.

Indigenous tourism can also be perceived as any form of direct or indirect involvement of indigenous people in tourism. This can be through entrepreneurship or passive displays (Hinch and Butler, 1996). It describes the collection of activities and enterprises owned or exploited by individual people. According to Erikson (2003), indigenous tourism revolves around exotic cultures which travellers seek to experience, gain insights into and collect in some form. Lindner (2014) explains that indigenous tourism encompasses performing arts, visual arts and crafts, festivals, museums and cultural centres, and historic sites. Maher (2009) argues that indigenous tourism is growing because tourists are steadily becoming more interested in indigenous culture.

Indigenous tourism in Kenya: key attractions and opportunities

According to Owuor, Knerr, Ochieng, Wambua and Magero (2017), indigenous communities in Kenya practise nature tourism, rural tourism, agricultural tourism and cultural tourism. They explain that the most predominant type of tourism amongst indigenous communities is cultural tourism, which is characterised by visits to local communities that preserve and practise their ancestral traditions and culture. They add that the main activities in community tourism in Kenya include participation in dance and music, festivals, buying souvenirs, artefacts and photography.

Kenya has several attractions which are exploited for indigenous tourism. Some of these attractions include the six UNESCO World Heritage sites in the country, namely, Mount Kenya National Park and natural forest, Fort Jesus, Old Town Lamu, Kenya lake system in the Great Rift Valley, the sacred Mijikenda Kaya Forest and the Turkana National Park. Kenya is also home to several prehistoric sites which are a great indigenous tourism attraction. One of these is Koobi Fora, where one of the earliest pieces of evidence of human habitation on earth was found. Other prehistoric and archaeological sites in Kenya include Olorgesailie, Enkapune Ya Muto, Hyrax Hill, *Jumba la Mtwana*, Ruins of Gedi, Manda Island, Namoratunga and Pate Island.

Kenya also has a number of sacred forests which serve as indigenous tourism attractions. According to Adam (2012), they include Karima Forest which is considered an *ihoero* (sacred natural site in the local Kikuyu culture). The forest is located in Othaya Division of Nyeri County in central Kenya. It is a tapering dome-shaped volcanic hill with its highest point at an altitude of 6000 ft above sea level. The forest is located between the sacred Kirinyaga mountain (Mt. Kenya) and the Nyandarua (Aberdare) ranges, about 150 kilometres north-east of the capital, Nairobi. There are two shrines, Kamwangi and Gakina, in Karima Forest, comprising 85 acres which are gazetted under the National Museums of Kenya. The other sacred site is the Mijikenda Kaya forests which are the most well-known of Kenya's cultural heritage sites. The area consists of several forest sites spread over 200 kilometres in the contiguous Kenyan coastal counties of Kwale, Mombasa, Kilifi and Malindi. The Mijikenda people respect the Kaya forests as the abodes of their ancestors and are revered as sacred natural sites. The sacred natural sites owe their continued existence largely to the cultural knowledge and practices of the nine coastal Mijikenda ethnic groups – the Giriama, Digo, Duruma, Rabai, Kauma, Ribe, Jibana, Kambe and Chonyi. Another sacred forest is Giitune, which is considered as an *irii* (sacred natural site in local culture) on the eastern side of Mt. Kenya and is one of the numerous sacred natural sites surrounding this UNESCO World Heritage site. Giitune lies in a high rainfall area with fertile and well-drained volcanic soils. It is a community forest under the governance of the community which is recognised and protected under the National Museums of Kenya. There are also Mathembo sacred natural sites in Ukambani in eastern Kenya where the Kamba community offers sacrifices during droughts and epidemics or to give thanks for a good harvest. The trees and bushes growing in these places are highly protected, and cutting them is prohibited. Kivaa sacred natural site in Masinga is an example of an *ithembo* (sacred natural site in local Kamba language) which has been rehabilitated by the local community through a revival of their cultural practices and governance systems related to ecosystems.

All the 42 ethnic groups living in Kenya have diverse cultural heritage which offer tourists a unique experience, from traditional dances and bull fighting to festivals and celebrations. The myths surrounding *kaya* on the coast and *Kit Mikayi* and *Simbi Nyaima* in the west are among cultural attractions in the country. Several museums preserving national cultural heritage are spread across the country in Nairobi, Kisumu, Kitale, Kapenguria, Lamu and Meru. Others are Fort Jesus in Mombasa, Gedi Ruins in Malindi, Thimlich Ohinga in South Nyanza and Jumba la Mtwana ruins in Kilifi. Every corner of Kenya has unique cultural features of tourist interest.

Indigenous tourism is being implemented in diverse forms in Kenya by the national government, county governments, communities and individuals to exploit the attractions highlighted above. Consequently, several examples of indigenous tourism projects exist in Kenya. Dunga tourism development project is located on the shores of the world's second largest fresh water mass, Lake Victoria in western Kenya. According to Jernsand (2017), the site attracts several domestic and international tourists who come to participate in traditional games such as canoe rides or tug of war; join in cultural music and dances; or enjoy local foods such as smoked fish and fermented milk. Also in western Kenya is an indigenous tourism circuit hinged around the production and sale of traditional artefacts and crafts. This circuit is predominant in Kisii where the locals produce soapstone carvings. Ondimu (2002) explains that besides the carvings, other tourist attractions in the region include pottery, traditional adornments and ornaments, initiation rites and songs, as well as traditional marriage ceremonies and homesteads.

Another form of indigenous tourism is what Okech (2014) calls culinary tourism. This type of tourism involves traditional food as the key attraction. Kenya boasts diverse indigenous cuisines which are reputed not only for being tasteful but also for their nutritional value. Culinary tourists swarm indigenous food centres dotting the entire country. For instance, in the coastal region there are *Swahili* dishes such as *pilau* (rice), *madafu* (coconut drink), traditional seafood, *kaimati* (donuts), and *bhajia* (coated potatoes). Other uniquely Kenyan cuisines include *nyama choma* (roasted meat), game meat, *mursik* (curdled milk), *aliya* (sun-dried meat), traditional vegetables and herbs, fermented porridge and *mukimo* (potatoes mashed with pumpkin leaves and beans). It is common to find these foods integrated as part of the allure of specific regions of Kenya.

Conclusion and recommendations

It is evident from the foregoing that communities in Kenya as well as the government have embraced indigenous tourism as a means of sustaining growth in the sector. Whereas good progress has been made, several challenges hamper effective execution of indigenous tourism in the country. The challenges include lack of adequate capital to develop products, market the attractions, build facilities and hire competent staff. A further challenge is the lack of relevant business skills amongst local communities to develop appropriate business models around indigenous knowledge and manage indigenous tourism ventures. Remoteness of indigenous tourist attraction sites also pushes up costs associated with visiting the attraction sites. The remoteness of some of the indigenous tourism territories also makes them vulnerable to insecurity and lack of basic services essential for hospitality. Given that some of the attractions are based on natural resources, the effects of climate change and the resulting environmental degradation also negatively affect the viability of indigenous tourism in those areas.

It is critical that indigenous tourism stakeholders formulate national policies and strategies on indigenous tourism. The strategy should identify the high potential niches and outline the means of harnessing them in both the short term and the long term. The government of Kenya would also need to create structures and institutional frameworks to facilitate indigenous tourism. One such structure could be a directorate dealing with indigenous tourism. These structures should percolate down to the devolved levels of government where most attractions are located. The stakeholders should also develop unique indigenous tourism products which can compete globally, rather than merely imitating their competitors. Importantly, the government of Kenya should develop the infrastructure essential for indigenous tourism, including telecommunication, transportation, accommodation and general services. Recognising that indigenous tourism relies greatly on cultures and natural habitats, the concerned communities should work to conserve and preserve these in perpetuity.

References

Adam, H. A. (2012). *Recognising natural sacred sites and territories in Kenya: An analysis of how the Kenyan constitution, national and international laws can support the recognition of sacred natural sites and their community governance systems.* Retrieved from https://cmsdata.iucn.org/downloads/gaiasns_1.pdf

Agrawal, A. (1995). Dismantling the divide between indigenous amd scientific knowledge. *Development and Change*, 413–439.

Akama, J. S. (2002). The role of government in the development of tourism in Kenya. *International Journal of Tourism Research, 4*(1), 1–14.

Chepchirchir, S., Kwanya, T., and Kamau, A. (2018). Maximising the socioeconomic value of indigenous knowledge through policies and legislation in Kenya. *Global Knowledge, Memory and Communication.* doi:10.1108/GKMC-03-2018-0026

Cohen, E. (1988). Authenticity and commoditization in tourism. *Annals of tourism research, 15*(3), 371–386.

Erikson, P. P. (2003). Welcome to this house: A century of Makah people honoring identity and negotiating cultural tourism. *Ethnohistory, 50*(3), 523–547.

Flavier, J. M., de Jesus, A., Navarro, C. S., and Warren, D. M. (1995). The regional program for the promotion of indigenous knowledge in Asia. In D. M. Warren, L. J. Slikkerveer, and D. Brokensha (Eds.), *The cultural dimension of development: Indigenous knowledge systems* (pp. 479–487). London: Intermediate Technology Publications.

Fleer, M. (1999). Children's alternative views: Alternative to what?. *International Journal of Science Education*, 119–135.

Hinch, T., and Butler, R. (1996). Indigenous tourism: A common ground for discussion. In R. W. Butler and T. Hinch (Eds.), *Tourism and Indigenous peoples* (pp. 3–19). London: International Thomson Business Press.

Ikiara, M. (2001). *Policy framework of Kenya's tourism sector since independence and emerging policy concerns* (No. 2). Nairobi: Kenya Institute for Public Policy Research and Analysis.

Jernsand, E. M. (2017). Engagement as transformation: Learnings from a tourism development project in Dunga by Lake Victoria, Kenya. *Action Research*, *15*(1), 81–99.

Johnson, M. (1992). Research on traditional environmental knowledge: Its development and its role. In *Lore: Capturing traditional environmental knowledge*. Ottawa, ON, CA: IDRC.

Kwanya, T. (2015, August). Indigenous knowledge and socioeconomic development: Indigenous tourism in Kenya. In *International conference on knowledge management in organizations* (pp. 342–352). Cham: Springer.

Kwanya, T., and Kiplang'at, J. (2016, July). Indigenous knowledge research in Kenya: A bibliometric analysis. In *Proceedings of the 11th international knowledge management in organizations conference on the changing face of knowledge management impacting society* (p. 48). ACM.

Langill, S. (1999). Indigenous knowledge: A resource kit for sustainable development researchers in dryland Africa. In *People, Land and Water Program Initiative*. Ottawa, Ontario, Canada: International Development Research Centre.

Lindner, M. H. (2014). *Indigenous tourism in North America and Sápmi*. Paper presented at the 29th American Indian Workshop (2007) in Tromsø, Norway. Retrieved from www.academia.edu/download/32851860/Indigenous_Tourism_2014.pdf

Maher, P. T. (2009). Tourism and indigenous peoples: Issue and implications. *Journal of Ecotourism*, *8*(2), 214–216.

Mayaka, M. A., and Prasad, H. (2012). Tourism in Kenya: An analysis of strategic issues and challenges. *Tourism Management Perspectives*, *1*, 48–56.

Moutinho, L. (2011). *Strategic management in tourism*. New York: CABI Press.

Ng'ang'a, L. W. (2018). *The perceived influence of strategic leadership on organizational performance of tourism government agencies in Kenya* (Doctoral Dissertation), JKUAT-COHRED, Nairobi, Kenya.

Njoya, E. T., and Seetaram, N. (2018). Tourism contribution to poverty alleviation in Kenya: A dynamic computable general equilibrium analysis. *Journal of Travel Research*, *57*(4), 513–524.

Ocholla, D. N. (2007). Marginalised knowledge: An agenda for indigenous knowledge development and integration with other forms of knowledge. *International Review of Information Ethics*, *7*(09/2007), 1–10.

Okech, R. N. (2014, July). Developing culinary tourism: The role of food as a cultural heritage in Kenya. In *Proceedings of the second international conference on global business, economics, finance and social sciences (GB14Chennai conference)* (pp. 11–13).

Ondimu, K. I. (2002). Cultural tourism in Kenya. *Annals of Tourism Research*, *29*(4), 1036–1047.

Onyancha, B. O., and Ocholla, D. N. (2005). The marginalized knowledge: An informetric analysis of indigenous knowledge publications. *South African Journal of Libraries and Information Science*, *71*(3), 247–258.

Owuor, G., Knerr, B., Ochieng, J., Wambua, T., and Magero, C. (2017). Community tourism and its role among agropastoralists in Laikipia County, Kenya. *Tourism Economics*, *23*(1), 229–236.

Semali, L., and Kincheloe, J. (1999). *Reclaiming education: Knowledge practices and Indigenous communities* (pp. 523–529). Chicago: The University of Chicago Press.

Semali, L. M. and Kincheloe, J. L. (2002). What is indigenous knowledge and why should we study it? In L. M. Semali and J. L. Kincheloe (Eds.), *What is indigenous knowledge?: Voices from the academy* (pp. 3–58). New York: Routledge.

Sindiga, I. (2000). Tourism development in Kenya. In Peter U. C. Dieke (Ed.), *The political economy of tourism development in Africa*. Putnam Valley, NY: Cognizant Communication.

Smart, D. (2018). 'Safariland': Tourism, development and the marketing of Kenya in the post-colonial World. *African Studies Review*, 1–24.

Smith, V. L. (1996). Indigenous tourism: The four H's. In R. W. Butler and T. Hinch (Eds.), *Tourism and Indigenous peoples* (pp. 283–307). London: International Thomson Business Press.

Steiner, A. (2008). *Indigenous knowledge in disaster management in Africa*. Nairobi: UNEP.

Wang, N. (1999). Rethinking authenticity in tourism experience. *Annals of Tourism Research, 26*(2), 349–370.

Warren, D. M. (1991). *Using indigenous knowledge for agricultural development*. World Bank Discussion Paper 127. Washington, DC: World Bank.

World Bank. (2004). *Indigenous knowledge: Local pathways to global development*. Washington, DC: World Bank.

World Travel and Tourism Council. (2015). *Travel and tourism economic impact: Kenya*. Retrieved from www.wttc.org/-/media/files/reports/economic%20impact%20research/countries%202015/kenya2015.pdf

World Travel and Tourism Council. (2017). *Travel and tourism economic impact: Kenya*. Retrieved from www.wttc.org/-/media/files/reports/economic-impact-research/countries-2017/kenya2017.pdf

Zeppel, H. (2006). *Indigenous ecotourism: Sustainable development and management*. Oxfordshire: CAB International.

Part III

Governance, integration and synergies

11 Regional integration

A lever for positive tourism development in Africa?

Bineswaree Bolaky

Disclaimer: The views and opinions expressed in this article are those of the author and do not necessarily reflect the official policy or position of her institution.

Introduction

The premise that regional integration and cooperation can be a lever for tourism development is not new, and attempts have been made in several parts of the world to promote an entire region as a tourist destination and to promote a single regional brand. The Caribbean, South East Asia and the South Pacific are cases in point. The Caribbean Tourism Organisation (CTO), for instance, has as its vision to 'position the Caribbean as the most desirable, year-round, warm weather destination' and to lead sustainable tourism in the region. In 1989, the 14 island nations of the South Pacific formed the South Pacific Tourism Organisation. In the Association of South East Asian Nations (ASEAN), tourism is a key sectoral body for regional cooperation and integration, with regional leaders sharing a common vision and having shared interests in integrating the tourism industry sector in regional cooperation frameworks (Chheang, 2013).

Specific examples of regional cooperation frameworks on tourism in ASEAN include (i) an ASEAN Tourism Strategic Plan (currently for 2016 to 2025) that identifies joint strategic areas of cooperation and whose implementation is backed by four tourism committees: the ASEAN Tourism Competitiveness Committee, the ASEAN Sustainable and Inclusive Development Committee, the ASEAN Tourism Resourcing, and Monitoring and Evaluation Committee and the ASEAN Tourism Professional Monitoring Committee; (ii) an ASEAN Mutual Recognition Agreement (MRA) on tourism professionals, whose objectives are to 'facilitate mobility of Tourism Professionals, to exchange information on best practices in competency-based education and training for Tourism Professionals, and to provide opportunities for cooperation and capacity building across ASEAN Member States' (ASEAN, 2013, p. vii); (iii) the adoption of ASEAN Tourism Standards; and (iv) an ASEAN Tourism Marketing Strategy (currently for 2017 to 2020), among others.

In Africa, the first Ten-Year Implementation Plan 2014–2023 of Agenda 2063 foresees the full implementation of an African tourism strategy and the establishment of an African tourism organisation (UNCTAD, 2017). However, regional cooperation initiatives on tourism and the inclusion of tourism in regional integration agreements remains under-developed, despite the fact that there is a strong nexus between regionalism and tourism. Among the eight Regional Economic Communities (RECs) of Africa (AMU, CENSAD, COMESA, EAC, ECCAS, ECOWAS, IGAD, SADC), the IGAD (consisting of Djibouti, Eritrea, Ethiopia, Kenya, Somalia, South Sudan, Sudan and Uganda) has a common tourism strategic plan – *the Sustainable Tourism Master Plan for the Inter-Governmental Authority on Development Region 2013–2023*, whose effective implementation remains fraught owing to political instability in the region and a lack of common adequate infrastructure (UNECA and IGAD, 2013). The only other REC with a common tourism development strategy is COMESA. While tourism in Europe and more recently Asia has been fuelled by intra-regional travel, in Africa the potential of intra-regional travel is under-developed, pending the expansion of a middle class. It is estimated that African tourists on the continent spend only a tenth of what an overseas tourist will spend (WEF, 2017). Furthermore, the full unleashing of extra-regional tourism as a development sector in Africa could be fostered by a more effective implementation of regional integration agreements on the continent. Regional integration and cooperation in Africa can be a lever for tourism development in Africa, supporting both intra-regional and overseas (extra-regional) travel and tourism, while tourism as a sector could also strengthen the overall effective operationalisation of African regional integration and cooperation agreements.

The African Continental Free Trade Agreement (AfCFTA) signals a new milestone in the history of regional integration in Africa, in principle planning for the creation of a single market for goods and services and the free movement of people, capital and businesses throughout the continent. Africa has a window of opportunity to harness its regional integration framework to usher in a new approach for developing tourism on the continent, building on comparative experiences and successes in other regions. At the recent African Travel Indaba 2018, held in South Africa, the South African Minister of Tourism called for an integrated and sustainable tourism framework for the region,[1] resting on a facilitation of synergies to develop regional tourism products. This will require increased commitment on the part of African states to implement their bilateral and regional integration agreements, with a mindset of joint development.

Regional integration: towards a new approach of tourism development in Africa?

There is a two-way relationship between regional integration (including in the form of regional cooperation) and tourism (both intra-regional and extra-regional). Regional integration and cooperation can facilitate market, institutional, regulatory and policy reforms that support the tourism sector, such as the free movement of African tourism professionals, and other specific African labour resources needed to operate a labour-intensive tourism sector. Visa removals and other business and trade facilitation measures in regional integration and cooperation agreements and protocols can also reduce operating and transaction costs for the tourism sector, both on the supply side for tourism business operators and on the demand side for tourists travelling to the region. The East African Tourist Visa within the EAC is an encouraging example of regional cooperation on tourism in Africa. It is a visa that allows foreign travellers to circulate between Kenya, Uganda and Rwanda on a single multi-entry visa, thereby stimulating tourism demand across all three countries and opening possibilities for tour operators to develop a regional tourism package. As an example of a multi-country regional tourism product, the tour operator 'Achieve Global Safaris' currently runs safari tours combining Rwanda, Uganda, Kenya and Tanzania, allowing it to position a product that is unique and to differentiate itself from other competitors while targeting high-end 'niche' consumers. Ethiopia announced in 2018 its intentions to introduce visa-free entry for all African nationals, in a bid to boost tourism, following a similar move by Rwanda.

Regional integration and cooperation can allow African countries to pool resources to address Africa's huge soft and hard infrastructure deficits. Africa's lagging infrastructure harms its tourism competitiveness (Bolaky, 2016). Based on the World Economic Forum (WEF) Travel and Tourism Competitiveness Report 2017, there are 26 African countries among the 50 least tourism-competitive countries in the world (WEF, 2017). Figure 11.1 shows the performance of the 33 African countries covered by the WEF Report on the 'International openness' indicator. On a scale of 0 to 7, with higher scores reflecting better performance, there are only eight countries with a score of 3 and above (Cabo Verde, Kenya, Madagascar, Mauritius, Mozambique, Tanzania, Tunisia and Uganda). On the other hand, the regional average in East Asia and the Pacific was 3.9 and in South-Eastern Asia 3.7. The lack of an 'open skies' policy in Africa, ineffective implementation of the 1988 Yamoussoukro Declaration, along with factors such as protectionist policies to favour national airline carriers, and an absence of competition and regulatory frameworks (WEF, 2017) render it difficult for national airline carriers to expand destinations abroad, unless they engage in bilateral airline services agreements that are lengthy and costly to negotiate with destination countries. Regional integration agreements and protocols within RECs and now within the AfCFTA can address these hurdles by facilitating the creation of a Single African Air Transport Market (SAATM). The African Union Agenda 2063 has the SAATM as one of its flagship projects in a bid to create a unified air transport market and liberalise civil aviation in Africa while catering for regulatory and institutional frameworks to support the emergence of an intra-African transport market (e.g. establishing safety and security standards and mechanisms for fair competition and dispute settlement as well as consumer protection). Another project is the issuance of an African Passport (AU, 2017). Progress in translating intent into actions and concrete results in such regional integration agreements will be critical in unleashing the full potential of intra-regional and overseas tourism as an engine of growth and development for Africa.

Regional integration, accompanied by a fostering of spatial development initiatives such as regional economic and business corridors, can promote regional

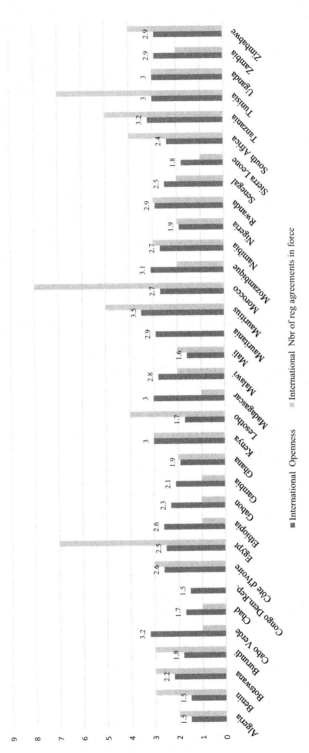

Figure 11.1 Tourism competitiveness indicator: international openness

investments in air transport, ground and port, and tourist service infrastructure that in turn can benefit tourism competitiveness for the region. Air, ground and port, and tourist service infrastructure are weak in many African countries (see Figure 11.2). Based again on the WEF Competitiveness Report 2017, it can be noted that only four countries (Cabo Verde, Mauritius, Namibia and South Africa) score above 3 on all three indicators. China's 'One Belt One Road Initiative' could, for instance, earmark infrastructure investments that support tourism as part of a developmental regionalism funding package for the region. China's investments in Africa could raise air, rail and road connectivity in the region, paving the way for the development of regional tourism products.

Regional integration and cooperation in building productive and trade capacities in Africa, such as through an accelerated implementation of regional trade and industrial policies and the implementation of the AU 'Action Plan for Boosting Intra-African Trade' can help to raise the economic and social benefits of tourism growth on the continent. The wider benefits of tourism development are partially contingent on the ability of countries and regions to reduce import leakages from their tourism sectors and to foster linkages between tourism and other sectors such as agriculture, local construction, creative industries and the retail sectors.

UNCTAD's research has shown that regional integration can be a launchpad for manufacturing development in Africa, given that intra-African trade tends to be more intensive in manufacturing than Africa's trade with the rest of the world (UNCTAD, 2013). Increased intra-African trade in agriculture and manufactures, spurred by regional integration, can contribute to reduced import leakages in the African tourism sectors as cheaper African imports replace more expensive international imports (for example by sourcing food and construction materials from regional sources rather than international ones and by opting for a tourism model based on the valuation of local resources and local heritage).

As regional integration advances, stimulating local and regional industrial and enterprise development, the possibilities for strengthening linkages between the tourism sector and other sectors at national and regional levels are enhanced. Auxiliary local and regional industries in sectors such as food and catering, sports and leisure, domestic travel, creative crafts, entertainment, fisheries, and apparel and fashion, propped up by increased regional demand, become more profitable and build competitiveness to service the local and regional tourism markets. A Mutual Recognition Agreement on tourism professionals, for instance, can support the set-up of tourism auxiliary industries that operate at a regional rather than national level, supported by larger tourism markets that allow them to reap economies of scale and enhance their competitiveness. A South African regional food and wine industry can service hotels in the SADC region, while a diamond industry in Botswana could export hand-made jewellery to service the shopping tourism segment of neighbouring tourism partners. Clothes manufactured in Mauritius could supply the shopping segment of other African tourism destinations, while cosmetics products made in Comoros service the spa segment. Regional cooperation in tourism allows countries to develop joint tourism products that can cut across multiple tourism market segments, in a way

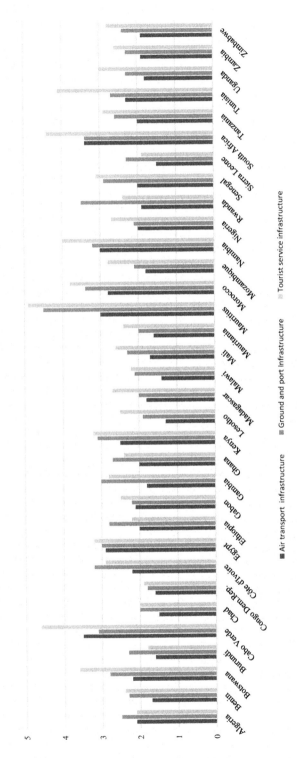

Figure 11.2 Tourism competitiveness indicator: infrastructure

■ Air transport infrastructure ■ Ground and port Infrastructure ▨ Tourist service infrastructure

that harnesses complementarities across individual country product offerings and that results in a sophisticated, branded, differentiated unique regional product characterised by income and price inelastic demand. A combined tour package, for instance, could cater to honeymooners, offering sea, sand and relaxation in the Seychelles, followed by a safari with their extended families to Kenya. Medical tourists travelling to Mauritius could end their journey in Seychelles for a relaxation and recuperation break. There are multiple permutations possible, combining different market segments, different countries for different lengths of stay and price categories.

While regional integration can support tourism development on the continent, tourism can also strengthen the effective implementation of regional integration and cooperation agreements. Tourism could be an 'easier' sector or 'entry point' over which countries can forge consensus when it comes to regional negotiations and cooperation. There may be a stronger political will among local and national leaders to cooperate with neighbouring countries and regions in promoting tourism cooperation either through joint marketing strategy, infrastructure connections or transport facilitation since cooperation on tourism may not involve a large surrender of national sovereignty (Chheang, 2013). Tourism can be a low hanging fruit in the regional integration and cooperation agenda. Tourism can be regarded as 'one of the softest and arguably least controversial means of cementing regional cooperation and integration' (Parnwell, 1993, p. 234). Tourism segments such as ecotourism, community-based tourism and cultural/heritage tourism, within intra-regional tourism, can play a critical role in fostering greater understanding and connections among peoples of the continent, laying the greater goodwill and cooperative spirit needed to progress on regional integration. Tourism can spearhead the building of a community of travel enthusiasts among Africans who are tolerant, understanding and supportive of the greater goals of regional integration in Africa. Intra-regional tourism can contribute to destroying myths and false perceptions among sections of African societies and instil a sense of community among diversity in the region.

Intra-regional African tourism is growing in Africa, but there is significant scope for increasing the contribution of tourism in total exports on the continent, not only by attracting more international travellers but also by developing intra-African tourism. However, data on intra-African tourism may be incomplete and should be interpreted with caution. Estimates of non-resident visitors[2] from the UN World Tourism Organization (UNWTO) are available either by nationality or by country of residence. The share of African nationals in total arrivals of non-resident visitors at national borders is high (above 70%) in countries such as Rwanda, Namibia, Senegal and Chad (Figure 11.3). The share of African residents in total arrivals of non-resident visitors at national borders is high (above 70%) in Lesotho, Botswana, Swaziland, South Africa, Uganda, Malawi, Mozambique and Zambia (Figure 11.4). In most cases, the destination countries attract African tourists mostly from neighbouring countries that belong to the same REC. These estimates confirm the potential for African countries to expand significantly intra-regional tourism by attracting larger numbers of arrivals from African host countries that are further away. Investments in airport and ground transportation

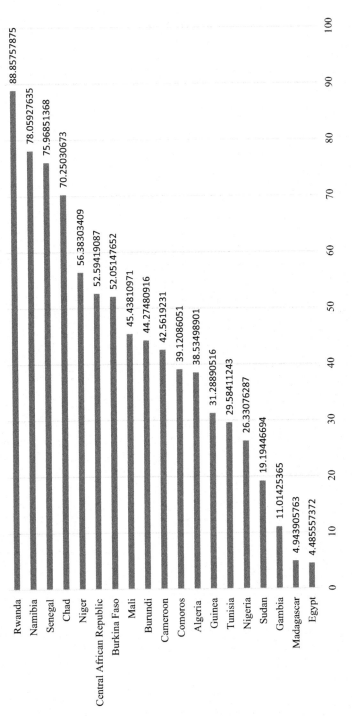

Figure 11.3 Share of Africans in total arrivals of non-resident visitors at national borders

2015

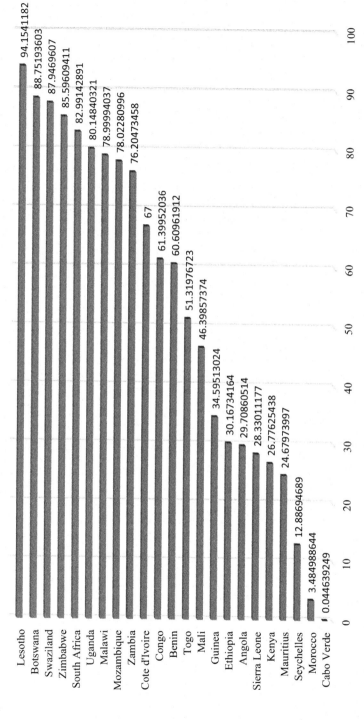

Lesotho 94.1541182
Botswana 88.75193603
Swaziland 87.9469607
Zimbabwe 85.59609411
South Africa 82.9914291
Uganda 80.14840321
Malawi 78.99994037
Mozambique 78.02280996
Zambia 76.20473458
Cote d'Ivoire 67
Congo 61.39952036
Benin 60.60961912
Togo 51.31976723
Mali 46.39857374
Guinea 34.59513024
Ethiopia 30.16734164
Angola 29.70860514
Sierra Leone 28.33011177
Kenya 26.77625438
Mauritius 24.67973997
Seychelles 12.88694689
Morocco 3.484988644
Cabo Verde 0.044639249

0   10   20   30   40   50   60   70   80   90   100

Figure 11.4 Share of residents in Africa in total arrivals of non-resident visitors at national borders

infrastructure to improve on connectivity on the continent is an important policy priority in that respect. These same estimates also suggest that there is a significant potential to attract international tourists arrivals in those countries where intra-African tourism occupies a large share of total tourist arrivals. Diversification of source markets in African countries should be a policy priority and will require significant investments in improving tourism competitiveness on the continent as well as accelerating regional cooperation and integration to enhance tourism competitiveness (Bolaky, 2016).

Positive integration: policy proposals

Adopting a regional tourism development approach on the continent is timely and should be scaled up. The advent of the AfCFTA could provide an opportunity to create momentum around an integrated and regional approach towards tourism development on the continent. Such a regional approach should rest on the implementation of common regional tourism development strategies and on policies to foster the development of regional tourism value-chains. Entire sub-regions can be marketed as unique destinations. Tourism clusters could be fostered both nationally and regionally. Regional solutions could be designed to tackle common competitiveness challenges across countries. Regional integration and cooperation on tourism, however, is challenging and has met with only some degree of success in other developing regions such as the Caribbean and South Pacific. There is an inherent dynamic of cooperation mixed with rivalry and competition at play that can impede the development of a genuinely cooperative culture across countries (World Bank, 2013), especially if the countries tend to depend on the same source markets and offer similar products. Other inhibiting factors include a lack of capacities within institutions and in policy making and implementation, shortage of political will and commitment, insufficient funding, limited private sector development and weak consultative mechanisms between the private and public sectors.

A region that has tried an integrated approach to tourism development are the Indian Ocean Islands of Comoros, Madagascar, Mauritius, Seychelles and Reunion Island, a French territory, all of which are members of the Indian Ocean Commission (IOC). Mayotte, another French territory, is also involved. The Vanilla Islands Organisation (VIO), established under the aegis of the IOC, has as its objective to raise tourism competitiveness among the islands of the Indian Ocean and unify them 'under one tourism brand through the valorization of each of the islands unique selling propositions' (UNWTO, 2013). The organization also aims to increase connectivity to and among intra islands, create new multi-destination products (UNWTO, 2013), harness complementarities and build on synergies across the islands in order to increase the number of high-end visitors to the region. Other objectives include providing tools for better efficiency and promoting quality standards and services. An 'AirPass' programme was set up to encourage island hopping for tourists. The current Vanilla Pass card offers discounts and benefits to tourists travelling to the islands and, in terms of multi-country packages, there is a combined ecotourism tour to Madagascar and the Comoros and an Indian Ocean cruise offer.

Policy proposals for regional tourism development in Africa

The successful development of regional tourism development approaches in Africa will necessitate a set of specific, practical and actionable public policies at regional and continental levels and policies that are developed in close consultation with private operators in the tourism sector. Tourism is essentially a private-led activity, and public-private partnerships are an effective driver of development in tourism (UNWTO, 2015). There are major areas in which public policy, backed by public-private partnerships, can promote regional tourism development in Africa, and these relate to improving transport and connectivity infrastructure, developing and implementing joint tourism development strategies that harness complementarities in offerings across countries and supporting the development of tourism value-chains and tourism clusters in the region.

Improve in air and ground connectivity and liberalise airspace to raise frequencies of flights and reduce costs of travelling

One area of regional cooperation lies in accelerating the implementation of the 1999 Yamoussoukro Declaration and the AU Single Air Transport Market project in order to create an 'open skies policy' on the continent that stimulates competition among airline carriers, drives down fares, increases flight frequencies, generates air traffic growth and sets safety and quality standards. The dream of creating a single unified common African market, marked by significant intra-African trade and investment, cannot be realised unless the continent significantly raises transport connectivity. The Yamoussoukro Declaration calls for:

- Full liberalisation of intra-African air transport services in terms of access, capacity, frequency and tariffs;
- Free exercise of first, second, third, fourth and fifth freedom rights for passenger and freight air services by eligible airlines (These rights, granted by most international air service agreements, enable, among others, non-national carriers to land in a state and take on traffic coming from or destined for a third state.);
- Liberalised tariffs and fair competition; and
- Compliance with established ICAO safety standards and recommended practices (World Bank, 2010).

More countries need to ratify the agreement and translate commitments into concrete actions. An observatory or scorecard monitoring and evaluating the ratification and implementation of the declaration across all RECs or within each REC could be a means of enhancing progress towards the objectives set in the declaration.

Develop and implement joint tourism development strategies within and across sub-regions based on existing complementarities

A good starting point for promoting regional tourism approaches in Africa is to accelerate the preparation of joint, integrated or common regional tourism development strategies in each REC or across geographical sub-regions. Such a strategy should aim at creating a unique quality, sustainable tourism brand for the region, based on the design of tourism products that exploits the complementarities that each destination offers (e.g. ecotourism combined with sea and beach tourism, community-based tourism combined with cruises, safaris combined with heritage tourism). A regional cruise tourism development strategy could also be a starting point to develop diverse products, especially along the coastlines of the continent. Other policy measures to address tourism competitiveness challenges include capacity building relating to the implementation of tourism strategies through technical assistance from more mature tourism destinations, human resource development involving the set-up and operationalisation of regional Tourism Training Institutes, operationalisation of MRA on tourism professionals across sub-regions to facilitate access to qualified tourism personnel, joint marketing campaigns across destinations, capacity building in tourism statistics collection and analysis to facilitate tourism market intelligence and resource mobilisation strategies to secure funding for the implementation of the regional development strategies (e.g. creation of Tourism Development Funds that are in part financed from donors and Southern partners such as China and India). The signing of Tourism Agreements in sub-regions and for the continent as a whole can provide a starting point to delineate areas for regional collaboration. ASEAN has had a Tourism Agreement since 2002 (see Box 11.1) that defines areas of regional cooperation in marketing, human resource development, and safety and security, among others.

Support the creation of regional tourism value-chains and tourism clusters in Africa

Policies to spur the creation of regional tourism value-chains and clusters in tourism could contribute towards promoting linkages and reducing leakages in the sector. This can be more effectively done if a regional tourism development strategy exists, that identifies sectors and activities where more private entrepreneurship is needed on a regional basis. Fiscal and monetary incentives can be tools for building productive capacities in specific tourism auxiliary industries matched by institutional support. Regional tourism development strategies have to be supported by a range of complementary strategies that include entrepreneurship strategies and Micro, Small and Medium-sized Enterprises (MSMEs) development policies, national and regional industrial policies, rural and agriculture development policies, private sector development strategies and gender development strategies to ensure that women have fair access to employment and entrepreneurship in the tourism industry. Effective state-business relations should guide the process. Consultative mechanisms between the public and private sector have to be encouraged on the continent in order to enhance effective tourism policy implementation, monitoring and evaluation. The development of national tourism clusters[3] within the regional tourism value-chain should be fostered and integrated in national rural and urban development policies to support private sector activities in a range of tourism auxiliary activities. Members of these clusters include tour operators, guides, hotels and restaurants, agricultural producers, transport services suppliers, financial services suppliers, entertainers, public authorities, tourism institutions, universities and training institutes. The potential for developing rural-based tourism must not be overlooked in regional tourism development in Africa. There is a potential for developing specific tourism niche segments in rural areas, involving community-based tourism, natural conservation projects and ecotourism based on authentic 'country' experiences.

Box 11.1 Regional cooperation in tourism in ASEAN

ASEAN has a Tourism Agreement that was adopted in Phnom Penh in November 2002. The objectives of the agreement are:

1   To cooperate in facilitating travel into and within ASEAN;
2   To enhance cooperation in the tourism industry among ASEAN Member States in order to improve its efficiency and competitiveness;
3   To substantially reduce restrictions to trade in tourism and travel services among ASEAN Member States;
4   To establish an integrated network of tourism and travel services in order to maximise the complementary nature of the region's tourist attractions;
5   To enhance the development and promotion of ASEAN as a single tourism destination with world-class standards, facilities and attractions;
6   To enhance mutual assistance in human resource development and strengthen cooperation to develop, upgrade and expand tourism and travel facilities and services in ASEAN; and
7   To create favourable conditions for the public and private sectors to engage more deeply in tourism development, intra-ASEAN travel and investment in tourism services and facilities.

The agreement contains 12 articles that deal, *inter alia*, with facilitation of intra-ASEAN and international travel, facilitation of transport services, market access, quality tourism, tourism safety and security, joint marketing and promotion, and human resource development.

Source: ASEAN (2002)

Regional integration in the context of 'Africa rising': a few remarks

There has been for some years a narrative around 'Africa rising': a narrative based on the fact that a few African economies were registering among the highest economic growth rates in the world (e.g. Cote d'Ivoire, Ethiopia, Ghana, Senegal and United Republic of Tanzania), driven in part by a commodity boom and increased foreign direct investment from the BRICS countries (Brazil, Russia, India, China and South Africa). Though that narrative came under attack with macro-political and economic shifts in several countries, the fact remains that the size of the middle class on the continent is expanding and opens up new opportunities (van Blerk, 2018). Africa's rising middle class is also an attraction for foreign investments on the continent. The narrative, however, is a fragile and vulnerable one. The region's dependence on world markets for mostly commodity-based exports leaves it vulnerable to the ups and downs of the global macro-economic cycle. The African continent needs to engage in economic diversification, structural transformation and source market diversification to keep its economic growth trajectory sustainable and inclusive. The strengthening of a regional integration-tourism nexus in Africa can contribute towards this goal. The development of regional markets can reduce the dependence of African countries on the vagaries of external markets, while high value-added tourism can be a key sector offering scope for significant diversification.

Nonetheless, the deepening of regional integration in Africa, to the extent that it is accompanied by inclusive growth that leads to economic gains distributed across different countries and income groups, has the potential to expand further the size of the middle class in Africa. Rising incomes in Africa, matched by inter-generational mobility, can generate additional demand for intra-regional tourism that should be met on the supply side by targeted investments to facilitate transport and to provide quality tourism services to Africans. Accelerated prosperity in African countries can spur a demand for 'made in Africa' goods and services that can stimulate demand for regional tourism in specific segments, such as shopping and business tourism. The policy message in this context is that the two-way relationship between regional integration and tourism strengthens when Africa is rising. If regional integration accelerates economic growth and is matched by socially inclusive policies that expand the middle class, this benefits demand for regional tourism in Africa. Sound macro-economic and social policies that support inclusive growth matter for intra-regional tourism expansion.

Within the Africa rising narrative, a potentially interesting development relates to the impact of increased digitalisation and e-commerce on regional integration and tourism development in Africa. E-tourism is 'a way of establishing commercial relationships (mainly sales) using the Internet for offering tourism related products: flights, hotel reservation, car rental and so on' (Condratov, 2013, p. 58). It also refers to the digitisation of all the processes and value-chains in the tourism, travel, hospitality and catering industries that enable organisations to maximise their efficiency and effectiveness (Buhalis, 2003). Regional integration in Africa should be accelerated through increased investments in infrastructure, including digital infrastructure. The African continent needs to harness digitalisation for increased economic gains. The AfCFTA has identified tourism among its five priority sectors, in addition to transport, communications, financial and business services. Phase 2 negotiations could include e-commerce while the preparation of an African e-commerce strategy is on the agenda. Should digitalisation become an investment priority for African countries as they brace for the advance of e-commerce and regional integration, opportunities will exist for the regional development of e-tourism in Africa. Digitalisation can be an additional force for boosting regional integration and tourism development. A continent-wide e-tourism strategy, matched by policies, institutions and incentives, could spur the development of a range of online African companies along a digitised tourism value-chain. Examples include indigenous online booking platforms, online travel agents, online catering services and online shopping, to name a few. Sustained economic growth and structural transformation, powered by digitalisation, should be priorities for the African continent. Africa rising through these processes and Africa's middle classes expanding are beneficial forces for the strengthening of a regional integration-tourism development nexus.

Entrepreneurship strategies and digital entrepreneurship policies targeting the tourism sector can also play a pivotal role in the creation of regional tourism value-chains in Africa and the digitisation of such tourism value-chains. Tourism is mostly a private sector activity that needs to be supported and regulated by the state. Without profit-oriented entrepreneurship driving the tourism industry, the sector cannot develop. Complementary policies are needed to support the emergence of entrepreneurship and the survival of private Small and Medium-sized Enterprises (SMEs) in the tourism sector and to facilitate their integration in digitised and non-digitised regional tourism value-chains. Targeted incentives towards the tourism sector in national entrepreneurship strategies and the fostering of partnerships between Multinational Enterprises (MNEs) and local SMEs in the tourism and hospitality industry in order to facilitate training and transfer of skills and knowledge are examples of policy actions. The earmarking funds to support tourism entrepreneurship, financed in part from tourism levies and taxes on operations of foreign companies in the tourism industry, could also be considered. The undertaking of surveys among tourism operators to understand the constraints to their survival, profitability and expansion and integration into value-chains merits further attention. The literature on tourism entrepreneurship in general is expanding but remains dispersed, and in the case of Africa, it needs greater space in policy discourse.

Conclusions

As regional integration gathers momentum in Africa, with ratifications of the AfCFTA proceeding and political heads of state confirming their commitment to the unification of the African goods and services markets, the continent has a window of opportunity to engage in the development of a regional tourism model, based on regional cooperation and collaboration in multiple spheres, such as transport facilitation and human resource development. The implementation of a common African tourism strategy and e-tourism strategy along with a Mutual Recognition Agreement among tourism professionals and operators, the creation of a Single African Air Transport Market and a single African Passport, supported by regional institutions such as an African tourism organisation, will be critical steps in that direction. More RECs could develop a common regional tourism strategy and foster intra-REC cooperation in tourism.

There is a regional integration-tourism nexus that needs to be better harnessed in Africa. Regional integration and cooperation in Africa can be a lever for tourism development, supporting both intra-regional and overseas (extra-regional) travel and tourism, while tourism as a sector could also strengthen the overall effective operationalisation of African regional integration and cooperation agreements. For instance, regional integration and cooperation can allow African countries to pool resources to address Africa's huge soft and hard infrastructure deficits that hamper its tourism competitiveness. Regional tourism packages, combining different segments across different countries, can be proposed to international tourists, offering a unique tourism product and experience at a higher value-added end of the global tourism market. Increased intra-African trade in agriculture and manufactures, spurred by regional integration and regional trade and industrial policies, can contribute to reduce import leakages in the African tourism sectors and foster the creation of linkages instead through the development of tourism auxiliary industries. On the other hand, tourism could be an 'easier' sector or 'entry point' over which countries can forge consensus when it comes to regional negotiations and cooperation. There may be a stronger political will among local and national leaders to cooperate with neighbouring countries and regions in promoting tourism cooperation through either joint marketing strategy, infrastructure connections or transport facilitation, since cooperation on tourism may not involve a large surrender of national sovereignty.

There are major areas in which public policy, backed by public-private partnerships, can promote regional tourism development in Africa, and these relate to improving transport and connectivity infrastructure, developing and implementing joint tourism development strategies that harness complementarities in offerings across countries and supporting the development of tourism value-chains and tourism clusters in the region. Regional tourism development strategies in turn have to be supported by a range of complementary strategies that include entrepreneurship strategies and MSME development policies, national and regional industrial policies, rural and agriculture development policies, private sector development strategies and gender development strategies to ensure that women have fair access to employment and entrepreneurship in the tourism industry. Effective state-business relations should guide the process. The potential for developing rural-based tourism must also not be overlooked in regional tourism development in Africa. In addition, sound macro-economic and social policies that support inclusive growth and a rising middle class in Africa, within an 'Africa rising' narrative, can contribute towards intra-regional tourism expansion.

Lastly, digitalisation can be an additional force for boosting regional integration and tourism development in Africa, and in this context, digital entrepreneurship can contribute towards the digitisation of regional tourism value-chains on the continent.

Notes

1 See www.indaba-southafrica.co.za/news/INDABA-2018-african-ministers-meet-to-dis cuss-integrated-regional-tourism.aspx
2 A visitor is classified as a tourist if his or her trip includes an overnight stay, or a same-day visitor (or excursionist) otherwise. The data presented in this paragraph are only approximate estimates to intra-African tourism, as both tourists and non-tourists are included in the data on visitors. For some countries, arrivals are not available by nationality but only by country of residence.
3 The tourism cluster consists of a group of resources and attractions, business and institutions directly or indirectly involved in tourism, concentrated in a particular geographic area (Fundeanu, 2015).

References

ASEAN. (2002). ASEAN tourism agreement. Unofficial text. Retrieved from https://cil.nus.edu.sg/wp-content/uploads/formidable/18/2002-ASEAN-Tourism-Agreement.pdf

ASEAN. (2013). *ASEAN Mutual Recognition Agreement (MRA) on tourism professionals handbook*. Jakarta, Indonesia: Association of South East Asian Nations.

AU. (2017). *The single African air transport market: An agenda 2063*. Retrieved from https://au.int/sites/default/files/newsevents/workingdocuments/33100-wd-6a-brochure_on_single_african_air_transport_market_english.pdf

Bolaky, B. (2016). Tourism for economic development in Africa. *Journal of Research in Business, Economics and Research, 7*(4), 1222–1248.

Buhalis, D. (2003). *eTourism: Information technology for strategic tourism management*. London: Pearson (Financial Times/Prentice Hall).

Chheang, V. (2013). *Tourism and regional integration in Southeast Asia. V.R.F series No.481. Institute of developing economies*. Chiba, Japan: Japan External Trade Organization.

Condratov, I. (2013). E-tourism: Concept and evolution. *Ecoforum, 2*(1), 10.

Fundeanu, D. D. (2015). Innovative regional cluster, model of tourism development. *Procedia Economics and Finance, 23*, 744–749.

Parnwell, M. J. G. (1993). Environmental issues and tourism in Thailand. In M. Hitchcock, V. King, and M. J. G. Parnwell (Eds.), *Tourism in South East Asia* (pp. 286–302). London: Routledge.

UNCTAD. (2013). *Economic development in Africa report 2013: Intra-African trade: Unlocking private sector dynamism*. Geneva and New York: United Nations.

UNCTAD. (2017). *Economic development in Africa report 2017: Tourism for transformative and inclusive growth*. Geneva and New York: United Nations.

UNECA and IGAD. (2013). *Sustainable tourism master plan for the Inter-Governmental Authority on Development (IGAD) region 2013–2023*. Kigali: United Nations Economic Commission for Africa.

UNWTO. (2013). *UNWTO shows full support to the Vanilla Islands*. Retrieved from http://media.unwto.org/press-release/2013-09-11/unwto-shows-full-support-vanilla-islands

UNWTO. (2015). *Affiliate members global reports, volume eleven – public-private partnerships: Tourism development.* Madrid: UNWTO.

UNWTO (2018a). *Compendium of tourism statistics*, 2018 edition. Madrid: UNWTO.

UNWTO (2018b). *Yearbook of tourism statistics*, 2018 edition. Madrid: UNWTO.

van Blerk, H. (2018). *African lions: Who are Africa's rising middle class?* IPSOS Views No. 15. IPSOS.

WEF. (2017). *The travel and tourism competitiveness report 2017: Paving the way for a more sustainable and inclusive future.* Geneva: World Economic Forum.

World Bank (2010). *Open Skies for Africa: Implementing the Yamoussoukro declaration.* Washington, DC: The World Bank Group. doi:10.1596/978-0-8213-8205-9.

World Bank. (2013). *The way forward for Indian Ocean Island tourism economies: Is there a role for regional integration?* Washington, DC: The World Bank Group.

12 Tourism progress in the SADC region

Postcolonial era milestones

Zibanai Zhou

Overview of the SADC region in the postcolonial era

The Southern African Development Community (SADC) region is an economic grouping that comprises 15 member countries, established in 1982. Its membership encompasses Angola, Botswana, Democratic Republic of Congo, Lesotho, Madagascar, Malawi, Mauritius, Mozambique, Namibia, Seychelles, South Africa, Swaziland, Tanzania, Zambia and Zimbabwe (Acheampong and Tseane-Combi, 2016). Most of the SADC countries attained political independence between the early 1960s and the 1990s. South Africa, the region's economic powerhouse, was the last country to attain self-rule in 1994. Given the above, it is apparent that the SADC region countries have relatively young democracies. Soon after attainment of self-rule, the countries painstakingly embarked on ambitious economic development trajectories aimed at revitalising their economies. One way of doing this was through the exploitation of the natural tourism resource base spread across the region.

However, years of brutal and protracted wars of political liberation left most of the region's infrastructural facilities in a dilapidated state. The postcolonial period therefore meant serious rebuilding work was critical. Economic emancipation and value addition grounded in citizens' empowerment and sustainable economic development were imperative. Nonetheless, in the political sphere, democracy is slowly being entrenched, despite some pockets of political instability which erupt intermittently, for instance in the case of Angola, Madagascar, Mozambique, Zimbabwe, Lesotho and the Democratic Republic of Congo. But broadly, on the socioeconomic front, there are positive signs: a growing middle class, improving literacy rates, as well as a revolution in information technology progressing at an unprecedented pace, spurring tourism development in turn. These factors combine to make the SADC region hopeful in the tourism space (Drummond, Thakoor, and Yu, 2014).

Arguably, the challenges faced by the region have been given a disproportionately large portion of academic space in tourism scholarship, at the expense of highlighting the many positive strides the region has made in the sphere of tourism. The core contribution of the current chapter therefore is to outline landmark tourism development milestones registered in the postcolonial era, thus painting a more optimistic picture of the region's tourism future.

Regional cooperation structures

RETOSA, formed in 1997, is the regional tourism marketing institution of SADC. The organisation aims to increase tourism to the region through sustainable development initiatives, effective destination marketing and improved regional cooperation, in collaboration with the public and private sectors. It also seeks to create greater investment awareness for tourism development and ultimately to reduce poverty in local communities. RETOSA works with SADC member countries' tourism ministries, business actors and international strategic partners such as the United Nations World Tourism Organisation (UNWTO).

The regional organisation is credited with strengthening tourism mechanisms and systems within member countries, formulating and developing marketing strategies and programs for the region, creating a concrete regional tourism image, initiating and coordinating targeted human resources development and training programs, implementation of a regional accommodation registration and grading scheme aiming at the development of high-quality products, and cooperating with regional conservation bodies and ecotourism operators to ensure a sustainable and high-quality product development (Manwa, 2011; RETOSA, 2010). Thus, the formation of RETOSA enabled member countries to compete more effectively against well-developed destinations, by pooling resources to create a regional synergy. Through its official advisory role, RETOSA has added value to National Tourism Boards such as the Namibia Trust Board, Zimbabwe Tourism Authority (ZTA), South African Tourism (SATOUR), Malawi Tourism Association (MTA) and Seychelles Tourism Marketing Authority (STMA).

RETOSA uses four pillars to promote and market the region to the target market: adventure, big game, affordability and diversity (RETOSA, 1998). To date, RETOSA's marketing spoors have been spread in the traditional source markets of western Europe and North America and also in emerging markets like China and Russia. RETOSA has maintained SADC's visibility at international marketing platforms such as the World Travel Market and the Shanghai Travel expo. RETOSA's multi-pronged trade strategy encapsulates corporate briefings, seminars, road shows, media blitz and publications, and corporate promotions aimed at stimulating conferences, sports and incentive business into the region, development of a tourism database accessible to stakeholders, commissioned research on customer attitudes and intensive networking with source marketing bodies. In addition, focused marketing strategies like the use of carnivals have been adopted by the region to boost tourism traffic into the region. The region hosts a number of travel trade shows, for example, the Travel Expo in Zimbabwe, the Great Indaba in Durban, South Africa, and the Namibia Travel Expo in Windhoek.

There are also engagements with multilateral development agencies in the SADC region who provide financial support and advice on tourism development issues. For example, the UNWTO, the United Nations Educational, Scientific and Cultural Organization (UNESCO), and the United Nations Development Program (UNDP) have been engaged at the highest level to provide technical and expert advice to the region. Furthermore, bilateral agreements on a country-by-country basis have been signed, giving effect to joint management of natural attractions and pooling of resources to achieve a range of outcomes, for example, to mitigate poaching.

Product development

Peace Parks

By definition, Peace Parks are biodiversity and wildlife conservation areas that straddle the boundaries of and are managed in common by two or more countries (Adams and Hulme, 2001). SADC has made significant strides in developing and commissioning Peace Parks as a way of alleviating poverty, fostering peace and stability within the SADC member states and enhancing ecological conservation. Examples include the Great Mapungubwe Transfrontier Park, Great Limpopo Transfrontier Park (GLTP), Kgalagadi Transfrontier Park and Ai/Ais Richtersveld Transfrontier Park (Büscher and Ramutsindela, 2015; Duffy, 2001; Godwin, 2002; King, 2010).

Transfrontier conservation areas are instrumental in promoting the Africa renaissance theme. These Transboundary Protected Areas initiatives foster more effective biodiversity management, allowing for the restoration of traditional wildlife migration routes and an ecosystem approach to conservation.

A diversified product portfolio

As with most countries on the African continent, the SADC region's tourism product revolves around safaris and the 'big five', as well as other nature-based activities, including sight-seeing, hiking, bird-watching and hunting gorillas and chimpanzees; resorts, which include beach, lake and water sports tourism; cultural tourism encompassing archaeology, village tourism, cultural heritage, historical architecture and traditional markets; and business products such as conferences, meetings and trade.

Further, SADC's destination managers have implemented a range of tourism development strategies aimed at understanding market tastes and trends, designating tourism development zones, extensive stakeholder consultation with local communities when pursuing flagship development opportunities like Peace Parks, world heritage sites, training and equipping personnel with requisite tourism technical skills and drawing up a marketing and promotion strategy to support the tourism product development (NASCO, 2008). Tourism development zones offer special concessions to tourism investors by way of tax holidays and other investment incentives (Aggarwal, 2007). Zimbabwe's Victoria Falls and Beitbridge areas, South Africa' Limpopo province, and Western Cape areas have been declared tourism development zones, for example.

World heritage sites

SADC is home to a large number of world heritage sites such as Tsodilo in Lesotho, Maloti-Drakensburg park, Lake Malawi National Park, Choigoni Rock art, Robben Island, Mapungubwe cultural landscape in South Africa, Victoria Falls, and the Great Zimbabwe in the Masvingo province of Zimbabwe (UNESCO, 2016), which have been leveraged by SADC to develop the tourism sector. With world heritage site status, these various attractions are positioned as important to the collective interests of humanity.

Community-based tourism initiatives

The region has developed and nurtured numerous community-based tourism initiatives whose goal is to give rural communities the rights to use wildlife at the local level (Turner, 2004; MET, 1995b). Examples include Namibia's Torra Conservancy Program in the North West, Zimbabwe's Community-Based Natural Resource Management (CBNRM) programme (for example, the Mahenye and Nyaminyami projects), Seychelles' National Climate Change Responsive Strategy, South Africa's Maluleke Ecotourism Project in Limpopo, a National Parks program for public-private partnerships and Botswana's Okavango ecotourism project, modelled and designed within a high-value and low-impact tourism policy.

The CBNRM construct emerged in the early 1990s as an alternative to the top-down, state-centred environmental protection regime. The central idea of CBNRM was devolution of control over natural resources from the state or other external agents to the community, with emphasis on participatory democracy (Li, 2002; Western and Wright, 1994). CBNRM thus quickly became a primary strategy for conservation action in the SADC region's rural communities, where the poorest segments of society have long inhabited and managed ecologically valuable regions. Participation of local communities led to a sense of ownership of and responsibility for the resources and a clearer understanding of purpose, thus contributing to improved outcomes. It further empowered local communities, giving them a sense of pride in their natural resources and control over their communities' development.

In Southern Africa, where wildlife is the key resource in CBNRM, a common mechanism for generating revenue for local communities is to develop contracts with professional safari operators. The operators manage sport hunting or game-viewing safaris on communal territory, with local communities receiving a share of the proceeds (Murphree, 1995). Community residents also receive benefits beyond direct income, including problem animal control, infrastructure improvements and job opportunities which further help to alleviate poverty. In turn, local communities are less likely to engage in activities that harm the ecological environment, such as poaching megafauna.

Notably, the United States Agency for International Development (USAID) played a particularly important role in the region, providing substantial funding for CBNRM programs in Botswana, Malawi, Namibia, Zambia and Zimbabwe (Agrawal and Gibson, 1999). In recent times, however, a number of these community projects are now severely curtailed by the shortage of international donor funding.

MICE tourism

SADC has become a recognised meetings, incentives, conventions and exhibitions (MICE) destination in the 21st century, as illustrated by the hosting of important events such as the 2010 FIFA World Cup, the UNWTO General Assembly, ATA congress, Commonwealth Heads of Government Meeting (CHOGM), Africa Cup of Nations (AFCON) and numerous travel shows (UNWTO, 2014). The hosting of sport events, especially high-profile mega events, has become an important component of promoting the international visibility and profile of Africa's tourism destinations. The hosting of the 2010 FIFA World Cup in Southern Africa was particularly significant, being the first time an event of such calibre had been hosted on the African continent (Tichaawa, 2014; Nicolau, 2012; Cornelissen, 2007).

The significance of mega events for growing tourism is widely recognised in the literature (du Plessis and Maennig, 2011). Mann (2008, p. 2) points out that 'the legacies of mega events involve ensuring that as many long term benefits are generated for the host city, region and nation well before, during and long after the event'. Giampiccoli and Nauright (2010) posit that mega events are considered important promoters of tourism and feature prominently in the development and marketing plans of most destinations that seek to host them. Similarly, Fouries and Santana-Gallego (2010), Kavetos and Szymannski (2008) and Barclay (2009) underscore that mega events attract tourist revenues and international media recognition for the host region.

Swart and Bob (2012) note that the SADC region has benefited immensely from hosting events. Of critical importance is presenting a new image of the SADC region to the global tourism market, dispelling many of the entrenched negative and misleading images of the region and its peoples. Harris (2011) opined that MICE tourism helped the SADC region to establish a higher international prominence for itself and gain international goodwill. It is critical that the good impression made by the hosting of the events in the SADC region be sustained and used to advance its position in relation to tourism and other economic development imperatives.

Accommodation

The region boasts world-class accommodation stock, offered by reputable international brand names such as the Accor group, Starwood, Intercontinental, Holiday Inns, and Crowne Plaza. The regional tourism body, RETOSA, harmonised accommodation facilities' star grading standards for member countries in an endeavour to maintain quality and benchmarking to reflect contemporary accommodation trends, including requirements of the expanding millennial market segment, new in-room technologies as well as responding to the persistent concern for security. Through the coordination of RETOSA, the region has developed specific minimum requirements on urban hotels, vacation resorts, guest houses, self-service apartments, nature lodges and campgrounds for quality assurance and universal accessibility of the region's tourism product. This has enabled the region to present a consistent and concrete tourism product that meets the expectations of the demanding customer of the 21st century.

Improvements in access

Increased accessibility is demonstrated by the growing number of countries in the region that are entering into bilateral, regional and international open skies agreements to facilitate travel, and at the same time implementing friendlier visa requirements and in certain circumstances removing the visa requirement entirely. SADC's key policy instruments and other enabling conditions such as air transport infrastructure, tourism service infrastructure, price competitiveness, ground and port infrastructure and international openness have been recalibrated with hindsight to enhance efficiency and ease of doing business in the region. Aviation plays a vital role in bringing visitors from all over the globe, and as such, facilitation of air connectivity with source markets has been prioritised in the collaborative tourism strategy.

Rail and air access

A supportive infrastructure is the backbone of any successful tourism destination. In that respect, significant investments have been made in the expansion and rehabilitation of aviation infrastructures within the SADC region including air, road and rail networks. Worth mentioning is the TAZRA railway network connecting Tanzania, Zambia and Zimbabwe. TAZRA is the longest railway linking Southern Africa and East Africa, built with the help of China to facilitate the movement of cargo. The railway serves as a trade route for Zambia, Zimbabwe and Malawi, and it has been described as the economic lifeblood of SADC (Brautigan, 2010).

SADC countries have also developed flight connections to long-haul destinations, with South Africa acting as the main hub linking the region with key source markets. The famous Oliver Tambo (O.R. Tambo) International airport has evolved to become the gateway into the whole of mainland Africa. SADC has taken steps to lift restrictions on air transport on a wider scale (Air Transport Action Group, 2003). The aerospace has been liberalised with a significant number of airline carriers now plying the region, including ComAir, Quantas, Lufthansa, Air Zimbabwe, South African Airways, Fastjet and Air Namibia. As a result, tourism in SADC has benefited immensely from the open skies policies through enhanced tourist choice on airlines, routes, schedules, frequencies and airports, and cheaper fares. The liberalisation of air services has also stimulated the creation and growth of low-cost airlines, charter airlines and airline alliances, which have in turn improved affordability of travel and led to increased tourist flows (Bieger and Wittmer, 2006; Turton and Mutambirwa, 1996; Schlumberger, 2010).

Tourist movement and the uni-visa initiative

Some SADC member countries have entered into bi- and tri-lateral agreements to ease the flow of tourists at immigration and customs points (Vanheukelon and Bertelsmann-Scott, 2016). For example, during the 2013 co-hosting of the UNWTO's General Assembly, Zimbabwe and Zambia had a bilateral agreement to use a single visa. This was a trial run, with a vision to implement the system to other SADC member countries. Another example is the KAZA visa, which tourists can now use for entry into Zimbabwe, Zambia, Botswana and Namibia (UNWTO, 2016).

These initiatives help to counteract the image of the region as having rigid, restrictive and chaotic border formalities. If implemented broadly, the universal visa regime would further enhance regional connectivity within the region and with the rest of the globe. The ultimate goal is for all member countries to be part of the unified travel identification system, making it easier for tourists to travel across the entire region without any restrictions (SADC, 2003). The potential impact of the proposed uni-visa would additionally resonate with the already established transfrontier conservation areas (TFCA), allowing movement of tourists across national parks.

However, bureaucracy and dithering among SADC member states in harmonising land use systems, in addition to political and economic instability in some countries, have stalled the implementation of the single visa.

Challenges

The preceding sections have outlined the major tourism development milestones for the SADC region over the course of the last few decades. It is important, however, to acknowledge that a number of challenges remain, including:

- SADC countries have found difficulty in attempting to balance the needs of the multiplicity of stakeholders in community-based tourism projects. It is clear that blueprint approaches do not work, as each community is unique, in respect of its resource endowment, politics and other situational factors (Agrawal and Gibson, 1999; Crocker, 1991).
- Not surprisingly, on the marketing and promotion front, RETOSA has been stifled by bureaucracy, which has meant very slow decision-making and implementation of agreed upon strategies, as demonstrated in the case of the uni-visa (Rannditsheni, 2008). The lack of consensus among member countries on costs, policy requirements, measures and requirements for the issuing of the uni-visa threaten to derail the process.
- Functional processes such as levy collection are still problematic among the SADC states, as some countries repeatedly fail to honour their obligations on time.
- Synergies are not fully exploited, leading to the duplication of duties and efforts in the public and private sectors of various countries.
- The region still lags behind in technological advancement, making it less attractive for technology savvy tourist market segments.
- The management of SADC's Peace Parks has been complicated by the domination of national interests, insufficient community consultation and sensitive border issues, such as the illicit flow of goods and economic migrants between neighbouring countries (most notably, between Zimbabwe and

South Africa from 2000). Inter-state differences in land use and legal systems across boundaries are increasingly becoming sources of conflict and controversy. For example, in the case of the region's flagship Peace Park, the GLTP, the harmonisation of land use remains a source of tensions. South Africa's Kruger Park observes a preservationist management regime, allowing no one to hunt in the park or to reside there. On the other hand, Mozambique's Limpopo Park is home to an estimated 15,000 people. Further complicating matters, Zimbabwe's Gonarezhou has been 'invaded' by local communities (Koch, 2001; Nielsen and Chikoko, 2002). Furthermore, there is uneven infrastructural development amongst member countries, making it difficult for all stakeholders to agree on how to equitably distribute revenues from the Peace Parks. The surges of global protectionism, coinciding with local currents of nationalism, are also impeding conservation projects.

Conclusion

The SADC region countries have made significant progress in harnessing their tourism potential over the last few decades, including the creation of regional integration synergies, product development and improvements in access. However, many challenges remain. To thrive in the 21st century, the region will need to keep strengthening its synergies and enhancing its competencies on various fronts, including accessibility, investment in technology and maintaining the integrity of its natural resources and other attractions.

References

Acheampong, K. V., and Tseane, G. (2016). Tourism BSR in the Western Cape communities as a strategy for sustainable development. *African Journal of Hospitality, Tourism and Leisure*. Retrieved from www.ajhtl.com/uploads/7/1/6/3/7163688/2016_article_13_vol._5__2_.pdf

Adams, W., and Hulme, D. (2001). Conservation and community: Changing innovations, policies and practices in Africa Conservation. In D. Hulme and M. Murphree (Eds.), *Africa wildlife and Livelihood: The promise and performance of community conservation*. Oxford: James Currey.

Aggarwal, A. (2007). *Impact of special economic zones on employment, poverty and human development*. Indian Council for Research on International Relations. Working Paper No. 194. Retrieved from https://icrier.org/pdf/Working_Paper_194.pdf.

Agrawal, A., and Gibson, C. L. (1999). Enchantment and disenchantment: The role of community in natural resource conservation. *World Development, 27*(4), 629–649.

Air Transport Action Group. (2003). *The contribution of air transport to sustainable development in Africa*, Oxford Economic Forecasting. Retrieved from https://www.icao.int/Meetings/wrdss2011/Document/JointWorkshop2005/ATAG_AfricaStudy1.pdf.

Barclay, J. (2009). Predicting the costs and benefits of mega-sporting events: Misjudgement of Olympic proportions? *Economic Affairs, 29*(2), 62–66.

Bieger, T., and Wittmer, A. (2006). Air transport and tourism- perspectives and challenges for destinations, airlines and governments. *Journal of Air Transport Management, 12*, 40–46.

Brautigan, D. (2010). *China, Africa and the international Aid Architecture.* Working paper Number 107. Africa.

Büscher, B., and Ramutsindela, M. (2015). Green violence: Rhino poaching and the war to save Southern Africa's peace parks. *African Affairs, 115*(458), 1–22.

Crocker, D. A. (1991). Insiders and outsiders in international development ethics. *Ethics and International Affairs, 5,* 149–173.

Cornelissen, S. (2007). Crafting legacies: The changing political economy of global sport and the 2010 FIFA world cup. *Politokon, 34*(3), 241–259.

Drummond, M. P., Thakoor, V., and Yu, S. (2014). *Africa rising: Harnessing the demographic dividend.* International Monetary Fund. IMF Working Paper, African Department, WP/14/143. Retrieved from https://www.imf.org/external/pubs/ft/wp/2014/wp14143.pdf.

Duffy, R. (2001). Peace parks: The paradox of globalisation. *Geopolitics, 6*(2), 1–26.

du Plessis, D., and Maennig, W. (2011). The 201 FIFA World Cup high-frequency data economics: Effects on international tourism and awareness for South Africa. *Development Southern Africa, 28*(3), 349–365.

Fouries, J., and Santana-Gallego, M. (2010). *The impact of mega events on tourist arrivals. Department of economics,* Working Paper Number 171, University of Stellenbosch, South Africa.

Giampiccoli, A., and Nauright, J. (2010). Problems and prospects for community-based tourism in new South Africa: The 2010 FIFA world cup and beyond. *African Historical Review, 42*(1), 42–62.

Godwin, N. (2002). Planned transborder nature park draws praise. *Travel Weekly, 61*(15), 36.

Harris, L. (2011). Mega events and the developing world: A look at the legacy of the 2010 soccer world cup. *South African Journal of International Affairs, 18*(3), 407–427.

Kavetos, G., and Szymannski, S. (2008). *National wellbeing and international sport events.* International Association of Sports Economics. Working paper Series Number 08–04.

King, B. (2010). Conservation geographies in Sub-Saharan Africa: The politics of national parks, community conservation and Peace Parks. *Geography Compass, 4*(1), 14–27.

Koch, E. (2001). Environmental Consultant and community representative 6, 7. Mafisa Consultancy, Midrand, Johannesburg, South Africa.

Li, T. M. (2002). Engaging simplifications: Community based resource management, market resources and state agendas in Upland Southeast Asia. *World Development, 30*(2), 265–283.

Mann, P. (2008, January 28–30). *Legacy best practice. An Introduction and global review.* Legacy lives 2008 conference report. Pump Legacy.

Manwa, H. (2011). Competitiveness of Southern African development community as a tourist destination. *Tourism Analysis, 16*(1), 77–86.

MET. (1995b). *Ministry of environment and tourism: Promotion of community based tourism: Policy document.* Windhoek, Namibia.

Murphree, M. (1995). *The lessons from Mahenye: Rural poverty, democracy and wildlife conservation* (No. 1). London, UK: International Institute for Environment and Development, Wildlife and Development Series.

NASCO. (2008). *Namibia's communal conservancies: A review of progress and challenges.* Windhoek: Namibia Association of CBNRM Support Organisation.

Nicolau, J. (2012). The effects of using the world cup on tourism market value. *The Spain Case, 40*(5), 503–510.

Nielsen, S., and Chikoko, H. (2002). The great Limpopo trans-frontier park, how great is the idea? *Newsletter of the South Africa TBNRM Network, 1,* 6–7/11.

Rannditsheni, R. (2008). *Southern African Development Community (SADC) close to establishing One Visa (Univisa) for tourists.* Retrieved from www.info.gov.za/speeches/2008/08032611451001.htm

RETOSA. (1998). *Regional tourism organisation of Southern Africa.* Marketing Strategy Plan 1998–2000. RETOSA, Midrand, Johannesburg, South Africa.

RETOSA. (2010). *Univisa passport marketing tool front runner to the real deal.* Retrieved from www.trademaekea.com/news/sadc-uni-visa-to-boost-regional-tourism/

SADC. (2003). *Southern Africa development community, protocol on the development of tourism in the Southern Africa development community,* SADC House, Central Business District, Gaborone, Botswana.

Schlumberger, C. E. (2010). *Open skies for Africa: Implementing the Yomoussoukro declaration.* Washington, DC. World Bank.

Swart, K., and Bob, U. (2012). Sport events and social legacies. *Alternation, 17*(2), 72–95.

Tichaawa, T. M. (2014). A tale of two regions: Stakeholder perceptions of tourism legacies and the 2010 FIFA world cup in Africa. *African Journal of Hospitality, Tourism and Leisure.* Retrieved from www.researchgate.net/publication/282862623_A_tale_of_two_regions_stakeholder_perceptions_of_tourism_legacies_and_the_2010_FIFA_World_Cup_in_Africa

Turner, S. (2004, August 9–13). *A Crisis in CBNRM? Affirming the commons in Southern Africa.* Paper presented at the 10th biennial conference of the International Association for the Study of Common Property (IASCP), Mexico.

Turton, B. J., and Mutambirwa, C. C. (1996). Air Transport services and the expansion of international tourism in Twining-Zimbabwe. *Tourism Management, 17*(6), 453–462.

United Nations Educational, Scientific and Cultural Organisation. (2016). *Annual report: Making the SDGs a reality for Southern Africa.* Harare, Zimbabwe UNESCO.

UNWTO. (2014). Global report on the meeting industry. Retrieved from http:// www.imexexhibitions.com/media/350548/UNWTO_meetingsindustry_am-report%20(2).pdf

UNWTO. (2016). *Visa openness Report.* Madrid, Spain: World Tourism Organisation.

Vanhen, K. J., and Bertelsman-Smith, T. (2016). *The political economy of regional integration in Africa.* SADC.

Vanheukelon, J., and Bertelsmann-Scott, T. (2016). *The political economy of regional integration in Africa, SADC.* Maastricht: ECDPM.

Western, D., and Wright, M. (1994). *Natural connections: Perspectives in community-based conservation.* Washington, DC, Covelo, CA: Island Press.

13 Tourism and economic wellbeing in Africa

*Ogechi Adeola, Olaniyi Evans
and Robert Ebo Hinson*

Introduction

Recognising the potential of tourism for enhancing economic wellbeing many countries are increasingly turning to tourism as a vehicle for development (Giaoutzi, 2017; Cornelissen, 2017; Singh, 2017; Bianchi, 2018). Africa is a particularly interesting case to study in light of the level of progress the continent has made in tourism development in the last few decades. However, economic wellbeing in terms of GDP per capita and consumption per capita is very low across most of the continent.

Tourism development brings benefits as well as costs for destination countries (Wang and Pfister, 2008). Benefits include enhanced business growth and the creation of jobs for the unemployed or underemployed, elevating them out of poverty. In addition, tourism has the potential to diversify an economy, making it less dependent on the volatility of one or two sectors. The increased tax revenues and economies of scale induced by tourism enable governments to improve public services (Reeder and Brown, 2005). On the other hand, many of the potential costs of tourism development are linked to the resulting rapid growth of the destination countries. The growth can erode both natural and cultural amenities, for example, by despoiling scenic views and historic sites. Tourism may lead to pollution, health-related problems, road congestion, higher housing costs, overcrowded schools, higher crime rates and strained public services (Archer, Cooper, and Ruhanen, 2005; Reeder and Brown, 2005).

With this tangle of positive and negative effects of tourism, it is understandable why experts and policy makers may be uncertain about the value of tourism for economic wellbeing. There are concerns about the potential effects on poverty, crime and other socioeconomic conditions. This study considers the validity of these concerns by analysing recent data on tourism and economic wellbeing in Africa.

Nonetheless, the literature on the relationship between tourism and subjective wellbeing has been expanding in recent years (Chen and Petrick, 2013; Uysal, Sirgy, Woo and Kim, 2016; Smith and Diekmann, 2017). Wellbeing can be studied at different levels of analysis: individual, community, country and regional (Sirgy, 2001; Mancini, George, and Jorgensen, 2012). The majority of studies in the literature, notably, consider wellbeing at the individual level. This study substantiates the individual-level findings with regional-level empirical evidence in a largely under-studied context, Africa.

The remaining sections are organised as follows. The next section discusses the conceptual and empirical literature on tourism and economic wellbeing. This is followed by a description of the data and the empirical methodology. The analysis section provides the empirical results using the fully modified least square estimation method. The final section provides a summary of the main findings and offers suggestions for future studies.

Literature review

Wellbeing is one of the popular keywords and concepts in fields as diverse as philosophy, management, economics, psychology, medicine and recently in tourist studies (Alexandrova, 2012). As Carlisle, Henderson, and Hanlon (2009) have argued, there is no unanimous definition of wellbeing. It is also safe to argue that the multiplicity of theoretical and conceptual treatments of wellbeing have led to quite blurred and rather broad definitions of the concept (Crisp, 2016; Jayawickreme, Forgeard, and Seligman, 2012). Wellbeing takes many forms and manifests in five central philosophical views, namely, hedonic, life satisfaction, eudaimonic, desire fulfilment and non-eudaimonic objective list (Armenta, Ruberton, and Lyubomirsky, 2015); it may also be categorised as physical, societal or economic wellbeing. In particular, economic wellbeing describes the capacity of individuals, families and communities to consistently meet their basic needs (including food, utilities, healthcare and education). It also includes the capacity to make economic choices and feel a sense of satisfaction with one's finances and employment pursuits, and sustain adequate income throughout the lifespan (Council on Social Work Education, 2018).

Tourism studies are increasingly focused on wellbeing in the last decade, both from a methodological and theoretical perspective. Wellbeing appeared in tourism studies through a range of terms inspired by philosophy and psychology, such as 'life satisfaction' and 'quality of life' (e.g., Pearce, Filep, and Ross, 2010; Dolnicar, Yanamandram, and Cliff, 2012), 'happiness' (e.g., Filep and Deery, 2010) and 'wellness' (Kelly, 2012; Voigt and Pforr, 2013). Quality of life appears to be the most frequently used in place of wellbeing in studies (e.g. Pukeliene and Starkauskiene, 2009; Sirgy et al., 2006; Theofilou, 2013).

According to Uysal et al. (2016), wellbeing is embedded in the very definition of tourism. That is, tourism affects the wellbeing of all in destination communities, not only those who participate in the production and consumption of tourism goods and services. Tourism is a multipart industry: it provides employment, revenues and economic diversity (Delibasic, Karlsson, Lorusso, Rodriguez, and Yliruusi, 2008). Tourism has many forms such as social, economic, cultural and environmental (Godfrey and Clarke, 2000) and is, therefore, a means of economic, social and cultural exchange (Mowforth and Munt, 2003).

Critics have argued that the tourism industry provides seasonal, unskilled, low-wage jobs, and thus negatively impacts local wages and income such that as the workforce in these jobs increases, tourism expands poverty and unfavourably affects health, education and other aspects of wellbeing (NaRanong and NaRanong, 2011). Tourism could also lead to rapid growth which puts a strain on infrastructure and leads to snags such as road congestion. Conversely, if tourism draws significant inflows of residents, it could improve the fortunes of the country. Development may spark a housing boom and higher demand for goods and services,

> resulting in a more diversified economy with more high-paying jobs. Even low-paid recreation workers could benefit if better employment became available. Income levels could rise, along with levels of education, health, and other measures of community welfare, and poverty rates could be expected to decline.
>
> (Reeder and Brown, 2005, p. 2)

In the past three decades, studies (e.g. Allen, Long, Perdue, and Kieselbach, 1988; Ivlevs, 2017; Sharpley, 2014; Woo, Kim, and Uysal, 2015) have investigated community residents' perception of tourism effects on their wellbeing. Allen et al. (1988) found that community wellbeing was perceived to drop as tourism development progressed. Similarly, Ivlevs (2017) in a study on European residents found that tourism negatively influenced residents' life satisfaction, particularly in countries with relatively highly intense tourism.

On the contrary, Milman and Pizam (1988) investigated the attitude of Central Florida residents towards tourism development and found that tourism indeed improves the overall quality of life. In the same vein, Perdue, Long and Kang (1999) examined the relationship between tourism development and several objective indicators of wellbeing in the US. Their study found that all the objective indicators (i.e. income per capita, per student education expenditure, quality of healthcare facilities) improved with increasing levels of tourism development. Woo et al. (2015) likewise found in their study that community residents' perceived value of tourism development positively affects the overall quality of life, and that overall quality of life greatly enhances tourism development.

In addition, Renda, Mendes and Valle (2012) found that tourism positively affects host community residents' quality of life. However, a negative relationship was found between tourism and their emotional and community wellbeing. Reeder and Brown (2005) assessed the effect of recreation and tourism development on socioeconomic conditions in rural recreation counties in the US. They found that recreation and tourism development contribute to rural wellbeing by improving education and health, increasing local employment, wage levels and income, and reducing poverty. Aref (2011) investigated the effect of tourism on quality of life in Iran and showed that tourism has a positive effect on the quality of life of residents. The most significant impacts of tourism were linked to community wellbeing, emotional wellbeing, income and employment.

In the literature, wellbeing is usually measured using objective or subjective indicators. Subjective indicators capture experiences that are important to the individual. Most studies in the literature use subjective indicators to capture well-being of tourists and residents of host communities. Conversely, objective indicators address social indicators such as income and standard of living, amongst others, which capture economic wellbeing. According to Uysal et al. (2016), there are only a few studies representing this type of research in tourism research, yet, from a practical perspective, studies relying on objective indicators could help better monitor and measure structural and physical changes over time, as well as how visitors and providers may respond to such changes.

Data and methodology

Data

The main data source for this study is the World Bank's (2018) World Development Indicators. These data are complemented with country-level data from the Economist Intelligence Unit on political stability. The data cover the period 1995–2016 and 44 countries in Africa. The countries include Algeria, Angola, Benin, Botswana, Burkina Faso, Burundi, Cabo Verde, Cameroon, Central African Republic, Comoros, Democratic Republic of Congo, Congo Republic, Cote d'Ivoire, Egypt, Ethiopia, Gabon, Gambia, Ghana, Guinea, Guinea-Bissau, Kenya, Lesotho, Madagascar, Malawi, Mali, Mauritius, Morocco, Mozambique, Namibia, Niger, Nigeria, Rwanda, Senegal, Seychelles, Sierra Leone, South Africa, Sudan, Swaziland, Tanzania, Togo, Tunisia, Uganda, Zambia and Zimbabwe.

Model

The dependent variable is a measure of the level of economic wellbeing in each country. Economic wellbeing is a multi-dimensional concept. This multidimensionality, however, leads to high correlations between the indicators and results in higher multi-correlations among them to the extent that using several indicators can lead to redundancy of information and likely cause a multi-collinearity problem, which can result in misleading inferences. To preclude these problems, this study employs the two most commonly used measures of economic wellbeing in the literature, namely, consumption per capita (from the household perspective) and GDP per capita (from the whole economy perspective) (Office of National Statistics, 2014). The two measures are combined into a robust index of economic wellbeing (*Wellb*) using principal component analysis. Note that higher values imply higher economic wellbeing.

The main explanatory variable is tourism. In the literature, there are two measures of tourism: international tourism arrivals and international tourism receipts. To guard against possible multi-collinearity problems, the two measures are combined into a robust index of tourism activities (*Tour*) using principal component analysis. Note that higher values imply higher tourism activities.

A more serious concern with the estimation results is the possibility of spurious correlation or omitted variable bias problem (Gujarati, 2003; Evans et al.,

2018; Evans, 2018a). That is, tourism could pick up the effects of other variables not controlled for in the model specification which are correlated with both the measures of economic wellbeing as well as tourism. To guard against the omitted variable bias problem, this study controls for a number of country-level variables including GDP growth, capital formation, FDI, trade openness, internet usage, government spending and political stability. It is natural to expect GDP growth, capital formation, government spending and political stability to be higher in countries with higher economic wellbeing (Barro, 2003; Ciccone and Jarociński, 2010; Evans, 2017; Evans and Alenoghena, 2017; Evans and Saibu, 2017; Moral-Benito, 2012; Petrakos and Arvanitidis, 2008). Further, the literature suggests that GDP growth, capital formation, FDI, trade openness, internet usage, government spending and political stability may reinforce tourism (Adeola, Boso, and Evans, 2018; Asrin, Pouya, and Khalid, 2015; Khoshnevis and Khanalizadeh, 2017).

The resulting function is:

$$Wellb_{it} = \rho_0 + \rho_1 Tour_{it-1} + \rho_2 Growth_{it} + \rho_3 Capf_{it} + \rho_4 Fdi_{it} + \rho_5 Trade_{it}$$
$$+ \rho_6 Internet_{it} + \rho_7 Govt_{it} + \rho_8 Polstab_{it} + \varepsilon_{it} \tag{13.1}$$

Where, i = 1, 2, . . ., N, that is, the 44 countries selected for the study; t refers to the year; *Wellb* is economic wellbeing; *Tour* is tourism; *Growth* is GDP growth; *Capf* is capital formation (% of GDP); *Fdi* is net inflows of foreign direct investment (% of GDP); *Trade* is trade openness; *Internet* is internet users (% of the population), *Govt* is government spending (% of GDP); and *Polstab* is political stability.

Estimation technique

The fully modified least square (FMOLS) is employed for analysis. A semi-parametric approach designed to provide optimal estimates of co-integrating regressions, FMOLS is robust to serial correlation and endogeneity problems (Adeola and Evans, 2017; Evans, 2018b; Evans and Kelikume, 2018). Hence, the estimates are robust and consistent. Furthermore, FMOLS is applicable to data series irrespective of their order of integration, i.e. whether they are purely I(0), purely I(1) or mixed (Phillips and Hansen, 1990). Extensive discussion of the FMOLS approach can be gleaned from Phillips and Hansen (1990) and Pedroni (1995, 2000).

Empirical analysis

The main regression results are summarised in Table 13.1 (for pre-estimates, see Appendix 1). The results are obtained using the FMOLS estimation method. To better assess the robustness of the parameter estimates to different specifications, the model is estimated using 1995–2016 and 2005–2016 as sample periods (Tables 13.1 and 13.2). Using the 1995–2016 sample period, the estimation results in Table 13.1 show a positive relationship between tourism and economic wellbeing, and the relationship is statistically significant at the 1% level (column 1). Higher levels of tourism are correlated with higher levels of economic wellbeing.

Table 13.1 Tourism and economic wellbeing (1995–2016)

	1	2	3	4	5	6	7	8
Tourism	0.014*	0.014*	0.012*	0.012*	0.012*	0.056*	0.053*	0.065*
GDP growth		0.005*	0.003***	0.003***	0.003***	0.005*	0.003**	0.003
Capital formation (% of GDP)			0.005**	0.004**	0.004**	0.004*	0.006*	0.006*
FDI (% of GDP)				0.005**	0.006*	0.005*	0.005*	0.005**
Trade openness					-0.008	0.006	-0.008	-0.002
Internet usage						0.009*	0.008*	0.006*
Government spending (% of GDP)							0.005**	0.007**
Political stability								0.001***
R Squared	0.993	0.993	0.994	0.993	0.995	0.995	0.996	0.997
Observations	652	698	684	676	646	630	659	458
No. of Countries	44	44	44	44	41	41	41	40

Notes: Significance level is denoted by * (1% or less), ** (5% or less) and *** (10% or less).

Table 13.2 Tourism and economic wellbeing (2005–2016)

	1	2	3	4	5	6	7	8
Tourism	0.093*	0.098*	0.069*	0.069*	0.069*	0.028*	0.032*	0.057*
GDP growth		0.003**	0.001***	0.001	0.001	0.004*	0.001	0.002**
Capital formation (% of GDP)			0.008*	0.007*	0.007*	0.005*	0.004*	0.005*
FDI (% of GDP)				0.002	0.002*	0.003*	0.003**	0.004**
Trade openness					-0.003	0.007	-0.005	-0.008
Internet usage						0.007*	0.006*	0.006*
Government spending (% of GDP)							0.002***	0.005***
Political stability								0.007***
R Squared	0.992	0.992	0.994	0.993	0.995	0.996	0.996	0.998
Observations	422	450	454	452	421	415	416	418
No. of Countries	44	44	44	44	41	41	40	40

Notes: Significance level is denoted by * (1% or less), ** (5% or less) and *** (10% or less).

However, this estimation may be spurious, as tourism may be spuriously picking up the effect of other variables, thus biasing the strength of the relationship. Columns 2 to 8 show that this is indeed the case. The estimated coefficient value of tourism increases substantially from .014 to .065 and is always significant at less than the 1% level. As expected, GDP growth, capital formation (% of GDP) and FDI (% of GDP) are associated with higher economic wellbeing, and the association is significant at the 1% level. There is no statistically significant impact of trade openness on the level of economic wellbeing in any of the specifications discussed in the chapter. Internet usage, government spending (% of GDP) and political stability are associated with higher economic wellbeing, and the association is statistically significant.

To better assess the robustness of the parameter estimates to different specifications, the model is re-estimated, using 2005–2016 as sample period. The regression results from the FMOLS regressions are summarised in Table 13.2. The outcome is qualitatively similar to the results above. These results show a positive and statistically significant (at less than the 1% level) relationship between tourism and economic wellbeing, and this holds regardless of the set of controls (columns 1–8, Table 13.2).

The primary objective of the study is to assess the effect of tourism on economic wellbeing. It is, therefore, appropriate to examine the causality between tourism and economic wellbeing, considering that, in the literature, if a pair of I(1) series are cointegrated, then there must be a unidirectional causality running in either way (Engle and Granger, 1987). The tourism and economic wellbeing variables are non-stationary, stationary after first differencing and cointegrated. Table 13.3 summarises the results of the short-run and long-run Granger causality. In the short run, there is causality running from tourism to economic wellbeing at the 5% level. In addition, there is causality running from economic wellbeing to tourism at the 1% significance level. Furthermore, the statistical significance of *Ect* implies the presence of long-run causality. In the long run, there is causality running from tourism to economic wellbeing at the 1% level. Also, there is causality running from economic wellbeing to tourism at the 1% significance level.

Discussion

The FMOLS estimations have shown a statistically positive association between tourism and economic wellbeing, meaning that increased tourism is associated

Table 13.3 Panel Granger causality test results

	Short-run causality	Long-run causality
	F-stat	ECT
Internet usage ⟶ Economic wellbeing	4.81**	−0.01*
Economic wellbeing ⟶ Internet usage	2.57*	−0.09*

Notes: Significance level is denoted by * (1% or less) and ** (5% or less). The optimal lag length was selected using the Schwarz information criteria.

with increased wellbeing. This finding is comparable with other studies in the literature (for example, Woo et al., 2015). According to Uysal et al. (2016), tourism affects the wellbeing of all in destination communities, not only those who participate in the production and consumption of tourism goods and services. Tourism provides employment, revenues and economic diversity (Delibasic et al., 2008), and therefore has various positive impacts on wellbeing.

The short-run and long-run causality has also shown bi-directional causal linkages between tourism and economic wellbeing. The causality analysis thereby implies that tourism leads to economic wellbeing while economic wellbeing also leads to the expansion of tourist activities in both the short and long run. The results, therefore, provide evidence that while tourism plays significant roles in increasing economic wellbeing, economic wellbeing also plays significant roles in the expansion of tourism, in both the short and long run. The implication is that once a country becomes a tourist destination, the wellbeing of the residents is affected by tourism, and the wellbeing of the residents is vital for the development, operation and sustainability of tourism (Kim, 2002).

In summary, tourism causes wellbeing, by its tourism contribution to the GDP generated by industries involved directly with tourists, including airlines, hotels, travel agents, and other transport services, and the activities of restaurant and other leisure industries (Bilen, Yilanci, and Eryüzlü, 2017; Roudi, Arasli, and Akadiri, 2018; Suhel and Bashir, 2018). It contributes employment within the travel and tourism industry and also boosts spending within the country by international tourists for both leisure and business trips, including spending on transport and hotels, as well as government spending on travel and tourism services directly linked to visitors, such as recreational (e.g., national parks) and cultural (e.g. museums) services, tourism promotion, visitor information services, public services and other administrative services (Allan, Lecca, and Swales, 2017; Kubickova and Li, 2017; Srakar and Vecco, 2017). Moreover, economic wellbeing is achieved by individuals, families and communities through tourism when tourist attractions and activities ensure their ability to access skills and economic resources, as well as opportunities for generating income and asset-building and providing opportunities for secure employment with ample compensation and benefits for all (Kim, 2002).

Conclusion

The significant effect of tourism on economic wellbeing suggests that promoting tourism for increased economic wellbeing is both strategic and urgent. African countries need more strategic focus on fostering tourism as a significant source of economic wellbeing. It is also imperative that stakeholders and policy makers have knowledge of the implications of their actions and inactions in the overall interest of the short-run and long-run effects of the tourism sector on economic wellbeing in Africa.

The study has also shown that the relationship between tourism and economic wellbeing is strengthened in magnitude by controlling for the large number of country-level variables. As expected, GDP growth, capital formation (% of GDP) and FDI (% of GDP) are associated with higher economic wellbeing. Further, internet usage, government spending (% of GDP) and political stability are associated with higher economic wellbeing. The implication is that enabling macroeconomic environment and political stability is important for the increased positive contribution of tourism to economic wellbeing. Governments of these African countries should, therefore, prioritise enabling macroeconomic environment and political stability in order to attract tourism development and, in turn, to boost economic wellbeing on the continent.

This study focused mainly on Africa. Further insights may come from extending the analysis to include other continents. Future research could also address issues related to tourism impacts on other aspects of economic wellbeing, such as public services. Our understanding of tourism effects might also benefit from different constructions of the econometric model. For example, future models could be fine-tuned to focus on individual countries or types of tourism activities. More sophisticated models may unravel specific transmission channels between tourism and economic wellbeing.

Appendix 1

The first step of the analysis is to assess the existence of unit root in the data and to determine the degree of integration of the series. Theoretically, a process is either I(0), I(1) or I(2). Therefore, this study applies panel data unit root tests: Im, Pesaran, and Shin (2003) and Levin, Lin, and Chu (2002). Im et al. (2003, hereafter IPS) allows for heterogeneity in the individual deterministic effects and heterogeneous serial correlation of the error terms (see Evans, 2015; Evans, 2016; Evans and Adeoye, 2016). In order to facilitate comparisons, the results of another panel unit root test, Levin et al. (2002, hereafter LLC), is also provided. Table 13.4 summarises the results of the IPS and LLC unit root tests. The test results show that the variables had unit root properties and had to be differenced. After differencing, the time series became integrated of order one and showed no unit root properties.

Having confirmed the non-stationarity of the data series, it is natural to test the existence of a long-run relationship between the series. Kao residual co-integration test is used to examine the co-integrating relationships among the variables. Table 13.5 summarises the results of the co-integration test. The test results

Table 13.4 Summary of panel data unit root tests

| | Level | | First Difference | |
	IPS	LLC	IPS	LLC
Wellb	2.23	−2.53	−15.59*	−18.77*
Tours	1.17	−3.06	−18.52*	−22.89*
Growth	2.46	2.41	−19.33*	−19.24*
Capf	−0.78	−2.54*	−24.02*	−32.34*
Fdi	−1.27	−1.52	−9.06*	−8.23*
Trade	0.03	0.37	−3.26*	−5.42*
Internet	40.96	30.27	−2.78*	−3.99*
Govt	−0.60	−0.43*	−3.59*	−3.99*
Polstab	−1.91**	−2.47	−8.70*	−17.38*

Notes: Significance level is denoted by * (1% or less) and ** (5% or less). The tests assume asymptotic normality.

Table 13.5 Kao residual co-integration test

	t-Statistic	Prob.
ADF	−2.686*	0.004
Residual variance	0.001	
HAC variance	0.002	

Notes: Significance level is denoted by * (1% or less); Newey-West automatic bandwidth selection and Bartlett kernel.

indicate the presence of long-run co-integrating relationships among the set of variables at the 1% level of significance.

References

Adeola, O., Boso, N., and Evans, O. (2018). Drivers of international tourism demand in Africa. *Business Economics, 53*(1), 25–36.

Adeola, O., and Evans, O. (2017). Financial inclusion, financial development, and economic diversification in Nigeria. *The Journal of Developing Areas, 51*(3), 1–15.

Alexandrova, A. (2012). Well-being as an object of science. *Philosophy of Science, 79*(5), 678–689.

Allan, G. J., Lecca, P., and Swales, K. (2017). The impacts of temporary but anticipated tourism spending: An application to the Glasgow 2014 Commonwealth Games. *Tourism Management, 59*, 325–337.

Allen, L. R., Long, P. T., Perdue, R. R., and Kieselbach, S. (1988). The impact of tourism development on residents' perceptions of community life. *Journal of Travel Research, 27*(1), 16e–21e.

Archer, B., Cooper, C., and Ruhanen, L. (2005). The positive and negative impacts of tourism. *Global tourism, 3*, 79–102.

Aref, F. (2011). The effects of tourism on quality of life: A case study of Shiraz, Iran. *Life Science Journal, 8*(2), 26–30.

Armenta, C. N., Ruberton, P. M., and Lyubomirsky, S. (2015). Psychology of subjective wellbeing. In J. D. Wright (Ed.), *International encyclopaedia of the social and behavioral sciences* (2nd ed., Vol. 23, pp. 648–653). Oxford: Elsevier.

Asrin, K., Pouya, F., and Khalid, A. R. (2015). Modeling and forecasting of international tourism demand in ASEAN countries. *American Journal of Applied Sciences, 12*(7), 479–486.

Barro, R. J. (2003). Determinants of economic growth in a panel of countries. *Annals of Economics and Finance, 4*, 231–274.

Bianchi, R. (2018). The Political Economy of tourism development: A critical review. *Annals of Tourism Research, 70*, 88–102.

Bilen, M., Yilanci, V., and Eryüzlü, H. (2017). Tourism development and economic growth: A panel Granger causality analysis in the frequency domain. *Current Issues in Tourism, 20*(1), 27–32.

Carlisle, S., Henderson, G., and Hanlon, P. W. (2009). 'Wellbeing': A collateral casualty of modernity? *Social Science and Medicine, 69*(10), 1556–1560.

Chen, C. C., and Petrick, J. F. (2013). Health and wellness benefits of travel experiences: A literature review. *Journal of Travel Research, 52*(6), 709–719.

Ciccone, A., and Jarociński, M. (2010). Determinants of economic growth: Will data tell? *American Economic Journal: Macroeconomics, 2*(4), 222–246.

Cornelissen, S. (2017). *The global tourism system: Governance, development and lessons from South Africa*. London: Routledge.

Council on Social Work Education (CSWE). (2018). Working definition of economic well-being. Retrieved March 6, 2018, from www.cswe.org/Centers-Initiatives/Initiatives/Clearinghouse-for-Economic-Well-Being/Working-Definition-of-Economic-Well-Being

Crisp. (2016). (2006) Well-being. In E. N. Zalta (Ed.), *The Stanford encyclopaedia of philosophy* (Summer ed.). Retrieved March 30, 2018, from http://plato.stanford.edu/archives/sum2016/entries/well-being

Delibasic, R., Karlsson, P., Lorusso, A., Rodriguez, A., and Yliruusi, H. (2008). *Quality of life and tourism in Budečsko*. Retrieved from www.cenia.cz/__C12572160037AA0F. nsf/$pid/CPRJ6WECYXIH/$FILE/SED%2

Dolnicar, S., Yanamandram, V., and Cliff, K. (2012). The contribution of vacations to quality of life. *Annals of Tourism Research, 39*(1), 59–83.

Engle, R. F., and Granger, C. W. (1987). Co-integration and error correction: Representation, estimation, and testing. *Econometrica: Journal of the Econometric Society,* 251–276.

Evans, O. (2015). The effects of economic and financial development on financial inclusion in Africa. *Review of Economic and Development Studies, 1*(1), 17–25.

Evans, O. (2016). The effectiveness of monetary policy in Africa: Modeling the impact of financial inclusion. *Iranian Economic Review, 20*(3), 327–337.

Evans, O. (2017). Back to the land: The impact of financial inclusion on agriculture in Nigeria. *Iranian Economic Review, 21*(4), 885–903.

Evans, O. (2018a). Digital agriculture: Mobile phones, internet and agricultural development in Africa. *Actual Problems of Economics, 7–8*(205–206), 76–90.

Evans, O. (2018b). Connecting the poor: The internet, mobile phones and financial inclusion in Africa. *Digital Policy, Regulation and Governance, 20*(6), 568–581. https://doi.org/10.1108/DPRG-04-2018-0018

Evans, O., and Adeoye, B. (2016). The determinants of financial inclusion in Africa: A dynamic panel data approach. *University of Mauritius Research Journal, 22*, 310–336.

Evans, O., and Alenoghena, O. R. (2017). Financial inclusion and GDP Per capita in Africa: A Bayesian VAR model. *Journal of Economics and Sustainable Development, 8*(18), 44–57.

Evans, O., and Kelikume, I. (2018). The effects of foreign direct investment, trade, aid, remittances and tourism on welfare under terrorism and militancy. *International Journal of Management, Economics and Social Sciences, 7*(3), 206–232.

Evans, O., Adeniji, S., Nwaogwugwu, I., Kelikume, I., Dakare, O., and Oke, O. (2018). The relative effect of monetary and fiscal policy on economic development in Africa: A GMM approach to the St. Louis equation. *Business and Economic Quarterly, 2*, 3–23.

Evans, O., and Saibu, O. (2017). Quantifying the impact of monetary and exchange rate policies on economic diversification in Nigeria. *Nigerian Journal of Economic and Social Studies, 59*(1), 131–152.

Filep, S., and Deery, M. (2010). Towards a picture of tourists' happiness. *Tourism Analysis, 15*(4), 399–410.

Giaoutzi, M. (2017). *Tourism and regional development: New pathways*. London: Routledge.

Godfrey, K., and Clarke, J. (2000). *The tourism development handbook: A practical approach to planning and marketing*. London: Continuum.

Gujarati, D. N. (2003). *Basic econometrics* (4th ed.). Boston: McGraw-Hill.

Im, K. S., Pesaran, M. H., and Shin, Y. (2003). Testing for unit roots in heterogeneous panels. *Journal of Econometrics, 115*(1), 53–74.

Ivlevs, A. (2017). Happy hosts? International tourist arrivals and residents' subjective well-being in Europe. *Journal of Travel Research, 56*(5), 599–612.

Jayawickreme, E., Forgeard, M. J. C., and Seligman, E. P. (2012). The engine of well-being. *Review of General Psychology, 16*(4), 327–342.

Kelly, C. (2012). Wellness tourism: Retreat visitor motivations and experience. *Tourism Recreation Research, 37*(3), 205–213.

Khoshnevis, Y. S., and Khanalizadeh, B. (2017). Tourism demand: A panel data approach. *Current Issues in Tourism, 20*(8), 787–800.

Kim, K. (2002). *The effects of tourism impacts upon quality of life of residents in the community* (Doctoral Dissertation), Virginia Tech.

Kubickova, M., and Li, H. (2017). Tourism competitiveness, government and tourism area life cycle (TALC) model: The evaluation of Costa Rica, Guatemala and Honduras. *International Journal of Tourism Research, 19*(2), 223–234.

Levin, A., Lin, C. F., and Chu, C. S. J. (2002). Unit root tests in panel data: Asymptotic and finite-sample properties. *Journal of Econometrics, 108*(1), 1–24.

Mancini, J., George, D. V., and Jorgensen, B. (2012). Relational tourism: Observations on families and travel. In M. Uysal, R. Perdue, and M. J. Sirgy (Eds.), *Handbook of tourism and quality-of-life research: Enhancing the lives of tourists and residents of host communities* (pp. 309–320). Dordrecht, Netherlands: Springer.

Milman, A., and Pizam, A. (1988). Social impacts of tourism on Central Florida. *Annals of Tourism Research, 15*(2), 191e–e204.

Moral-Benito, E. (2012). Determinants of economic growth: A Bayesian panel data approach. *Review of Economics and Statistics, 94*(2), 566–579.

Mowforth, M., and Munt, I. (2003). *Tourism and sustainability: Development and new tourism in the third World*. London, UK: Routledge Publishing.

NaRanong, A., and NaRanong, V. (2011). The effects of medical tourism: Thailand's experience. *Bulletin of the World Health Organization, 89*(5), 336–344.

Office of National Statistics. (2014). *Economic well-being – framework and indicators*. Retrieved from www.ons.gov.uk

Pearce, P., Filep, S., and Ross, G. (2010). *Tourists, tourism and the good life*. London: Routledge.

Pedroni, P. (1995). *Panel co-integration: Asymptotic and unite sample properties of pooled time series test with an application to the PPP hypothesis*. Indiana University Working Papers in Economics No. 95–013.

Pedroni, P. (2000). Fully modified OLS for heterogeneous co-integrated panels. In B. Baltagi (Ed.), *Non-stationary panels, panel co-integration, and dynamic panels, advances in econometrics* (Vol. 15, pp. 93–130). Amsterdam: JAI Press.

Perdue, R. R., Long, P. T., and Kang, Y. S. (1999). Boomtown tourism and resident quality of life: The marketing of gaming to host community residents. *Journal of Business Research, 44*(3), 165–177.

Petrakos, G., and Arvanitidis, P. (2008). Determinants of economic growth. *Economic Alternatives, 1*, 49–69.

Phillips, P. C. B., and Hansen, B. E. (1990). Statistical inference in instrumental variable regression with I (1) processes. *The Review of Economic Studies, 57*, 99–125.

Pukelienė, V., and Starkauskienė, V. (2009). Quality of life concepts, measurement and challenges. *Taikomoji Ekonomika: Sisteminiai Tyrimai*, *3*(2), 51–65.

Reeder, R. J., and Brown, D. M. (2005). *Recreation, tourism, and rural well-being* (No. 7). Washington, DC: US Department of Agriculture, Economic Research Service.

Renda, A. I., da Costa Mendes, J., and do Valle, P. O. (2012). *A structural model approach of residents' perception of tourism impacts in their own quality of life: The municipality of Loulé.* Algarve: Tourism and Management Studies, pp. 1088–1091.

Roudi, S., Arasli, H., and Akadiri, S. S. (2018). New insights into an old issue – examining the influence of tourism on economic growth: Evidence from selected small island developing states. *Current Issues in Tourism*, 1–21.

Sharpley, R. (2014). Host perceptions of tourism: A review of the research. Tourism Management, *42*, 37e–49e.

Singh, T. V. (2017). Tourism and development: Not an easy alliance. In *Tourism and economic development* (pp. 30–41). London: Routledge.

Sirgy, M. J. (2001). *Handbook of quality-of-life research: An ethical marketing perspective.* Dordrecht: Springer.

Sirgy, M. J., Michalos, A. C., Ferriss, A. L., Easterlin, R. A., Patrick, D., and Pavot, W. (2006). The quality-of-life (QOL) research movement: Past, present, and future. *Social Indicators Research*, *76*(3), 343–466.

Smith, M. K., and Diekmann, A. (2017). Tourism and wellbeing. *Annals of Tourism Research*, *66*, 1–13.

Srakar, A., and Vecco, M. (2017). Ex-ante versus ex-post: Comparison of the effects of the European Capital of Culture Maribor 2012 on tourism and employment. *Journal of Cultural Economics*, *41*(2), 197–214.

Suhel, S., and Bashir, A. (2018). The role of tourism toward economic growth in the local economy. *Economic Journal of Emerging Markets*, *10*(1), 32–39.

Theofilou, P. (2013). Quality of life: Definition and measurement. *Europe's Journal of Psychology*, *9*(1).

Uysal, M., Sirgy, M. J., Woo, E., and Kim, H. L. (2016). Quality of life (QOL) and wellbeing research in tourism. *Tourism Management*, *53*, 244–261.

Voigt, C., and Pforr, C. (2013). *Wellness tourism.* London: Routledge.

Wang, Y., and Pfister, R. E. (2008). Residents' attitudes toward tourism and perceived personal benefits in a rural community. *Journal of Travel Research*, *47*(1), 84–93.

Woo, E., Kim, H., and Uysal, M. (2015). Life satisfaction and support for tourism development. *Annals of Tourism Research*, *50*, 84–97.

World Bank. (2018). *World development indicators.* Retrieved from http://databank.worldbank.org/data/reports.aspx?source=world-development-indicators

14 The positive interaction between tourism development and human development

Evidence from Mauritius

Boopen Seetanah and Sheereen Fauzel

Introduction

The World Tourism Organization's (2016) statistics indicate that tourism accounts for around 10% of the world's GDP (USD 7.2 trillion), supporting 284 million jobs, and remains one of the largest sectors in the world. Tourism is predicted to have a growth rate of around 4% annually for the next 10 years. Tourism is thus one of the most important economic activities in the world today, generating services, products, foreign currency, employment and investments and catalysing national development. The sector also highlights and conserves cultural heritage and acts as a bridge in international harmony and peace.

Tourism activities may also have additional effects on residents' welfare, both positive and negative. Positive impacts include a rise in employment as well as an increase in local income. In addition to that, the local population may enjoy lifestyle benefits with the presence of a tourism industry, such as additional recreational facilities built to cater for tourists. However, there can be negative effects as well, such as an increase in the cost of living due to the presence of tourists (Biagi, Lambiri, and Faggian, 2012), intensification of local crime (Schubert, 2010; Biagi and Detotto, 2014) and possible problems related to crowding and environmental pressures on the urban and natural equilibrium (Lindberg, Andersson, and Dellaert, 2001; Andereck, Valentine, Vogt, and Vogt, 2007).

There exists a wide literature on the impact of the tourism sector on economic growth (see Sinclair, 1998; Durbarry, 2004; Katircioglu, 2009; Seetanah, 2011 among others). The majority of these studies concentrate on testing the tourism-led growth (TLG) hypothesis, which refers to the economic impact of international tourism in the context of developed or developing countries. Generally, a positive and significant relationship is obtained between tourism and economies (Vanegas and Croes, 2003; Brau, Lanza, and Pigliaru, 2007). It is also noteworthy that an overwhelming portion of the literature has explored the relationship between tourism and development by means of an economic indicator, namely real GDP or the growth rates. The main assumption of the studies is that wealth is strongly associated with human development (HD), wellbeing and quality of life. Although some scholars recognise that tourism development (TD) may directly impact on HD (see Tecle and Schroenn, 2006; Jordan, Havadi-Nagy, and Marosi, 2016), applied research has largely ignored this possible impact, except for a few recent works (for example, Croes, 2012; Biagi, Ladu, and Royuela, 2017). Moreover, current studies have largely ignored potential endogenous and dynamic links that may exist in the tourism development–human development index (HDI) nexus.

The aim of this research is thus to further understand the impact of TD on HD by presenting evidence from a Mauritian case study. The study uses dynamic time series econometric analysis, namely a vector autoregressive framework which caters for potential dynamic and endogenous relationships in the hypothesised link, over the period 1988–2016. Mauritius is a good case study given that it is one of Africa's best economic performers and, moreover, is a tourist-dependent economy similar to a number of small island developing states (SIDS) (see Sannassee, Seetanah, and Lamport, 2014). The study also derives valuation implications for both the African continent as well as from a SIDS viewpoint.

The chapter is organised as follows: the next section delves briefly into the theoretical underpinning and empirical links between TD and HD, followed by a contextual analysis of the case of Mauritius. The main section presents the methodology and discusses the results from the analysis, before summarising the key insights in the conclusion.

Literature review

Theoretical underpinnings

Tecle and Schroenn (2006) argue that growth in the tourism industry promotes human capital development through the positive spill-over effect of improvement in human resources necessary to drive that growth. Further, TD could enhance human capital in the following ways. First, it serves as a source of livelihood to those working in the sector as well as those rendering services to international tourists during their visit (Sinclair, 1998; Christie, Fernandes, Messerli, and Twining-Ward, 2013; Jordan, Havadi-Nagy, and Marosi, 2016). Through their employment, they are better able to acquire the necessities of life and a better quality of life, which may in turn lead to an increased life expectancy. In addition, since TD contributes to government revenues, it serves as additional finance that governments can utilise to subsidise both health and educational services for their citizens. Other indirect impacts are also realisable; for example, the number of child enrolment in schools might improve, from primary level to tertiary level. Better healthcare may also reduce infant mortality (Hertz, Hebert, and Landon, 1994).

In addition, tourism growth complements other sources of foreign exchange. The additional foreign exchange earned can be used to procure essential drugs and import healthcare facilities, which would in turn lead to better health outcomes for the population. Also, local businesses benefit from the additional business created by tourism and related industries, generating higher taxable income for governments as a result (Christie et al., 2013; UNWTO, 2015).

Interestingly, TD has also often been associated with increased foreign inward investment which in turn stimulates both physical and human capital development. TD may indeed be related to increased demand for goods and services such as food, accommodation, entertainment and transportation, which would necessitate further investment including foreign direct investment (FDI) (Tang, Selvanathan, and Selvanathan, 2007). Moreover, Sandford and Dong (2000) posit that investment opportunities could be identified, as potential foreign investors are likely to obtain first-hand knowledge and information related to the economic and business environment of the host country, enhancing their confidence, during their stay as tourists. Increased FDI may have a potential impact on education, for example through the offer of scholarships to individuals of the host countries or to local employees (Egger, Egger, Falkinger, and Grossmann, 2005). The most significant impact of FDI on education is via employment creation. Multi-national companies (MNCs) provide attractive employment opportunities to skilled labour, and this creates an incentive for individuals of the host countries to seek improvement in their education levels. Furthermore, FDI flowing in the host countries contributes taxes to the government which can act as an incentive to use these for education investment. Previous studies have indeed reported a positive link between FDI and human capital (for example, Nunnenkamp, 2002).

Empirical studies

Research on the impact of TD on HD has been quite scant. There is, however, extensive research on the impact of human capital development on TD (Baum, 2015; Marchante and Ortega, 2012; Singh, 1997; Tecle and Schroenn, 2006), concluding that deficiency in the HD constrains TD. Another strand of the literature is related to the impact of TD on quality of life (QoL) and employment. Andereck and Vogt (2000), Fredline, Deery, and Jago (2005), Kim (2002), Gjerald (2005), Andereck et al. (2007), Marzuki (2009), Aref (2011), Mai, Rahtz and Shultz (2013) and Bakri, Jaafar and Mohamad (2014) have found that TD, in some way or another, had an impact on the QoL and employment of either individuals or the community.

Among the few empirical works focusing on the effect of TD on HD is that presented by Croes (2012), who analysed the link between tourism and HD in Nicaragua and Costa Rica over the period 1990 to 2009 using co-integration techniques. He observed that, overall, TD has a significant effect on HD. Ridderstaat, Croes, and Nijkamp (2016) subsequently found such a connection in the case of the island of Aruba in the short run using multivariate co-integration analysis and Granger causality testing. Bhutia (2014) studied the role of tourism on human resource development in Darjeeling District of West Bengal, based on secondary sources, literature search and discussions with key stakeholders and interactions with the tourists. The study recommended that it is particularly important to promote tourism as an instrument for human resource development in the region.

More recent evidence is available from Folarin, Oladipupo, Ajogbeje and Adeniyi (2017) and Biagi et al. (2017). Folarin et al. (2017) examined the effect of TD on human capital development in Africa using data on a panel of 25 African countries for the period 1998 to 2014. They used the general moment method (GMM) to account for dynamism. The study reported that TD had a positive and significant effect on human capital development in Africa overall. Biagi et al. (2017) also extended the role of tourism to HD and studied 63 countries comprising developed and developing countries over the period 1996 to 2008. They found that TD on average is a factor for HD, flagging however the existence of a threshold effect with respect to the level of TD.

In summary, although scholars have assessed the role of human capital in TD, the effect of tourism growth on HD has been relatively neglected in research. Moreover, current studies have largely ignored potential endogenous and dynamic links that may exist in the TD–HDI nexus.

Overview of HDI and tourism in Mauritius

According to the Human Development Report (2016), the HDI for Mauritius is 0.781 for the year 2015, and this places the country in the high HD category. In addition, there has been an increase of 26% in the country's HDI from 1990 to 2015. From decomposing the HDI and assessing the three dimensions in isolation, it is observable that the performance for the disaggregated variables has been significant for Mauritius. For instance, the standard of living as measured by Gross National Income (GNI) per capita has improved by about 141.5% between 1990 and 2015. Moreover, Mauritius' life expectancy at birth increased by 5.2 years, mean years of schooling increased by 3.4 years and expected years of schooling increased by 4.7 years.

The country has made considerable progress in terms of access to education and the provision of health services. Mauritius has been aiming at building a knowledge society and becoming a regional knowledge hub. This has been pursued through the provision of free education for all. The country also provides free health services in its public hospitals and health centres. These incentives have improved health services in the country, in turn boosting life expectancy.

With specific reference to the tourism sector, statistics indicate that the sector has contributed 7.8% to GDP in 2016. Tourist arrivals in 2016 grew by 10.8%, exceeding the growth of international tourist arrivals, which according to the United Nations World Tourism Organisation (UNWTO) reached 3.9%.[1] Figure 14.1 shows the increase in tourist arrivals and tourism receipts over the period 1983–2016.

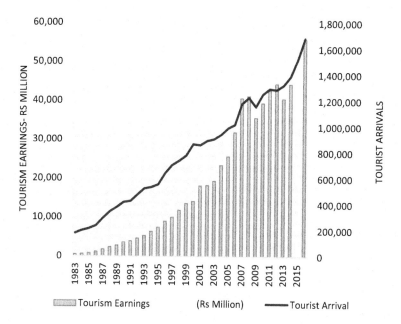

Figure 14.1 Tourist arrivals and tourism receipts 1983–2016
Source: Authors' computation – data extracted from Statistics Mauritius

Methodology and analysis

Model specification and variables

Drawing on the work of Croes (2012) and Biagi et al. (2017), the following regression equation is used:

$$HDI = f\left(TOU, UNEM, OPEN, GOVTSP, GDFCF\right)$$

The dependent variable in the study was the HD index. This proxy has been used by various scholars as a social welfare index and to account for poverty reduction (see Gohou and Soumaré, 2012; Croes, 2012; Biagi et al., 2017). Indeed, the HD index is a composite index of economic performance, education and health. According to the UNDP, the HD index is a summary composite index that measures a country's average achievements in three basic aspects of HD: health, knowledge and a decent standard of living. Health is measured by life expectancy at birth; knowledge is measured by a combination of the adult literacy rate and the combined primary, secondary and tertiary gross enrolment ratio; and standard of living by GDP per capita (PPP US$). Data were extracted from the UNDP website.

In reference to the TD variable (TOU), various proxies have been used in the literature, namely tourism arrivals, nights of stay and tourism receipts, among others. In this study, we follow the literature on tourism demand and development (Naude and Saayaman, 2005; Khadaroo and Seetanah, 2009; Seetanah and Sannasee, 2015 ; Durbarry and Seetanah, 2015; amongst others) in using the number of tourist arrivals to measure tourist development. The data were extracted from the Statistics Mauritius database.

An additional control variable is unemployment (UNEM). This is a phenomenon that affects social welfare to a great extent and is seen as a social evil (Landais, 2015). Government spending (GOVTSP) is included in the model as it is argued (see Alexiou, 2009) that higher government expenditure in a country will boost welfare of the population. The level of openness (OPEN), measured by the sum of imports and exports to GDP, is considered an HDI-enhancing factor because when the economy opens up, there is a wider range of goods available to the population, and as a result the social welfare in a country improves (Winters, 2000; Polodoo, Seetanah, and Sannassee, 2016). For instance, trade openness and reform increases the revenue of the poor as a group, and the transition costs are normally small relative to the overall benefits, at least in the long run. Finally, gross fixed capital formation (GDFCF) is also included to capture the impact of local investment on HD. Investment has a multiplied effect on the economy and helps to boost HD (Srinivasan, 2005; Gohou and Soumare, 2012).

The econometric specification can be written as follows:

$$ln\ HDI_t = \alpha_0 + \beta_1 ln\ TOU_t + \beta_2 ln\ UNEM_t + \beta_3 ln\ OPEN_t$$
$$+\ \beta_4 ln\ GOVTSP_t + \beta_5 ln\ GDFCF_t + \mu_t \qquad \qquad \dots (1)$$

where t denotes the time dimension and the logarithm is applied to the variables for ease of interpretation and comparison (as interpretation will be percentage change terms).

Estimation issues

A vector autoregressive approach (VAR) is used to explain the relationship between TD and HDI. The VAR resembles a simultaneous equation modelling, whereby several endogenous variables are considered together. This method therefore does not impose *a priori* restrictions on the dynamic relations among the different variables and takes into account possible endogeneity issues. It is noteworthy that HD is dynamic in nature (Folarin, 2017) and should be modelled accordingly. Moreover, the hypothesised relationship may also be endogenous in nature given the possibility of reverse causation, since tourism arrivals and development may also be determined by the human capital and the development level. Indeed, such a mutually reinforcing effect is likely to occur as improvement in HD performance would imply tourism services enhancement and thus yielding higher tourism and revenues (Tecle and Schroenn, 2006; Croes, 2012). As Amoah and Baum (1997) posit, the tourism industry is labour intensive, depending on capable personnel to deliver, operate and manage the tourist product.

We first of all investigate the time series properties of the data, as applying regression on time series data may generate spurious results (Granger and Newbold, 1974; Phillips, 1986) given the possibility of non-stationary data. Thus, undertaking a check of data stationarity is a prerequisite for applying the co-integration test. As a result, the augmented Dickey-Fuller (ADF) test and the Phillips-Perron test were applied. All the variables are integrated of order 1 (I(1)) and thus stationary in first difference. We subsequently employed the Johansen maximum likelihood test to test for the presence of co-integration in the vector error correction model. The trace statistics and maximal eigenvalue confirm the presence of the same. Hence, we conclude that a long run relationship exists in all the above specifications.

Empirical results

The long run estimates are shown in Table 14.1.

From the LHDI equation and the LTOU, it may be observed that tourism arrivals have a positive and significant impact on the HD index in the long run. More precisely, a 1% increase in tourist arrivals in the country leads to a 0.13% increase in HD. This result is consistent with the findings of Croes' (2012) study of Nicaragua and Costa Rica, Folarin et al.'s (2017) study of a sample of African countries and Biagi et al.'s (2017) analysis of a number of developed and developing country scenarios. Thus, TD may have boosted human capital as expansion of the Mauritian tourism sector led to employment creation, and in turn creating better livelihoods for the workers (Christie et al., 2013; Jordan et al., 2016)). Income generation from the sector for households can be linked to better living standards and an increase in life expectancy. Moreover, TD generated increased government tax and other revenues thereby allowing the Mauritian government to subsidise the welfare state, yielding positive broad health and education outcomes.

Table 14.1 The long run estimates

	MODEL 1 HDI Equation	MODEL 2 Tourism Equation
DEPENDENT VARIABLES →	LHDI	LTOU
Independent Variable		
LTOU	0.13***	
LHDI		0.254**
LUNEM	−0.097**	0.034
LOPEN	0.235*	0.236**
LGOVTSP	0.46**	0.125*
LGDFCF	0.209**	0.323**
CONSTANT	6.028	2.324*

Notes: * Indicates the significance at 10%, ** significance at 5% and *** significance at 1%.

From the control variables, and as expected, we can observe that unemployment has a negative and significant impact on HD. Interestingly, a VAR framework also enables us to draw insights with respect to reverse causality. From the tourism equation (LTOU), it can be observed that HD is an important element in TD as witnessed by the positive and significant coefficient of LHDI. This confirms the existence of a bicausal relationship between TD and HD and suggests a mutually reinforcing effect, at least in the long run. Croes (2012) found similar results for the case of Nicaragua.

The short run estimates

In the presence of co-integration, a vector autoregressive error correction model (VECM) is subsequently specified and estimated, and this allows for an investigation of the dynamic nature of the model as well as the determination of the short run estimates. In this study, the VECM is estimated using an optimum lag length of 1. The empirical results of the short run estimates for model 1 of the VECM are displayed in Table 14.2.

With the HDI equation as the dependent variable, it may be argued that TD is still a contributor to HD in the short run, although with a smaller coefficient compared to the long run scenario. This implies that TD may take some time to register its full potential on HDI. Similar observations have been made in previous studies (for example, Croes, 2012). Local investment and unemployment are shown to be significant factors in explaining HDI in the short run while the remaining explanatory variables are insignificant, suggesting only long run effects. It is also clear that tourist arrivals influence HD, although, as reflected in Table 14.3, the reverse does not hold true, at least for the short run.

Table 14.2 also shows that the lagged value of the dependent variable is positive and significant, implying that lagged tourism arrivals contribute positively towards the current levels of tourism. This confirms the existence of dynamism in tourism modelling and presents some evidence of the persistence in arrival from certain countries, following the positive experience of tourists. It is also interesting to note that the adjustment parameter (ECM) is -0.36 (second column), which indicates a relatively rapid adjustment speed of the system to its long-run equilibrium. This reflects the speed at which the disequilibrium is made up for in the next period, i.e. nearly 36% of the discrepancy between long-term and short-term HD is corrected within a year. This adjustment speed coupled with the fact that the short run parameter is smaller than the long run parameter might indeed also suggest that tourism may take time to attain its full impact on the HD.

Conclusion

The study investigated the impact of TD on HD in Mauritius over the period 1988–2016, using dynamic time series econometric analysis, namely a vector autoregressive framework which caters for potential dynamic and endogenous relationships in the hypothesised link. The results showed that TD has a positive

Table 14.2 Short run estimates (dependent variable: LHDI)

	D(LHDI) HDI Eq.	−D(LTOU) Tourism Eq.	D(LUNEM) Unemployment Eq.	D(LOPEN) Openness Eq.	D(LGSP) Govt Spending Eq.	D(LGDFCF) Investment Eq.
ECM	−0.359**	−0.279**	−0.328*	−0.116	−0.3917*	−0.4174
D(LHDI(−1))	0.2859**	−0.0601	2.240	0.515	0.3591	−1.657
D(LTOU(−1))	0.053*	0.333**	0.2572	0.2072	0.0019	0.479
D(LUNEM(−1))	−0.014**	0.102	0.139**	0.1036	−0.0064*	−0.332
D(LOPEN(−1))	−0.0282	0.093	−0.031	0.1242*	−0.0659**	0.510
D(LGSP(−1))	0.102	0.564*	−1.011*	0.624	0.097	0.224*
D(LGDFCF(−1))	0.0244***	−0.0874	−0.253	−0.134	−0.0056*	0.1479**
C	0.018***	0.087**	−0.0223**	−0.034**	0.0011***	0.0395**

Notes: * Indicates the significance at 10%, ** significance at 5% and *** significance at 1%.

and significant influence on HD in the long run. A 1% increase in tourist arrivals in the country led to a 0.13% increase in HD. Interestingly, it was also observed that HD is an important element in TD as well. In other words, the study confirms the existence of a bicausal relationship between TD and HD. Analysis of the short run estimates revealed that TD is still a contributor to HD in the short run, although with a small coefficient as compared to the long run coefficient. This implies that the impact of TD on HDI is only realised after a period of time. Our results further show that tourist arrivals influence HD. However, the reverse did not hold true, at least for the short run. Our findings imply that social policy makers should consider TD as a valid development tool.

Note

1 http://tourism.govmu.org/English/Tourism%20sector/Pages/Tourism-Sector.aspx

References

Alexiou, C. (2009). Government spending and economic growth: Econometric evidence from the South Eastern Europe (SEE). *Journal of Economic and Social Research, 11*(1), 1.

Amoah, V., and Baum, T. (1997). Tourism education: Policy versus practice. *International Journal of Contemporary Hospitality Management, 9*(1), 5–12.

Andereck, K., Valentine, K., Vogt, C., and Vogt, R. (2007). A cross-cultural analysis of tourism and quality of life perceptions. *Journal of Sustainable Tourism, 15*(5), 483–502.

Andereck, K., and Vogt, C. (2000). The relationship between residents' attitudes toward tourism and tourism development options. *Journal of Travel Research, 39*(27), 27–36.

Aref, F. (2011). The effects of tourism on quality of life: A case study of Shiraz, Iran. *Life Science Journal, 8*(2), 26–30.

Bakri, N. M., Jaafar, M., and Mohamad, D. (2014). Perceptions of local communities on the economic impacts of tourism development in Langkawi, Malaysia. In *SHS web of conferences* (Vol. 12, p. 01100). EDP Sciences.

Baum, T. (2015). Human resources in tourism: Still waiting for change? – A 2015 reprise. *Tourism Management, 50*, 204–212.

Bhutia, S. (2014, June). The role of tourism for human resource development in Darjeeling district of West Bengal. *India Journal of Tourism and Hospitality Management, 2*(1), 113–128.

Biagi, B., and Detotto, C. (2014). Crime as tourism externality. *Regional Studies, 48*(4), 693–709.

Biagi, B., Ladu, M. G., and Royuela, V. (2017). Human development and tourism specialisation. Evidence from a panel of developed and developing countries. *International Journal of Tourism Research, 19*(2), 160–178.

Biagi, B., Lambiri, D., and Faggian, A. (2012). The effect of tourism on the housing market. *Handbook of Tourism and Quality-of-Life Research*, 635–652.

Brau, R., Lanza, A., and Pigliaru, F. (2007). How fast are small tourism countries growing? Evidence from the data for 1980–2003. *Tourism Economics, 13*, 603–613.

Christie, I. T., Fernandes, E., Messerli, H., and Twining-Ward, L. (2013). Tourism in Africa: Harnessing tourism for growth and improved livelihoods. Washington, DC: The World Bank. *Research, 19*(2), 160–178.

Croes, R. (2012). Assessing tourism development from Sen's capability approach. *Journal of Travel Research*, *51*, 542–554.

Durbarry, R. (2004). Tourism and economic growth: The case of Mauritius. *Tourism Economics*, *10*, 389–401.

Durbarry, R., and Seetanah, B. (2015). The impact of long haul destinations on carbon emissions: The case of Mauritius. *Journal of Hospitality Marketing and Management*, *24*(4), 401–410.

Egger, H., Egger, P., Falkinger, J., and Grossmann, V. (2005). *International capital market integration, educational choice and economic growth*. IZA Discussion Paper No. 1863, Institute for the Study of Labor IZA.

Fredline, L., Deery, M., and Jago, L. (2005). *Social impacts of tourism on communities*. Retrieved December 9, 2010, from http://www.surfcoast.vic.gov.au

Folarin, O., Oladipupo, E., Ajogbeje, K., and Adeniyi, O. (2017). Does tourism development contribute to human capital development in Africa? *Tourism*, *65*(3), 314–329.

Gjerald, O. (2005). Sociocultural impacts of tourism: A case study from Norway. *Journal of Tourism and Cultural Change*, *3*(1), 36–58.

Gohou, G., and Soumaré, I. (2012). Does foreign direct investment reduce poverty in Africa and are there regional differences? *World Development*, *40*(1), 75–95.

Granger, C. W., and Newbold, P. (1974). Spurious regressions in econometrics. *Journal of Econometrics*, *2*(2), 111–120.

Hertz, E., Hebert, J. R., and Landon, J. (1994). Social and environmental factors and life expectancy, infant mortality and maternal rate: Results of a cross-national comparison. *Social Science Medical*, *39*, 105–114.

Human Development Report. (2016). *Human development for everyone*. Briefing note for countries on the 2016 human development Report.

Jordan, P., Havadi-Nagy, K. X., and Marosi, Z. (2016). Tourism as a driving force in rural development: Comparative case study of Romanian and Austrian village. *Tourism*, *64*(2), 203–218.

Katırcıoğlu, S. (2009). Revisiting the tourism-led growth hypothesis for Turkey using the Bounds test and Johansen approach for cointegration. *Tourism Management*, *30*(1), 17–20.

Khadaroo, A. J., and Seetanah, B. (2009). An analysis of the relationship between transport capital and tourism development in a dynamic framework. *Tourism Economics*, *15*(4), 785–802.

Kim, K. (2002). *The effects of tourism impacts upon quality of life of residents in the community* (Dissertation), Faculty of the Virginia Polytechnic Institute and State University.

Landais, C. (2015). Assessing the welfare effects of unemployment benefits using the regression kink design. *American Economic Journal: Economic Policy*, *7*(4), 243–278.

Lindberg, K., Andersson, T. D., and Dellaert, B. G. C. (2001). Tourism development. Assessing social gains and losses. *Annals of Tourism Research*, *28*, 1010–1030.

Mai, N. T. T., Rahtz, D. R., and Shultz II, C. J. (2013). Tourism as a catalyst for quality of life in transitioning subsistence marketplaces: Perspectives from Ha Long, Vietnam. *Journal of Macromarketing*, *34*(1), 28–44.

Marchante, A. J., and Ortega, B. (2012). Human capital and labor productivity: A study for the hotel industry. *Cornell Hospitality Quarterly*, *53*, 20–30.

Marzuki, A. (2009). Impacts of tourism development. Anatolia: *An International Journal of Tourism and Hospitality Research*, *20*(2), 450–455.

Naude, A. W., and Saayaman, A. (2005). Determinants of tourist arrivals in Africa: A panel data regression analysis. *Tourism Economics*, *11*(3), 365–391.

Nunnenkamp, P. (2002). *Determinants of FDI in developing countries: Has globalization changed the rules of the game?* (No. 1122). Kiel Working Paper.

Phillips, P. C. B. (1986). Understanding spurious regressions in econometrics. *Journal of Econometrics, 33*, 311–340.

Polodoo, V., Seetanah, B., and Sannassee, R. V. (2016). Exchange rate volatility and manufacturing trade: Evidence from Africa. *The Journal of Developing Areas, 50*(6), 133–148.

Ridderstaat, J., Croes, R., and Nijkamp, P. (2016). The tourism development – quality of life nexus in a small island destination. *Journal of Travel Research, 55*(1), 79–94.

Sandford, D., and Dong, H. (2000). Investment in familiar territory: Tourism and new foreign direct investments. *Tourism Economics, 6*(3), 205–219.

Sannassee, R. V., Seetanah, B., and Lamport, M. J. (2014). Export diversification and economic growth: The case of Mauritius. In M. Jansen, M. S. Jallab, and M. Smeets (Eds.), *Connecting to global markets: Challenges and opportunities* (pp. 11–23). Geneva: World Trade Organization.

Schubert, S. F. (2010). Coping with externalities in tourism: A dynamic optimal taxation approach. *Tourism Economics, 16*(2), 321–343.

Seetanah, B. (2011). Assessing the dynamic economic impact of tourism for island economies. *Annals of Tourism Research, 38*(1), 291–308.

Seetanah, B., and Sannassee, R. V. (2015). Marketing promotion financing and tourism development: The case of Mauritius. *Journal of Hospitality Marketing and Management, 24*(2), 202–215.

Sinclair, T. M. (1998). Tourism and economic development: A survey. *The Journal of Development Studies, 34*(5), 1–51.

Singh, S. (1997). Developing human resources for the tourism industry with reference to India. *Tourism Management, 18*, 299–306.

Sr, M. V., and Croes, R. R. (2003). Growth, development and tourism in a small economy: Evidence from Aruba. *International Journal of Tourism Research, 5*(5), 315–330.

Srinivasan, G. (2005). Improving overall climate key to FDI flows: IMF, *Businessline*, 1.

Tang, S., Selvanathan, E. A., and Selvanathan, S. (2007). The relationship between foreign direct investment and tourism: Empirical evidence from China. *Tourism Economics, 13*(1), 25–39.

Tecle, Y. H., and Schroenn, J. L. (2006). The contribution of HRD to tourism-led development in an African context. *South African Journal of Economic and Management Sciences, 9*(4), 444–457.

United Nations World Tourism Organization (UNWTO). (2015). *Tourism in Africa: A tool for development- affiliate members regional reports, Volume four*. Madrid: UNWTO.

Winters, L. A. (2000). *Trade, trade policy and poverty: What are the links*, CEPR Discussion Paper No. 2382, London.

World Tourism Organization. (2016). *UNWTO annual report 2015*. Madrid: UNWTO.

15 Tourism governance and organisational infrastructure in the East African Community

A baseline analysis

Bernard Kitheka and Agnes Sirima

Acknowledgements

We are grateful to Dr. Carmen Nibigira, formerly with the East Africa Tourism Platform (EATP), for her insights and for supporting this study.

Introduction

Organisations are an integral part of modern society. At their best, organisations enhance the performance of human institutions (Lusthaus, 2002). Efficient and effective organisations are the heart of a nation's progressive and sustainable development (OECD, 2001), and their performance is a function of the organisation's enabling environment, capacity and motivation (CIDA, 2006). Organisations thus need to exploit opportunities to build work environments, knowledge bases, skill sets and capacities for efficient delivery of their promises. Similarly, people working within organisations need to learn to set, review and reach common goals (Vinzant and Vinzant, 1996). However, in a fast modernising world, most organisations, at local and global scales, are experiencing an unprecedented wave of environmental changes occasioned by globalisation forces, technological advances and changes in governance models (Schneider, 2002). These forces compel organisations to continually learn, grow and adapt in order to remain relevant.

Organisational capacity assessment (OCA) is a common tool used to provide details about an organisation's performance, enabling environment, capacity and motivation to achieve its stated mission (Egan, Yang, and Bartlett, 2004; Lusthaus, 2002). OCA plays a valuable role in creating the foundation for institutional learning, institutional strengthening and investment decision-making (Pact, 2012). The current baseline study was conducted to assess the organisational capacities of tourism associations in the East African Community (EAC) states of Burundi, Rwanda, Uganda, Tanzania and Kenya. The study also gives an overview of the public and private organisational climate of EAC tourism. The target organisations are responsible for championing tourism development in their respective countries.

An OCA is a systematic, participatory approach of measuring organisational performance and challenges with the goal of improved strategies and results (Lusthaus, 2002). Conducted either internally or by external reviewers, OCA draws upon a tradition of applied organisational research for supporting organisational change, continuous learning and development. OCA can enable organisations to track changes over time and benchmark performance against organisations engaged in similar activities. It can also be employed as a collaborative, self-assessment process to offer organisations opportunities to reflect on their current status against recognised best practices (USAID, 2012).

The OCA approach was originally developed to help engage staff and stakeholders of non-governmental agencies in order to measure the organisation's unique capacities and guide future development (Pact, 2012). OCA's breakthrough was its ability to help organisations identify perceived organisational strengths and weaknesses and explore differences of opinions across staff, boards and stakeholders, and then use the insight to build consensus around future development. In an attempt to understand the organisational climate and organisational performance in member states, this study employs two conceptual lenses, namely, organisational capacity and organisational leadership.

Organisational capacity

Organisational capacity is the ability of an organisation to fulfil its mission as enabled by organisational infrastructure (e.g. finance resources), capabilities (e.g. leadership and competencies), knowledge and learning (to enable adaptive capacity), collaboration (e.g. access to financial resources) and a persistent rededication to achieving results (Kibbe, 2003; Yu Lee, 2002).

Organisational capacity is critical to the development and implementation of policy. Beyond the passage of laws and policies, the outcomes of organisational goals largely depends on the agency's training and allocation of human power, and the policy-making process (Ting, 2009). Ting asserts that capacity determines whether regulations are enforced, revenues are collected, benefits are distributed and programmes are completed. Further, Fredericksen and London (2000) underscore the importance of visionary leadership and vision-sensitivity. Both leadership and vision require presence of directorship and oversight bodies to manage day-to-day operations and to facilitate organisational evolution (Barnett and Hansen, 1996).

An organisation evolves not only in what it does, but also in how it operates (Zollo, Cennamo, and Neumann, 2013). After formation, organisations must allow periods of incremental changes interspersed by discontinuous reorientation and transformations rather than making changes whenever there is a crisis (Tushman, Newman, and Romanelli, 1986). Mature organisations should be able to sustainably fulfil promises and responsibilities to primary stakeholders and the society (Clarkson, 1995; Jawahar and McLaughlin, 2001). However, if an organisation does not learn how to adapt and evolve into changing systems and viewpoints, it is unlikely to remain relevant, economically, socially and environmentally (Zollo et al., 2013).

Organisational leadership

Organisational leadership plays a big role in facilitating system-wide momentum and directing reorientation. During periods of incremental changes and convergence, executive leadership's role is to re-emphasise strategy, mission and core values, to be alert to external opportunities and threats, and to motivate constructive organisational behaviour. Similarly, the presence and active involvement of senior management is crucial in providing foresight during the evolution process (Tushman et al., 1986). Creativity and innovation are also tied to the organisation's leadership; they are critical competencies in improving organisational performance and staying power (DiLiello and Houghton, 2006). Creativity theory suggests that when the leadership and working environment facilitates idea generation, problem solving and knowledge sharing, individuals working for the given organisation are more likely to be innovative (Kozbelt, Beghetto, and Runco, 2010).

Geo-historical context of study site

The East African Community (Figure 15.1) is a regional intergovernmental organisation consisting of six states: Burundi, Kenya, Rwanda, Tanzania, Uganda and South Sudan. The idea of regional cooperation between individual states dates back to the colonial period (Reith and Boltz, 2011), but the first semblance of the community was formed in 1967 by Kenya, Uganda and Tanzania. This maiden treaty was dissolved in 1977, revamped in 1993 and fully endorsed in 1999 (Ogola, Njengaa, Mhando, and Kigundu, 2015). In 2000, the current regional body was enacted with a secretariat based in Arusha, Tanzania. Rwanda and Burundi became members in 2007, followed by South Sudan in 2016. South Sudan has considerable endowment of natural resources and biodiversity and enormous potential to develop a viable tourism industry. However, because of lack of data on South Sudan's tourism, the country was excluded from the current study.

Overview of EAC tourism

Tourism plays significant economic and development roles in East Africa: it is a means of alleviating poverty, a major source of foreign exchange, a driver for natural resources conservation and an incentive for cultural preservation (Okello and Novelli, 2014). It employs more than one million people and accounts for 4% of the region's gross domestic product, ranking it only behind agriculture (Nibigira, Sabuhoro, and Kitheka, 2017). It is estimated that in 2016 nearly four million foreigners visited the region, maintaining a relative consistency in arrivals over the last five years.

East Africa, boasting a rich and varied concentration of wildlife, is a natural destination for tourists (Honey and Gilpin, 2009). Its tourism, usually categorised as ecotourism or nature-based (Watkin, 2003; Western, 2008), is founded on a flourishing natural heritage complemented by diverse cultures and the hospitality of local communities. The most notable tourism offerings include wildlife tourism, beach tourism, gorilla tourism, cultural tourism and mountaineering. Kenya and Tanzania

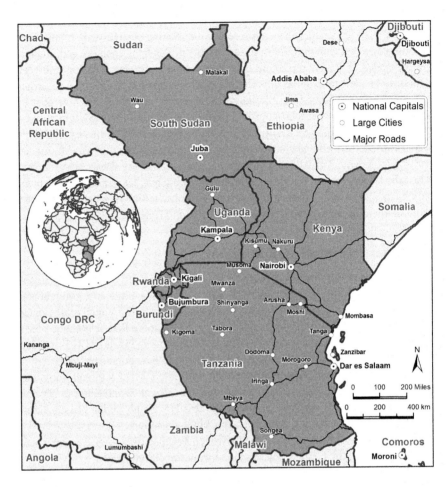

Figure 15.1 EAC member states

Source: Map by Bernard Kitheka

are the preferred destinations for safari tourism and beach tourism (Van der Duim, Peters, and Akama, 2006), whereas in Uganda and Rwanda tourists can experience the unique gorilla tourism (Van der Duim et al., 2006). Culture and heritage tourism are major attractions in all five countries, though it is least tapped in Burundi because of prolonged internal conflicts (Nibigira et al., 2017). Kenya has a relatively more developed business, convention and conference tourism (Christie, Fernandes, Messerli, and Twining-Ward, 2014; Rogerson and Visser, 2014), but Rwanda is rapidly emerging as a competitive destination (Nielsen and Spenceley, 2010). Currently, most EAC long-haul tourists originate from Europe and North America, with leading sources being the UK, USA, France and the Netherlands (Christie et al., 2014). The majority of tourists visit protected areas such as national parks, game reserves, marine parks and wildlife sanctuaries.

Taking advantage of the shared borders, ecosystem and history, the regional geopolitical and economic bloc aims to jointly diversify tourism products, promote tourism and attract more tourists from traditional and new source markets. Specific areas of collaboration include management of tourism and wildlife resources, formation of a tourism and wildlife coordination agency and drawing of joint tourism marketing plans. In pursuit of these goals, some short-term strategic interventions include marketing and promotion of EAC as a single tourist destination, single criteria for classifying hotels and restaurants, harmonisation of policies and legislation on wildlife conservation, and capacity building in tourism and wildlife sectors (EAC Secretariat, 2015).

Methods

The current study, conducted between November 2015 and June 2016, employed part total and part convenient sampling methodology. All participating organisations and participants were based in the EAC's largest cities: Nairobi (Kenya), Kampala (Uganda), Kigali (Rwanda), Dar es Salaam and Arusha (Tanzania). Arusha was included because it is the seat of the EAC Secretariat. A pre-study plan had been made to visit and interview participants in Bujumbura (Burundi), but following political and social unrest, alternative arrangements were made to interview one participant by phone while a second one was interviewed in person in Kigali.

The survey instrument was developed through a collaborative effort involving the lead author and staff of the East African Tourism Platform (EATP). Questions elicited information on organisational capacities (including management/leadership and staffing capacities), organisational mission and mandates, active membership, funding levels, opportunities for in-country and regional partnerships, challenges and opportunities, and perspectives on country and regional tourism. Semi-structured interview questions were used to complement, and in some cases mirror, the survey questionnaire.

Sampling procedure

Selection of participants was based on their position in tourism at country or regional levels. Participants occupied management and leadership roles in the organisation they were associated with, or they had been recommended by a person in a leadership role, either an executive director, president, or chairperson of the trustee board. Most interviews were conducted one-on-one, but in two cases (Kenya Association of Tour Operators and Uganda Tourism Association), two sets of two participants were interviewed together.

The list of participating agencies and tourism associations was developed by the researcher in collaboration with the EATP coordinator. Only private non-profit organisations were targeted. However, to shed light on the government's role in tourism, three participants (one each from Kenya, Uganda and Rwanda) from government tourism agencies were also interviewed. The original plan was to visit and interview at least one person from each state's public tourism agency, but officers from Burundi and Tanzania were not available. Table 15.1 lists

Table 15.1 Target organisations and their management environment

Country	Organisation/Association	Secretariat present (size)	Board present	Participate in study
Uganda	Uganda Tourism Association*	Yes (2)	Yes	Yes
	Association of Uganda Tour Operators	No	Yes	Yes
	Uganda Safari Guides Association	No	Yes	Yes
	Uganda Travel Agents Association	No	Yes	Yes
	Uganda Community Tourism Association	No	Yes	No
	Uganda Hotel Owners Association	Yes (2)	Yes	Yes
Rwanda	Chamber of Tourism*	Yes (1)	Yes	Yes
	Rwanda Tours and Travel Association	Yes (2)	Yes	Yes
	Rwanda Hospitality Association	No	Yes	No
	Rwanda Drivers & Safari Guides Association	No	Yes	Yes
	Rwanda Tourism Educators Association	No	No data	No
Burundi	Hotel Association of Burundi	No	Yes	Yes
	Tour Operators Association of Burundi	No	Yes	Yes
Tanzania	Tourism Confederation of Tanzania*	Yes (5)	Yes	Yes
	Hotel Association of Tanzania	Yes (1)	Yes	Yes
	Tanzania Society of Travel Agents	No data	No data	No
	Tanzania Air Operators Association	No data	Yes	No
	Tanzania Association of Tour Operators	Yes (3)	Yes	yes
	Tanzania Tour Guides Association	No data	No data	No
	Tanzania Association of Cultural Tourism	No data	No data	No
	Zanzibar Association of Tour Operators	No data	No data	No
	Zanzibar Association of Tourism Investors	No data	No data	No
Kenya	Kenya Tourism Federation*	Yes (8)	Yes	Yes
	Kenya Association of Hotelkeepers & Caterers	Yes (9)	Yes	Yes
	Kenya Association of Tour Operators	Yes (15)	Yes	Yes
	Kenya Professional Safari Guides Association	Yes (No data)	Yes	No
	Kenya Association of Travel Agents	Yes (6)	Yes	No
	Ecotourism Kenya	Yes (5)	Yes	Yes
	Sustainable Travel & Tourism Agenda	Yes (2)	Yes	No

Notes: * National tourism apex body

organisations that were targeted, as well as the actual participants, and the five in-country tourism apex organisations that sit in the EATP board.

Data collection and analysis

The lead author travelled to the EAC states and visited all participating organisations. Data were collected through surveys, face-to-face semi-structured interviews, phone interviews, visits to participants' places of work and a review of grey literature. The lead author made all the appointments and conducted all the interviews. The interviews lasted an average of 36 minutes and involved detailed note taking. Structured surveys were administered in-person or through email. Thirty-six key informants were interviewed, 19 (52.8%) men and 17 (47.2%) women. Kenya had the largest number (15) of participants followed by Uganda (8), Rwanda (6), Burundi (4) and Tanzania (3). Most (20) participants had at least a bachelor's degree. Data analysis involved manually organising notes and constructing narratives around pre-determined themes of organisational capacities, tourism management and political climate, and organisational challenges. Survey and interview data were corroborated by field visits, consultation with the EATP coordinator, and review of grey literature. For reliability, codes and themes were verified by the EATP coordinator.

Results

Study findings are summarised into four main sections. The first section outlines the associations involved in this study. The second section analyses the governments' role in tourism. The third section summarises the private sector's role in tourism, including notes on each member state. The last section highlights some organisational capacity challenges facing tourism associations in EAC.

EAC tourism is increasingly on the global radar due to recently intensified political alignments, regional infrastructural developments and projected tourism growth. States, communities, businesses and individuals are all interested in a share of the tourism perks. However, it was evident that many entities were ill-informed about the intricacies of tourism beyond the short-term financial gains.

Overview of participating organisations

It was observed that public and private organisations play crucial roles in developing and managing tourism in member states. Their mandates and goals differ, but their roles are largely complementary. The level of effectiveness of each, and partnerships between the two sectors, vary from country to country. Similarly, knowledge, skill and experience levels in managing tourism undertakings differ substantially across states. However, the level of performance and competitiveness of each state hinges on how the government, as the lead agency, prioritises the tourism industry in its agenda. At the time of this study, only five associations reported five or more staff members (Table 15.1): Kenya Association of Tour Operators, Kenya Association of Hotelkeepers & Caterers, Kenya Association of

Travel Agents, Kenya Tourism Federation, Tourism Confederation of Tanzania and Ecotourism Kenya. It is possible that other associations have more staff, but there was no available data to suggest so.

Public sector involvement

The findings also revealed that governments' involvement in tourism development is usually through a designated ministry and a state agency. The ministry, either stand-alone or an amalgamation with other sectors (e.g. wildlife, trade, etc.), is the nodal organ for tourism development and promotion in-country. Usually headed by a cabinet minister, the ministry plays a crucial role in coordinating all state efforts, making policy, catalysing private investment, strengthening promotional and marketing efforts and developing human resources. The lead tourism agency in each state is headed by a director general or someone at a similar level of authority. Table 15.2 shows the respective government ministries and tourism state agencies as of the time of this study. At a regional level, the EAC Assembly also includes a tourism portfolio based in Arusha, Tanzania.

Private sector involvement

Across the bloc, most tourism professionals and businesses align under interest groups or membership organisations: tour operators, tour and safari guides, hotel owners and caterers, travel agents, air operators, and restaurants, pubs and entertainment. All the states have tourism apex or umbrella bodies that bring together all tourism associations under one roof (Table 15.1), but notably, those in Rwanda and Burundi lack functional secretariats.

Table 15.2 EAC state tourism portfolios

Country	Umbrella Ministry		Lead Agency	
	Institution	Head	Institution	Head
Uganda	Tourism, Wildlife and Antiquities	Cabinet Minster	Uganda Tourism Board	Director General
Rwanda	Foreign Affairs and Cooperation	Cabinet Minister	Department of Tourism	Chief Executive Officer
Burundi	Commerce, Industry and Tourism	Cabinet Minister	Burundi National Tourism Office	Director General
Tanzania	Natural Resources and Tourism	Cabinet Minister	Tanzania Tourist Board	Director General
Kenya	Commerce, Tourism and East Africa Region	Cabinet Secretary	Kenya Tourism Board	Director General

The tourism associations are member-driven credibility organisations whose main purpose is to represent, promote and protect the common interests of its members. Membership is ideally through registration and payment of a regular fee. Members are charged with developing standards and codes of conduct that participants must adhere to. The associations are overseen by boards and have some form of networking platforms such as a periodical and/or a website. However, this study established that many associations lack physical offices, functional secretariats, sustainable funding and active boards.

The East Africa Tourism Platform is the regional umbrella body for all non-profit organisations involved in tourism. Established in 2011, the EATP's mandate is to facilitate private and public sector engagement to foster regional tourism development and promotion. As the tourism apex body, the EATP works closely with relevant ministries, the EAC Secretariat, the East African Business Council and private sector entities in partner states. To date, the EATP has played a key role in lobbying for a single EAC tourist visa and use of national identification cards as valid travel documents for EAC residents (Nibigira et al., 2017).

Private sector highlights

Rwanda: Private sector businesses in tourism, travel and hospitality are organised under the Rwanda Chamber of Tourism (RTC). The RTC is an umbrella organisation under the Rwanda Private Sector Federation, which was formed in 2006 to lobby for tourism, travel and hospitality sectors and to represent tourism in sector-specific reforms aimed at improving the tourism business environment in Rwanda. Tourism associations also operate as vetting bodies, monitoring operators in the industry. The Chamber of Tourism members are organised into associations such as tours and travel, hospitality, safari guides and tourism educators. Data reveal that most tourism associations in Rwanda are severely underfunded and understaffed (Table 15.1).

Uganda: The tourism and hospitality private sector is organised under the Uganda Tourism Association (UTA). The UTA was created in the 1960s and revamped in 2013. The UTA brings together trade associations in tourism, travel and hospitality sectors under one umbrella organised along tour operators, safari guides, community tourism, hotel owners and travel agents, respectively. The UTA's specific mandate is to conduct policy research and advocacy on behalf of their members, provide a forum for policy discussions, engage the government and conduct capacity building training for their members. Most tourism associations in Uganda are underfunded and do not have a functional secretariat (Table 15.1).

Burundi: The Sectoral Chamber of Hotels and Tourism of Burundi (HTB), under which the tourism and hospitality private sector is organised, was created in 2009 following the restructuring of the Federal Chamber of Commerce and Industry. The HTB's mission is to initiate and support all efforts aimed at promoting the tourism sector as well improving the business environment. Each year HTB organises training for their members to improve their capacity. It also represents the industry in relevant national, regional and international events. Data reveal that HTB's main challenges include political instability in the country and a lack of tourism and hospitality training institutions and funds to run action plans for the Chamber.

Tanzania: The Tourism Confederate of Tanzania (TCT) was created in 2000 with the aim of bringing together sectoral associations organised under tour operators, cultural tourism, travel agents, hotel owners, air operators, professional hunters, tour guides and Zanzibar tourism investors, among others. The aim of the TCT is to enforce high standards in the tourism industry, engage government in constructive policy formulation and implementation as well as build the capacity of industry members in a bid to provide quality services.

Kenya: The Kenya Tourism Federation (KTF) was created in 1999 as an umbrella organisation to advocate and bring together various associations in tourism, travel and hospitality industries. Tourism and hospitality associations in Kenya coalesce along seven subsectors including tour operators, hotel keepers and caterers, travel agents, air operators, ecotourism and pubs, entertainment and restaurants. Unlike in other EAC states, most tourism associations in Kenya have functional secretariats, boards and large membership bases, which are indicators of the maturity of the tourism sector.

Discussion

The *Economic Road Map* and *Vision 2050* of the East African Community views tourism as a key pillar for national and regional development (EAC, 2016). The current study clearly identifies various organisational capacity strengths and challenges for tourism organisations in EAC states. Strengths and achievements were mentioned in the areas of cross-agency regional integration in cross-border management of natural resources, partnership between member states in tourism superstructure development, formation of EATP to oversee member states tourism associations, the spirit of volunteerism among board members to ensure associations continue operating especially where staffing was inadequate, flow of funding to support research and human resource development across the region, and establishment of region-faced networking forums including conferences, workshops and online platforms. Besides each state having its own agency and/or ministry in charge of tourism, the formation of a tourism ministry to the East African Community Assembly was also acknowledged as a move in the positive direction.

On the other hand, participants highlighted organisational capacity challenges in some critical areas. The most frequently mentioned challenges faced by the majority of the associations included lack of leadership including either or both directorship and oversight boards; poor staffing levels; poor funding levels; lack of harmony between board members and the management; poorly trained personnel and limited understanding of regional and global tourism issues and trends; bureaucratic bottlenecks from government agencies in implementing projects and tourism-friendly policies; and lack of clarity on the roles and responsibilities of the EATP.

Nonetheless, tourism is recognised as an important tool for poverty alleviation, a driver for wildlife conservation, a provider of millions of jobs, a catalyst for rural development and a major generator of foreign revenue for the government (Okello and Novelli, 2014). To realise tourism's full potential in that regard, better destination management and organisational leadership are imperative. The key tourism stakeholders could learn from the progress in other African regions, in terms of how geopolitical and economic integration arrangements can be leveraged to enhance members' individual performance. In particular, the Southern African Development Community (SADC), which has similar natural endowments as the study context, has made significant strides in integrating tourism into regional development plans in various areas, including travel facilitation, tourism training and education, joint marketing and promotion, service standards, environmental sustainability, tourism research, transportation and provision of incentives for tourism development. Other regions that have given tourism a sustainably viable regional outlook include the European Union and the Association of Southeast Asian Nations (ASEAN).

Conclusion and implications

The current study reveals that tourism associations in the EAC play crucial roles as destination marketing organisations but also suffer serious organisational capacity deficiencies. The results further point to a number of challenges, including the lack of effective leadership, poor funding and poor staffing, which make a strong case for the need to strengthen the EAC's tourism associations. Strong national and regional organisations are crucial for joint stewardship of natural resources, cross-border monitoring of resources, coordination of tourism stakeholders and harmonisation of regional tourism policies. The need for robust tourism associations in the region is also crucial in order to build globally viable products and brands. Strong associations can also complement public sector efforts in managing the tourism sector and providing a forum for tourism stakeholders to exchange ideas and work toward a competitive tourism industry.

Nonetheless, there were notable strengths in areas of networking, goodwill in coalition building for regional development, increased donor funding for research and human resource development, and government investment infrastructure development, among others. Future opportunities lie in strengthening partnerships among the associations under EATP and ensuring sustainable funding for EATP's operations, capacity building among staff and the board in areas of institutional development and organisational strategic management, accelerated development and implementation of the proposed regional tourism master plan, and consultative stakeholder approaches in identifying and solving key regional issues.

To optimise synergies in the future, the region's tourism industry requires better inter-agency coordination and public-private partnerships. Challenges in creating a conducive environment for tourism businesses often relate to a country's public and private institutional set-up as well as governance, as evidenced in some of the EAC states. Secondly, administrative barriers are hindering the movement of people. The growth potential of tourism is being hampered by the outdated practices of visa and border controls. Some of these challenges could be overcome if the states develop strong tourism associations to challenge existing policy barriers towards a sustainable tourism sector. Lastly, member states and the EAC bloc should take advantage of opportunities presented by the UN Sustainable Development Goals and the 'Africa rising' environment, as well as the potential presented by technological innovations, to advance the agenda for sustainable, competitive regional tourism. As a region, EAC will only become a competitive destination if individual states implement their part of the strategy, as espoused in the *Economic Road Map* and *Visions* of the East African Community.

References

Barnett, W. P., and Hansen, M. T. (1996). The red queen in organizational evolution. *Strategic Management Journal, 17*(1), 139–157.

Christie, I., Fernandes, E., Messerli, H., and Twining-Ward, L. (2014). *Tourism in Africa: Harnessing tourism for growth and improved livelihoods*. Washington, DC: International Bank for Reconstruction and Development, World Bank Publications.

CIDA (Canadian International Development Agency). (2006). *Organization assessment guide*. Accessed at: http://www.acdi-cida.gc.ca/INET/IMAGES.NSF/vLUImages/Performance review6/.

Clarkson, M. E. (1995). A stakeholder framework for analyzing and evaluating corporate social performance. *Academy of Management Review, 20*(1), 92–117.

DiLiello, T. C., and Houghton, J. D. (2006). Maximizing organizational leadership capacity for the future: Toward a model of self-leadership, innovation and creativity. *Journal of Managerial Psychology, 21*(4), 319–337.

EAC Secretariat. (2015). *East African Community facts and figures: EAC statistics portal*. Arusha, Tanzania: EAC Secretariat.

EAC. (2016). *Regional vision for socioeconomic transformation and development*. Retrieved September 25, 2018, from www.africa-platform.org/sites/default/files/resources/eac_vision_2050_february_2016.pdf

Egan, T. M., Yang, B., and Bartlett, K. R. (2004). The effects of organizational learning culture and job satisfaction on motivation to transfer learning and turnover intention. *Human Resource Development Quarterly, 15*(3), 279–301.

Fredericksen, P., and London, R. (2000). Disconnect in the hollow state: The pivotal role of organizational capacity in community-based development organizations. *Public Administration Review, 60*(3), 230–239.

Honey, M., and Gilpin, R. (2009). *Tourism in the developing world: Promoting peace and reducing poverty* (Vol. 233). Washington, DC: United States Institute of Peace.

Jawahar, I. M., and McLaughlin, G. L. (2001). Toward a descriptive stakeholder theory: An organizational life cycle approach. *Academy of Management Review, 26*(3), 397–414.

Kibbe, B. D. (2003). *Funding effectiveness: Lessons for building nonprofit capacity*. San Francisco: John Wiley and Sons.

Kozbelt, A., Beghetto, R. A., and Runco, M. A. (2010). Theories of creativity. In J. C. Kaufman and R. J. Sternberg (Eds.), *The Cambridge handbook of creativity* (pp. 20–47). New York: The Cambridge University Press.

Lusthaus, C. (2002). *Organizational assessment: A framework for improving performance*. Washington, DC: IDRC.

Nibigira, C., Sabuhoro, E., and Kitheka, B. (2017). Regional tourism development within East African Community. In R. Butler, and W. Suntikul (Eds.), *Tourism and political change*. Oxford: Goodfellow.

Nielsen, H., and Spenceley, A. (2011). The success of tourism in Rwanda: Gorillas and more. *Yes Africa Can: Success Stories from a Dynamic Continent*, 231–249.

OECD. (2001). *The DAC guidelines strategies for sustainable development: Guidance for development co-operation*. Paris, France: Organisation for Economic Co-operation and Development.

Ogola, F. O., Njengaa, G. N., Mhando, P. C., and Kigundu, M. N. (2015). A profile of the East African community. *African Journal of Management, 1*(4), 333–364.

Okello, M. M., and Novelli, M. (2014). Tourism in the East African Community (EAC): Challenges, opportunities, and ways forward. *Tourism and Hospitality Research, 14*(1–2), 53–66.

Pact. (2012). *Organizational Capacity Assessment (OCA) Handbook: A practical guide to the OCA tool for practitioners and development professionals*. Washington, DC: Pact.

Reith, S., and Boltz, M. (2011). *The East African community regional integration between aspiration and reality*. Berlin, Germany: KAS International Reports.

Rogerson, C. M., and Visser, G. (2014, December). A decade of progress in African urban tourism scholarship. *Urban Forum, 25*(4), 407–417.

Schneider, M. (2002). A stakeholder model of organizational leadership. *Organization Science, 13*(2), 209–220.

Ting, M. M. (2009). Organizational capacity. *Journal of Law, Economics, and Organization, 27*(2), 245–271.

Tushman, M. L., Newman, W. H., and Romanelli, E. (1986). Convergence and upheaval: Managing the unsteady pace of organizational evolution. *California Management Review, 29*(1), 29–44.

USAID. (2012). *Organizational capacity assessment for community-based organizations: New Partners Initiative Technical Assistance (NuPITA) Project*. Boston, MA: John Snow, INC.

Van der Duim, R., Peters, K., and Akama, J. (2006). Cultural tourism in African communities: A comparison between cultural Manyattas in Kenya and the cultural tourism project in Tanzania. In *Cultural tourism in a changing world* (p. 104). Toronto, CA: Channel View Publications.

Vinzant, D. H., and Vinzant, J. C. (1996). Strategy and organizational capacity: Finding a fit. *Public Productivity and Management Review*, 139–157.

Watkin, J. R. (2003). *The evolution of ecotourism in East Africa: From an idea to an industry* (No. 15). London, UK: International Institute for Environment and Development.

Western, D. (2008). *Ecotourism, conservation and development in East Africa: How the philanthropic traveler can make a difference*. Paper commissioned for travelers' philanthropy conference, Arusha, Tanzania.

Yu-Lee, R. T. (2002). *Essentials of capacity management* (Vol. 17). New York, NY: John Wiley & Sons.

Zollo, M., Cennamo, C., and Neumann, K. (2013). Beyond what and why: Understanding organizational evolution towards sustainable enterprise models. *Organization and Environment, 26*(3), 241–259.

16 The contribution of the law to tourism

The case of Mauritius

Roopanand Mahadew and Krishnee Appadoo

Introduction

Mark Twain once wrote, 'Mauritius was made first and then heaven, heaven being copied after Mauritius'. Mauritius has been touted as one of the world's finest tourist destinations in the world. Apart from its natural assets such as white, sandy beaches, great tropical weather, and tropical fauna and flora, Mauritius also boasts 'well-designed and run hotels, and reliable operational services and infrastructures' (Ministry of Tourism, 2015). Successive governments in Mauritius have endeavoured to ensure that the tourism industry meets international standards and continues to attract scores of tourists every year. With these two aims in mind, several pieces of legislation have been enacted with a view to making Mauritius one of the most viable tourist destinations in the world.

Tourism is one of the main pillars of the Mauritian economy (Gooroochurn and Sinclair, 2005, p. 478) and has contributed immensely to the economic growth of the country (Naidoo, Munhurrun, and Ladsawut, 2010). Its geographical position, stable political climate, an abundance of sea and sand and a hospitable and warm Mauritian population are a few of the reasons for the remarkable success of the tourism sector in Mauritius (Atilgan, Akinci, and Aksoy, 2003). However, the role of the law in the country's success has been overlooked. Indeed, Mauritius has a very strong legal framework for regulating various critical aspects of the tourism sector (Dieke, 2003). A combination of acts of parliament, regulations, policies and international instruments forms the foundation of the legal framework on tourism. This chapter highlights aspects of this legal framework. It is argued that the Mauritian case can be a useful best practice example for other African states seeking to develop their own tourism industries.

The impact of legislation on tourism in Mauritius

Arguably, the cornerstone of any legal framework for tourism should be based on the treatment of tourists in a destination country (Higgins-Desbiolles, 2006). To this end, it is worth noting that the Constitution of Mauritius is premised on the rule of law, separation of powers and human rights principles, resulting in a stable and progressive socioeconomic and political situation (Kasenally, 2011).

The Bill of Rights of the Constitution ensures the fundamental liberties and freedoms of everyone, including all tourists. Concepts of dignity, non-discrimination, fair treatment and protection of the law are all applicable to tourists visiting the country. In addition, the Mauritian Civil Code provides for reciprocity of the law, which implies that any tourist of whatever nationality is given the same treatment as the country of nationality would give to a Mauritian.

However, Mauritius has often been criticised for failing to practice sustainable tourism (Ritchie and Crouch, 2003), that is, for not taking proper consideration of various social, economic and environmental factors in pursuing its tourism development agenda. For example, recently, the Mauritian government has been 'accused of violating property rights afforded to the local citizens to favour the private sector to build hotels or other infrastructures for the tourism sector' (Beebeejaun, 2017, p. 3). This happened when the Road Development Authority allegedly granted permission to a private hotel in its attempt to privatise part of a public road so that tourists could gain access to the Mon Choisy Beach, a popular public beach in Mauritius. Conflicts between hoteliers and Mauritian beach goers are common in Mauritius, the former accusing members of the public of encroaching on their property, and the latter asserting that their right to enjoy the 'beach', which should be a 'free and public good', is interfered with (Business Mega, 2013).

Moreover, critics have pointed out that although the Mauritian government, in its National Periodic Report 2009–2015, announced that it would take active steps to review the Beach Authority Act 2002 and the Environmental Protection Act 2002 to create a legal and regulatory pathway towards a more 'rational development and sustainable use of resources' (Beebeejaun, 2017). To date, the right to development, placing citizens at the very heart of development strategies, has not been properly integrated in ensuing amendments to the above legislation, which are key to the tourism sector. Additionally, it has been put forward that environment impact assessments (EIAs) are not conducted with the level of rigour required under the law (Chatarayamontri, 2009), especially for hotelier projects, thus disregarding environmental concerns in setting up infrastructure in the tourism sector, with the government tending to grant EIAs in a very lenient manner.

As Mauritius continues on its tourism development trajectory, it is important to re-assess whether the current national legal framework in Mauritius is effective and adequate to guarantee sustainable futures (Sobhee, 2006), in terms of citizens' environmental, economic and social rights. The next sections analyse the existing laws, namely the Tourism Authority Act 2006, the Beach Authority Act 2002, the Mauritius Tourism Promotion Authority Act 1996 and the Environmental Protection Act 2002.

The Tourism Authority Act 2006

The aim of the Tourism Authority Act 2006 is to strive towards making Mauritius a world-class holiday and business destination for travellers, through developing an attractive tourism product, enhancing tourism services and continuing the country's tradition of warm hospitality (Tourism Authority, 2018). In this vein, the

Act is the repository of an effective legal framework, containing mechanisms and processes to ensure the protection of the natural environment in Mauritius. The Act contains a well-detailed plan for environmental management and coordination of all pervasive environmental concerns, leads the way towards the implementation of governmental policies and creates a trail for robust enforcement strategies for upholding social, economic and environmental rights in Mauritius.

The need for a tourism authority – aims, objectives and functions

Section 5 of the Act provides that the objectives of the Authority shall be manifold, namely, for the promotion of a sustainable tourism industry (Tosun, 2001); for fostering and encouraging the conduct of activities in the tourism sector in a responsible way, conducive to preserving the integrity of the Mauritian destination; for coordinating, supporting and interacting with stakeholders, namely institutions and organisations, for the development of the tourism industry; for encouraging research leading to the robust implementation of policies relating to tourism; for leading the way towards public understanding, interest and engagement in the tourism sector; for developing and implementing tourism and by-products of tourism activities and projects; and, finally, for enhancing cooperation and coordination between the public and private sector stakeholders directly or indirectly engaged in the tourism arena.

In relation to its functions, Section 6 of the Act caters for the following: licensing, regulating and supervising tourist enterprises and activities; registering, licensing and regulating the use of pleasure craft; licensing and supervising of activities of canvassers and skippers; managing and developing tourist sites across the handful of islands making the Republic of Mauritius; carrying out investigations and taking measures to suppress illegal, dishonourable, unsound and improper practices in relation to all the activities provided under the Act; establishing standards, guidelines and codes of practice concerning the carrying on or running of a tourist enterprise or activity, the operation of pleasure craft and the activities of a skipper and a holder of a canvasser permit; preparing effective action plans for developing and improving the tourism industry; collecting, compiling and publishing information and statistics on any matter related to the tourism sector; carrying out research and commission studies in the relevant field; taking appropriate measures for the protection of consumers of the tourism industry; and advising the minister generally on any matter relating to the tourism sector.

In the discharge of its functions, it is worth noting that the Tourism Authority and its officials have a wide range of powers, including, as provided by Section 7 of the Act, the issue, renewal, suspension, revocation or variation of licences and canvasser permits; the granting of exemption or partial exemption regarding compliance with any standard or guideline imposed by the Authority; the enlistment of services of consultants; the imposition of requirements of any licensee to furnish information relevant to a tourist enterprise or activity; and the publication and dissemination of any relevant information obtained in the course of its research in this field.

Complaint mechanisms procedures

The Tourism Authority has been equipped with due processes and mechanisms to deal with complaints made regarding any issue relating to licences and permits granted to operators in the tourism industry, to ensure compliance with the overarching provisions of the Act. For instance, under Section 24 of the Act, any person who feels dissatisfied with the level of services offered from a licensee or canvasser, or who is aggrieved by any act or omission of any licensee or canvasser, may make an official complaint in writing to the director of the Tourism Authority. This mechanism ensures that operators in the tourism industry provide a high level of service to consumers of tourist services, and that the operators conduct themselves in an ethical, responsible and accountable manner.

The Act further provides safeguards for ensuring that tourist operators on the island comply with specific standards and requirements. For instance, Section 26 regulates licensing of tourist activities such as running or carrying out a tourist enterprise and the usage of pleasure craft for commercial purposes. In 2017, a Mauritian citizen set up business activities on a public beach in Mauritius, erecting a stall for purposes of selling foodstuffs to tourists and the public on the beach of Trou aux Biches. After a public outcry and several complaints made by concerned Mauritian citizens to both the directors of the Tourism Authority and the Beach Authority, it was found that the individual had constructed the stall without the appropriate official authorisation from the Tourism and Beach authorities. The Tourism Authority issued an order for the individual to stop the erection of the stall, and consequently, the individual was reprimanded by the Authority for the illegal construction and had to take down the building.

Failure to comply with the provisions of Section 26 of the Tourism Authority Act can lead to a conviction, making the guilty party liable to a fine not exceeding MUR 100,000 and to imprisonment for a term not exceeding two years, which is an effective deterrent for practising illegal tourism activities on the island. Subsection 9 of the Act also provides that 'in the case of a second or subsequent conviction, the offender shall be liable to a fine not exceeding MUR 200,000 and to imprisonment for a term not exceeding five years'.

Safeguarding the interest of the tourist as consumer

In seeking to protect the interests of consumers of tourism services, the Tourism Authority also provides various safeguards. Section 27 restricts the issue of tourist enterprise licences to persons who have been convicted of any fraud or dishonesty offences, within three years of the date of application of the licence. Moreover, the Authority also seriously considers tourist enterprise licence applications, where the Authority has revoked licences from previous holders of a tourist enterprise licence: in these cases, the Authority is more likely than not to grant new and fresh tourist enterprise licences to these applicants. Additionally, the Authority has the power to refuse the granting of a tourist enterprise licence if it finds that the nature of the business activity is contrary to public order or morality, is likely to deceive any person as to the nature of the enterprise, or is identical or confusingly similar to another licensee who is already operating.

Section 30 addresses the variation, revocation or refusal to renew tourist enterprise licences where any information given to it by the licensee for the purpose of obtaining the issue of the licence is false in any material particular; where the licensee, without lawful excuse, fails to dutifully comply with a requirement under the relevant Act or any regulation made under it, or standard, guideline, code of practice or direction issued by the Authority under the Act or regulation made under it; or fails to pay any fee or charge levied in accordance with the Act or any regulation made under it; or in the case of the licensee being convicted of an offence under the Act or any regulation made under it; or finally in such circumstances where the licensee has acted in a dishonourable, improper, fraudulent, dishonest, disorderly or immoral manner, or is engaging in a violent conduct on the premises to which the licence relates.

Similarly, Section 31 of the Tourism Authority Act requires that a 'person who runs or carries on a tourist enterprise shall, at the request of an authorised officer, produce his tourist enterprise licence or a copy thereof to that office'. The penalty for failing to dutifully produce such a licence to an authorised officer upon inspection is a fine not exceeding MUR 5,000 and to imprisonment for a term not exceeding three months. In case a licensee fails to produce his/her tourist enterprise licence within five days at the office of the Authority, that person will be found guilty of an offence under the Act and, on conviction, be liable to pay a fine not exceeding MUR 25,000 and to imprisonment for a term not exceeding one year. Other corrective measures under this section include the suspension or even revocation of the said licence.

Moreover, Section 33 provides that every holder of a tourist enterprise licence shall keep a record of his/her business transactions during the course of the validity of the licence. Contravention of this requirement leads to a fine of MUR 10,000 and to imprisonment for a term not exceeding six months.

Additionally, Section 34 specifically contains provisions regarding the limitations of transferring a business enterprise licence without express authorisation from the Authority. Breach of this requirement makes the individual liable to a fine not exceeding MUR 25,000 and to imprisonment for a term not exceeding one year. According to Section 36 of the Act, regarding inspection and seizure on grounds of reasonable suspicion by the Tourism Authority that an individual is unlawfully using a dwelling house as a tourist enterprise in contravention of the Act, a magistrate may grant authorisation for an authorised officer to carry out investigations on the premises.

The director of the Tourism Authority, or any authorised officer duly designated by the director for that purpose, may also, under Section 37 of the Act, make a closing order pending judgment, in respect of any tourist enterprise where he/she is satisfied that any of the grounds by virtue of which a tourist enterprise licence may be revoked under Section 30 are met. Likewise, Section 38 of the Act provides that any person, who carries on or runs a tourist enterprise under a suspended licence, or in breach of a closing order, shall commit an offence and shall, on conviction, be liable to a fine not exceeding MUR 100,000 and to imprisonment for a term not exceeding two years. Section 38(2) further provides that in the case of a second or subsequent conviction, the offender shall be liable to a fine not exceeding MUR 200,000 and to imprisonment for a term not exceeding five years.

Regulating water sports as a tourist attraction

Section 40 contains provisions in relation to the proper and lawful registration of pleasure craft to operate in a navigational area within the waters of Mauritius. Section 47 prescribes that the Authority may refuse to register a pleasure craft where it is informed by the commissioner of police that the pleasure craft has been stolen; or that it is reasonably believed that the pleasure craft is not seaworthy; or that the pleasure craft does not comply with the requirements of the Act or any regulation made under it; or that the applicant has furnished inaccurate particulars in the application for the registration of the pleasure craft.

Section 79 regulates the granting of skipper licences. Sections 80 to 105 of the Act prescribe the conduct of a skipper licensee to ensure that tourists can practice tourist activities requiring a pleasure craft in a safe environment. Under these sections, subsequent breaches by a licensed skipper can lead to fines as heavy as MUR 300,000 and terms of imprisonment as robust as a maximum of five years.

In addition, the Ministry of Tourism introduced a new policy framework for a Pleasure Craft Management System. To ensure that the safety and security of tourists are given top priority, the new policy framework requires that (1) the design and construction of pleasure craft is based on ISO 12 2017 standard, (2) non-ISO-certified pleasure craft's carrying capacity to be determined in a scientific manner taking into account weather conditions and rough seas and (3) classification of skippers into categories of ocean going, up to 24 nautical miles and up to 12 nautical miles, based on their competence.

Managing public beaches – the Beach Authority Act 2002

The Beach Authority was set up in 2002 to create a robust institution that would effectively manage and control public beaches in Mauritius. The aim of the Beach Authority Act was thus to 'establish a Beach Authority and to provide for a legal framework for the management and control of public beaches in Mauritius'. The functions of the Beach Authority, as enunciated in the Act, are to implement projects relating to the conservation and protection of the environment of public beaches in Mauritius; the landscaping works on public beaches; infrastructural development, including provision of amenities for the use of the public and their maintenance on public beaches; the provision of leisure facilities on public beaches; the enhancement of the quality of sea water; and the day-to-day management of public beaches. Another function is to provide a regulatory framework for the proper management activities on public beaches and ensure the security and safety of users of public beaches on the island. Other functions include the granting of beach traders' licence for beach activities; the setting of standards and establishment of guidelines for beach management to enable beach users to derive maximum enjoyment from clean, safe and well-equipped beaches while safeguarding the environment; and also the provision of advisory services to the minister on all matters relating to the management and development of public beaches.

Environmental integrity – the Environmental Protection Act 2002

The Environmental Protection Act 2002 is particularly relevant for ensuring that the tourism industry is respectful of environmental concerns and standards. Environmental impact assessments, as provided under Part IV of the Act, are a safeguard against tourism activities which can harm the environment, and tourism projects have to undergo strict scrutiny under the EIA rules to make sure, for example, that new projects do not have a negative impact on waterways, air quality and the fauna and flora. Indeed, Chatarayamontri (2009) argues that conventional tourism in an uncontrolled way has significant threats to nature around the world. It has the potential to put pressure on an area and lead to problems such as soil erosion, land degradation, pollution, loss of natural habitat, endangering of species and destruction of forest.

It should be noted that the legislative framework on the protection of the environment does not only cater for large businesses such as five-star hotels but also other minor undertakings and activities that can affect the environment. The EIA licence for more significant undertakings such as the construction of five-star hotels and entertainment parks is in line with international standards of impact assessment on the environment as prescribed by the Convention of Environment and Development, commonly known as the Rio Declaration 1992. The procedure also requires public consultation and protects citizens' right to challenge and protest the granting of licences.

Promoting tourism through law – the Mauritius Tourism Promotion Authority Act

While there are various promotional campaigns that are organised by the Ministry of Tourism with various other stakeholders, the critical aspect of tourism promotion is well regulated by the law. The Mauritius Tourism Promotion Authority Act 1996 sets the foundational basis for the promotion of tourism in Mauritius. The main focus of this law is the establishment of the Mauritius Tourism Promotion Authority (MTPA) which is a body corporate. According to Section 4 of the Act, the objectives of the MTPA are (a) to promote Mauritius abroad as a tourist destination through advertising campaigns, tourism fairs and promotional campaigns, (b) to provide information on facilities, infrastructure and services available to tourists in Mauritius, (c) to initiate necessary actions towards the promotion of cooperation with other tourism agencies, (d) to conduct studies and research into market trends and opportunities and (e) to advise the Minister of Tourism on all relevant matters.

Section 5 establishes the board of the MTPA, and it is noteworthy that all members of the board must have relevant experience and proven ability in the field of tourism, trade, industry or administration as per Section 5(3) of the Act. Having such an authority enhances legal accountability and responsibility. The board and all members are under a legally binding obligation to ensure that their functions are discharged properly. Such a mechanism is more effective and efficient compared to a policy paper or an executive decision on tourism promotion.

Ensuring high service standards – incentivising employees of the tourism sector

The Tourism Employees Welfare Fund Act 2002 establishes a Tourism Employees Welfare Fund, which is a body corporate. As per Section 4 of the Act, the objective of the Fund is to 'set up schemes and projects and, generally, to carry out such other activities as may be considered desirable for promoting the welfare of employees of tourism enterprises and their families'. The Fund is administered by the Tourism Employees Welfare Fund Board, which has the following powers and functions: (a) carry out such activities and do all such acts and things as appear requisite and advantageous for the furtherance of the objects of the Fund, (b) grant loans from the Fund to employees for such purposes and on such terms and conditions as it may determine, (c) without prejudice to the generality of paragraph (a), invest any surplus remaining in the fund in such manner as the Board may determine, (d) acquire, purchase, take on lease, hire, hold, enjoy movable and immovable property of every description and mortgage, transfer or otherwise dispose of, or deal in any movable or immovable property belonging to the Fund upon such terms as the Board may think fit, (e) receive payment in consideration of the services provided by the Fund and (f) take or otherwise acquire and hold shares, debentures or other security in any company.

The main aim of the Act is ensuring the social and economic wellbeing of not only employees of the tourism sector, but also their relatives and families. The Act demonstrates a holistic approach taken by the State of Mauritius to ensure maximum efficiency and quality service in the tourism sector. There are 15 schemes in operation that are designed towards educational grants, social grants and soft loans to assist the employees in enhancing their quality of life and accessing education for their children. This creates a positive experience for tourism sector employees, which in turn leads to better work performance in the tourist service sector.

Conclusion

While flawed in some respects, the robust legal framework is a key factor in the relative success of the Mauritian tourism sector. The legislature and executive branch of government, since independence in 1968, have successfully driven forward the agenda of having effective laws and regulations as the foundation of the tourism industry. It is also noted that the state has shown the required political will to enforce these laws and to convict those in breach, to ensure consistency and compliance. The establishment of mechanisms, authorities, licensing offices and other institutions related to tourism have enhanced legal accountability. Other states in the region could draw lessons from Mauritius in this regard, to drive the growth of their own tourism industries.

References

'Access to public beaches: Obstructs the misunderstanding', Business Mega. (2013). Retrieved November 14, 2018, from https://business.mega.mu/2013/03/04/access-public-beaches-obstructs-misunderstanding/

Atilgan, E., Akinci, S., and Aksoy, S. (2003). Mapping service quality in the tourism industry. *Managing Service Quality: An International Journal, 13*(5), 412–422.

Beebeejaun, A. (2017). Human rights and environmental issues: The effectiveness of a legal framework for sustainable tourism in Mauritius. *African Journal of Hospitality, Tourism and Leisure, 6*(2), 1–10.

Chatarayamontri, N. (2009). *Sustainable tourism and the law: Coping with climate change, S.J.D.* (Dissertation), Pace University School of Law, Retrieved February 23, 2017, from http://digitalcommons.pace.edu/lawdissertations/6/

Dieke, P. U. (2003). Tourism in Africa's economic development: Policy implications. *Management decision, 41*(3), 287–295.

Gooroochurn, N., and Sinclair, M. T. (2005). Economics of tourism taxation: Evidence from Mauritius. *Annals of Tourism Research, 32*(2), 478–498.

Higgins-Desbiolles, F. (2006). More than an 'industry': The forgotten power of tourism as a social force. *Tourism management, 27*(6), 1192–1208.

Kasenally, R. (2011). Mauritius: Paradise reconsidered. *Journal of Democracy, 22*(2), 160–169.

Naidoo, P., Ramseook Munhurrun, P., and Ladsawut, J. (2010). Tourist satisfaction with Mauritius as a holiday destination, *Global Journal of Business Research 4*(2) 113–123.

Orams, M., and Lueck, M. (2016). Tourism. *Encyclopedia of Tourism,* 585–586.

'Overview of the tourism sector', Ministry of Tourism. (2015). Retrieved November 14, 2018, from http://tourism.govmu.org/English/Tourism%20sector/Pages/Tourism-Sector.aspx

Ritchie, J. B., and Crouch, G. I. (2003). *The competitive destination: A sustainable tourism perspective*. Cabi.

Sobhee, S. K. (2006). Fisheries biodiversity conservation and sustainable tourism in Mauritius. *Ocean and Coastal Management, 49*(7–8), 413–420.

Tosun, C. (2001). Challenges of tourism development in the developing world: The case of Turkey. *Tourism Management, 22*(3), 289–303.

Tourism Authority (2018). *Overview and scope.* Retrieved October 10, 2018, from http://www.tourismauthority.mu/en/about-2/overview-3.html

United nations environment programme, environmental impacts of tourism: Tourism's three main impact areas. Retrieved November 14, 2018, from www.unep.fr/scp/tourism/sustain/impacts/environmental/mainareas.htm

Part IV

Crises, controversies and the future

17 Terrorism and tourism recovery cases

A study of Tunisia and Egypt

David Adeloye and Neil Carr

Tourism and terrorism

On September 11, 2001, at about 8.45 a.m., four coordinated terrorist suicide attacks were carried out against the United States of America, leaving 2996 dead (Morgan, 2009). While these terrorist attacks (also referred to as the 9/11 attacks) were unprecedented in terms of their scale and the global attention they commanded, terrorism in general and the targeting of travel and tourism in particular are nothing new. The later part of the 20th century, often referred to as the *wave of international terrorism*, witnessed various terrorist attacks on tourists which included kidnappings, hijackings of commercial airplanes, the taking of hostages and killings. This period saw the rise of the Irish Republic Army (IRA), the Palestine Liberation Organization (PLO) and the Irgun sect who carried out several attacks (Laqueur, 2012). Studies on terrorism and tourism carried out by D'Amore and Anunza in the 1980s showed an increase in terrorism events from 206 in 1972 to 3010 in 1985, with some terrorist attacks specifically targeted at international tourists and hotels (Stafford, Yu, and Armoo, 2002).

Between the mid-1980s and the early 1990s, the Sendero Luminoso terrorist group in Peru deliberately targeted, attacked, kidnapped and killed international tourists (Stafford et al., 2002). Other examples of terrorism include the massacre during the 1972 Munich Olympic Games, the killing of 16 Greek tourists in Egypt by the al Jihad terrorist group in 1996 and the killing of 58 international tourists by Islamic militants at Luxor, Egypt, in 1997 (Lepp and Gibson, 2003).

More recently, there was the Bali bombing in 2002, where 202 tourists from over 20 countries were killed, and the Manchester bombing in 2017 with 22 casualties (Baker and Coulter, 2007; Press Association, 2017). These incidences serve as an unpleasant reminder of how fragile and vulnerable the tourism industry is to terrorism. The impact of terrorism on tourism was particularly vivid after the September 11 attacks. By the end of 2001, the global tourism industry recorded a 10% loss of its business, with some countries recording up to 30% losses (Crawford, 2012). At the start of 2001, the global tourism industry was growing at over 3.8%. However, by the end of the same year, the industry recorded a 1.3% decline in growth and an 8.6% drop in international tourist arrivals (Crawford, 2012).

Terrorism has become one of the main factors influencing tourists' perception of risk and their resultant travel decisions (Adeloye and Brown, 2018). Although there is a wide range of risks a tourist or destination could be exposed to, the impact of terrorism on destination image and tourist arrivals has posed a significant threat to the tourism industry nationally, regionally and globally. This is particularly true of countries that have a record of repeated terrorist attacks. Egypt and Tunisia are two such countries that have had to battle with the presence and impact of terrorism over the years, with many of the attacks targeted towards tourism, particularly international tourists.

Targeting tourism

Tarlow (2014) described some of the reasons why tourism has become a target for terrorist attacks:

1   Tourism provides an opportunity for mass casualties given the density of tourists at attractions or destinations.
2   Tourism often represents a variety of the values that terrorism abhors (e.g. celebration of differences, gender equality and capitalism).
3   Tourists on vacation are usually in a relaxed mood, are insufficiently protected and give little thought to security, which makes them an easy target. However, this is changing as tourists have become more aware of terrorism and safety concerns.
4   Attacks on tourists, especially international ones, normally provide global media coverage, which terrorism thrives on.
5   The tourism industry has significant economic benefits. Therefore, an attack on tourism is an attack on a destination's economy. An attack on tourism negatively affects the various industries directly and indirectly connected to tourism (e.g. hospitality, banking and airline).
6   As tourism involves iconic sites that symbolise a people or the global community at large, an attack on such icons will receive global publicity.

Of course, terrorism in general and that targeting tourism in particular is not evenly distributed across the world. Instead, terrorist attacks are focused in particular places. Such places include Egypt and Tunisia, both of which have a significant history of terrorist attacks (Essouaid and Rejeb, 2017).

The case of Egypt

The tourism industry is one of Egypt's most important economic sectors, in terms of employment, foreign exchange revenue and contribution to its total GDP. The sector supports 8.5% of total employment (2,425,500 jobs) and contributes 11% of its GDP ($21.1 billion) (World Travel and Tourism Council (WTTC), 2018a). Egypt's tourism ranges from historical and monumental attractions (the pyramids, great sphinx, temples) to beach and sea activities. However, a long series of terrorist attacks and threats targeting foreign visitors at beach resorts and other tourist attractions have repeatedly adversely affected Egypt's tourist trade over the past 30 years.

Tourism and terrorism in Egypt

The first recorded attack on foreign tourists in Egypt was on October 1, 1992, when a group of terrorists opened fire on a cruise boat carrying 100 German tourists (Aly and Stazicich, 2004). Three weeks after this event, another terrorist group (al-Gama'a al-Islamiyya) killed a British tourist and injured two others. This led to a series of other attacks by the same terrorist group over a period of four years. Al-Gama'a al-Islamiyya repeatedly ambushed and attacked passenger trains, buses and Nile cruise boats carrying foreign tourists (Crawford, 2012). Between 1992 and 1996, over 30 attacks were carried out, resulting in 12 deaths. The attacks intensified around mid-1996. On April 18, 1996, members of al-Gama'a al-Islamiyya opened fire on a group of 150 Greek tourists waiting for a bus near the Europa hotel in Cairo, leaving 18 dead and several injured (Crawford, 2012). A tour bus carrying Germans was also attacked in September 1997, leaving nine dead. Just two months after the tour bus attack, on November 17, 1997, 62 tourists were killed and several injured by terrorists in Luxor (Crawford, 2012).

Terrorist attacks continued in the early 2000s, with three bomb attacks targeting tourist hotels in the Sinai Peninsula, on October 7, 2004, leaving 34 tourists dead and 171 others injured (Crawford, 2012). A similar bomb attack, also targeting tourists, at the Sharm el-Sheikh resort city, killed 88 people. Attacks and kidnappings have continued and include the downing of Metrojet Flight 9268 on October 31, 2015 (Shapiro, 2015). The flight crashed, killing all 224 passengers on board, most of whom were tourists from Russia (219), Belarus and Ukraine (Shapiro, 2015). ISIS later claimed responsibility for the incident. Following the 2015 Metrojet disaster, Egypt saw a significant decline (47.2%) in its tourist arrivals the following year (Saleh, 2016). However, since 2016, the tourism industry has experienced a gradual recovery (see Figure 17.1).

Impact of terrorism on tourism

Analysis of the impact of terrorism on Egypt's tourism industry and economy suggests fluctuations in tourism growth due to the frequency of attacks. Despite the terrorist activities, tourism in Egypt is resilient. One year after the 1992 terrorist attack, tourism revenue fell by 11%. However, tourism revenue increased for two consecutive years in 1994 and 1995 (Crawford, 2012). Following the attack on Greek tourists in 1995, the Egyptian tourism sector experienced a relapse with a 15% decline in tourism revenue. This decline continued into 1997 with a further 3% decline. After the Luxor attacks in 1997, the tourism sector experienced a significant fall in tourism revenue of US$1.17 billion, a 50% decline (Crawford, 2012). After the attack, the Egyptian government and tourism businesses offered

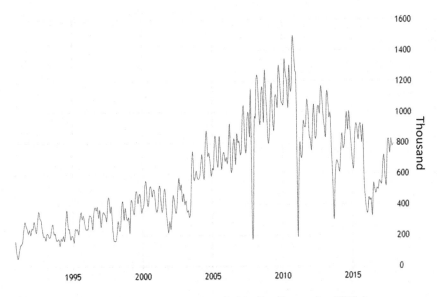

Figure 17.1 Egypt tourist arrivals (1990–2017) (Trading Economics, 2018a)

incentives and cheaper prices for prospective customers (Saleh, 2018). These tools have been used repeatedly to aid post-crisis recovery (Butscher, Vidal, and Dimier, 2009). Two years after the Luxor attack, the industry rebounded with tourism receipts reaching US$3.9 billion and $4.3 billion in 2000.

The case of Tunisia

Tunisia is one of Africa's most popular tourist destinations, with its 800-mile coastline, climate, history and shopping designed to create an all-round experience for visitors (Essouaid and Rejeb, 2017). Tunisia has been an attractive destination for many tourists since the 1960s. The Tunisian tourism industry is one of the country's most significant sectors, representing $5.6 billion (14.2%) of GDP in 2017 (WTTC, 2018b). The sector also supports 13% (464,000 jobs) of total employment (WTTC, 2018b). As with Egypt, Tunisia has struggled a great deal with a series of terrorist attacks over the last two decades. These attacks coupled with political instability have affected the Tunisian tourism industry and its destination image.

Tourism and terrorism in Tunisia

On April 11, 2002, a gas truck fitted with explosives was detonated at the ancient El Ghriba synagogue in Djerba. This event left 19 tourists dead, 14 of whom were German (Helm, 2002). After this attack, there were no recorded terrorist events. However, Tunisia struggled with political instability, which peaked in 2011 during the Tunisian revolution. This incorporated a period of intensive civil resistance that saw the longtime president, Zine El Abidine, ousted.

Following the revolution in 2015, a series of terrorist attacks on tourists left a significant dent in the image of the country. On March 18, 2015, the Bardo National Museum in Tunis was attacked by terrorists who took tourists (among others) hostage and ended up killing 22 tourists, most of whom were European, and left another 50 injured (Essouaid and Rejeb, 2017). Three months later, on June 26, Tunisia experienced its deadliest terrorist attack. A gunman attacked a tourist resort, killing 38 tourists, most of whom were British (Essouaid and Rejeb, 2017). This incident received widespread global media attention and condemnation. The Tunisian government later acknowledged responsibility for lack of a quick police response to the event. These two events in 2015 saw a significant decline in tourist arrivals (see Figure 17.2). Following the 2015 events, the Tunisian government made efforts to respond by enhancing security. Since 2015, as noted in Figure 17.2, the tourism industry has experienced a gradual recovery.

Impact of terrorism on tourism

Although the Tunisian tourism industry went into decline after the 2002 attacks, Tunisia recorded few terrorist threats and remained relatively calm for the remainder of the decade. During this period, Tunisia enjoyed a steady growth in its tourism industry. The 2011 Tunisian revolution provided a platform for jihadist groups to exploit socioeconomic grievances that encouraged the embracing of radical ideologies (Macdonald and Waggoner, 2018). This resulted in violent extremism and terrorist acts. The tourism industry experienced a significant decline of about 28% in tourism revenue, 40% in tourist arrivals, and 40.90% in tourism investments which lasted until after the revolution in 2012 (Essouaid and Rejeb, 2017). With the new government in power, measures were immediately taken to improve security, which included extra security at hotels, a request for hoteliers to install

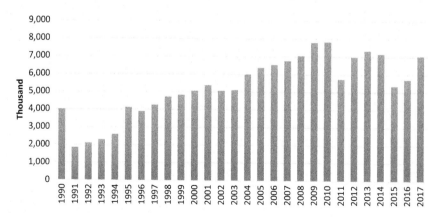

Figure 17.2 Tunisia tourist arrivals (1990–2017)
Source: Trading Economics (2018b)

new security equipment and security trainings for hotel staff. Between 2013 and 2014, the tourism industry gradually recovered with a 6.25% increase in tourism revenues and a 26.85% growth in tourist arrivals (Essouaid and Rejeb, 2017).

However, this recovery was undermined by the 2015 Bardo and Sousse attacks. As a result of this attack, 270 out of 570 (48%) Tunisian hotels closed temporarily (Essouaid and Rejeb, 2017). In 2015, tourist revenue declined by 54% and tourist arrivals fell by 36% (Essouaid and Rejeb, 2017). The Tunisian government responded immediately with a security overhaul with the help of British security services, financial support for tourist institutions, reduced taxes and relaxed visa requirements (Monks, 2017). Data for the first quarter of 2018 suggests that the industry has begun to recover from the events of 2015, with an increase of 23% in tourist arrivals and a 16.3% rise in tourism revenues (Amara, 2018).

Dealing with terrorism crisis: recovery strategies

Despite the increasing and unpredictable shocks from terrorist attacks, the tourism industry has shown remarkable capacity for recovery. One of the prime reasons for the tourism industry's ability to bounce back is due to the shelf life of the fear of terrorism risk. Studies have shown that people tend to forget and ignore terrorist attacks (especially one-off cases) in the long term (Adeloye and Brown, 2018). Other reasons, such as increased media coverage and a destination's recovery efforts, also play significant roles. However, as terrorist incidents occur, along with their impact, it is important to develop strategies proactively for recovering from such incidents.

Recovering from a terrorism crisis (or any kind of crisis) involves much more than crisis communication. The affected country requires conscious and continuous efforts to change the actual situation, or the new image being portrayed will be regarded as a fraud. One mistake often made by destinations during a crisis is to wholly focus on the negative public image without necessarily changing the reality. Jamaica, for instance, launched an expensive campaign to recover from its negative image by stressing friendliness and safety. The campaign caused more damage, however, as many unsatisfied tourists who had visited went back home and told their friends about their unpleasant experiences in Jamaica (Avraham and Ketter, 2006). In dealing with tourism crises, while image modification is important, actual tangible change is paramount (e.g. improvement in security infrastructures) at the destination. Anything short of real changes can further damage the image of a country once tourists realise the campaigns were all facades.

Tunisia and Egypt have made considerable efforts over the years to recover from tourism decline and the stereotypes associated with being identified as an unsafe destination (Avraham and Ketter, 2016). They improved and, in some cases, overhauled security infrastructures, adopted message strategies such as acknowledging the negative image and delivering a different message, sought new markets and relaxed visa requirements to encourage international tourism. The crisis recovery strategies implemented have proven to be effective despite the frequency of terrorist attacks experienced.

Improving ground security

Each terrorist incident reminds tourists of the existing dangers in a country and provides a good reason to shun the country, either on a short-term or long-term basis. Therefore, most countries find it most logical to focus on rebuilding a positive public image through various media strategies, in order to get tourists back as soon as possible. This, however, when implemented without proper security measures, can be disastrous for a country's image in the long run. In addition, improved security can be a self-promoting tool when trying to recover from a terrorism and image crisis. When a country promotes itself as 'safe', such a claim demands further explanation (Avraham and Ketter, 2006). Tourists will want to know just how safe it is and what has been done or is being done to improve security.

A study conducted by Adeloye and Brown (2018) on British domestic tourists highlights the importance of improved security. Tourists were interested in ascertaining whether there was a physical security presence (security agents and security equipment) such as CCTV cameras, scanners and bomb detectors at airports, ports, borders and hotels. They revealed that they felt much more confident travelling back to a destination that had previously been attacked if there was evidence of actual efforts to improve ground security at the destination (Adeloye and Brown, 2018).

As mentioned earlier, in 2015, the Tunisian government, in collaboration with Britain, overhauled all its security at its main airports, including Tunis and Djerba. This included installing the latest security systems such as explosive detectors (Tunisia Online, 2018). America and Germany also helped by installing patrol drones at the borders, x-ray scanners and a 120 km wall running along the Tunisian-Libyan frontier (Tunisia Online, 2018). As part of the Tunisian recovery effort, hotel staff in the main tourist locations were trained by the Metropolitan Police to look out for suspicious activities. Egypt undertook similar steps to improve security (Saleh, 2018). While these countries have done a good job to upgrade security (specifically for tourists), some of the underlying reasons behind the terrorist attacks (such as religious conflicts and economic conditions) have not been totally resolved.

Acknowledging the negative image

Terrorism crises (and other forms of crises) influence people's perceptions, beliefs, ideas, impressions and images of a tourist destination. According to the integrated model of destination image, these ideas (cognitive component) and feelings (affective component) gradually become representative of the identity of a destination and eventually inform the image of the destination in the minds of tourists (Matiza and Oni, 2014). While some places enjoy a positive image, others do not. Places that have a negative image in the minds of tourists may have suffered from repeated crises. As a result, they are generally avoided by tourists. Tourist destinations such as Tunisia and Egypt, as well as other developing countries, have suffered from negative images, perceptions, stereotypes and generalisations and require marketing strategies to alter such images (Avraham and Ketter, 2016). In tackling the image crisis, the multi-step model offers a strategic response to the challenge. This model suggests clear message strategies for marketing destinations during crises, one of which is acknowledging the negative image and delivering a message of change (Avraham and Ketter, 2016). Avraham and Ketter (2016) argued that this strategy plays an important role in the crisis recovery process, as it provides an efficient means by which a destination can regain a trustworthy, positive image following a crisis event. However, Matiza and Oni (2014) added that such messages should go hand-in-hand with concrete improvements aimed at guarding against repetition of the crisis.

This strategy was adopted by both the Tunisian and Egyptian governments, as they understood the tendency of Western markets to perceive their countries as dangerous after any terrorism-related event. The strategy is used to portray the transformation of a destination from a challenging past to a promising future. After a series of terrorist events, Egypt's Minister of Tourism stated, 'Egypt is in a transition period. It happened to other countries. . . . It seems like we're a divided society but we're going to get together' (eTurbo News (eTN), March 6, 2013). He later went on further to state, 'The violence that you may have seen in your television screens, I assure you that level of violence is dwindling down very fast. The security and safety is now currently even better by the day' (eTN, September 1, 2013). The aim of these statements was to cushion the effect of the incidents by highlighting that the events were not unique to Egypt, and that improvements had been made to the security situation so that a much better future lay ahead.

In confronting a negative destination image, several other countries (such as Oman, Jordan, Algeria, Lebanon, Pakistan and Iraq) have also adopted this strategy by admitting to the existence of a terrorism crisis. While acknowledging a problematic past and/or difficult present, these destinations have applied this strategy by presenting it as the start of a 'new era' (Avraham and Ketter, 2016). This was the case with Algeria, whose tourism marketers were aware of how their destination was perceived unfavourably by Westerners. Its tourism minister suggested, 'I think this is an image which is out of touch, because the black years are behind us . . . all that is left in the mind is a certain number of traces, which [of course] must be absolutely rubbed out' (eTN, December 2, 2009). The strategy was similarly used by Pakistan after a series of terror incidents, but also followed up with a counter-message. Pakistan's Minister of Commerce, in an official visit to London, held a press conference and stated, with regards to the issue of terror: 'Yes, such attacks are a matter of concern, but we are confident we will handle terrorism in Pakistan. . . . Pakistan is a safe country' (eTN, March 26, 2009).

The case of Pakistan shows how several strategies can be used together when managing a destination's image during crisis recovery. The minister directly related to the negative image of Pakistan, acknowledged it and tried to change the narrative by delivering a counter-message – Pakistan is safe. The delivery of a counter-message is in itself another recovery strategy.

Delivering a counter-message

A country not only needs to acknowledge the negative image. Rather, it also needs to follow up this recognition with a counter-message. This strategy focuses on delivering information contrary to the dominant messages surrounding the crisis (Avraham and Ketter, 2006). The strategy was adopted by the Tunisian Tourism Board after a terrorist attack in 2002 which left 20 people dead. They produced an advertising campaign with the aim of inspiring 'peace and tranquility'. Repositioning Tunisia away from the unsafe label is an effective way to change the negative image of the country (Avraham and Ketter, 2006). When adopting this strategy, it is important to ensure that actual efforts are made to improve security at the destination, as noted above. This made Tunisia's counter-message effort much more efficient, as tourists could see that the new image portrayed was backed up by actions (Saleh, 2018).

The challenge for many countries with issues of terror attacks or other negative occurrences is that the image crisis tends to last much longer than the physical crisis. Within this context, it can take a significant period (months in many cases) before the new reality or efforts made to tackle such crises are recognised by the market audience and international media (Avraham and Ketter, 2006). As a result, the multi-step model highlights the importance of message strategies, including the delivering of a counter-message.

The multi-step model firstly describes this strategy as a medium for correcting misperceptions. In essence, counter-messages are not only used to shatter the negative image, but also to correct misconceptions which could include those generated by lurid media headlines. Secondly, the multi-step model describes this strategy as a way to show business is in operation and to distance the destination in general from the specific affected area. An example is Tunisia's advertising campaign that sent out a counter-message of peace and tranquility within Tunisia rather than addressing specific areas (such as Tunis) where terror attacks have previously occurred. This is because, although incidents may happen in specific areas of a country, they influence the perception tourists have towards the country as a whole. Lastly, the model suggests this strategy is a way of communicating the change (or new reality) quickly and effectively. Overall, it is a way to return the destination to the global tourism map (Avraham and Ketter, 2016).

Changing the target market

Times of crisis can be good moments to explore new markets aside from existing ones, as there are potential markets that may have limited knowledge about the crisis or may be less concerned about the events reported (Hansen, 2010). In some instances, an attack could be severe within the existing market that there is little chance of overcoming it in the short term. An example is the 2015 tourist resort attack in Tunisia that saw 36 British tourists killed. There was a sharp decline in the number of British tourists to Tunisia for a period of two years (Essouaid and Rejeb, 2017). Destinations, therefore, could aim at new markets or markets previously considered as secondary (Avraham and Ketter, 2016). This does not mean, however, that existing markets should be ignored. Egypt and Tunisia have adopted this strategy by shifting some of their focus from the existing European audience and focusing on new target markets during crises. Egypt, for instance, re-directed its marketing towards regional tourism to compensate for the absence of Western tourists, while also seeking new markets from Japan, Brazil, Russia, India and China (Avraham and Ketter, 2016). Tunisia, on the other hand, developed domestic tourism which was less sensitive to terrorism crises. The aim in both cases is to diversify the tourist market.

In the case of Tunisia, after the 2015 attacks, efforts were made by the government to develop and strengthen its domestic tourism market in an attempt to offset losses from the international market. One of the major concerns for the domestic market was the high prices of tourism products and exclusion from the low-price packages offered by European tour operators to international tourists (Jeffery and Bleasdale, 2017). Alternative forms of tourism and hospitality infrastructure were developed (and are still being developed) to attract the local market (Oxford Business Group (OBG), 2018). This alternative infrastructure included bed and breakfast accommodation, as well as guestrooms and lodgings that came at affordable prices for the domestic tourist. Furthermore, more family theme park attractions have been developed to attract domestic tourists (Jeffery and Bleasdale, 2017). This appealed to the majority of the domestic market who travel as a family for vacations. These efforts yielded an immediate result as domestic tourists arrivals increased by 85% between 2015 and 2016 (OBG, 2018). Between 2015 and 2016, domestic spending as a proportion of the total tourist spending also grew considerably from 41.4% to 54% (WTTC, 2018b). While this strategy has led to an increase in domestic tourist numbers, it is doubtful whether the spending by these tourists has entirely offset the money lost from a downturn in international visitors. Certainly, any increase in domestic tourism has done nothing to offset the foreign exchange lost by the decline in international visitors.

Diversifying the tourist market seems to have been largely successful, though it has not been without its own challenges. One of the main challenges is competition. Other countries offer similar products and compete for the same market. For example, China is one of Egypt's target market. This is the same for Tunisia, Algeria, Libya, Morocco and neighbouring European countries such as Spain, who all offer similar products focused around the sun and beaches. To deal with this challenge, price reduction techniques have been adopted (Jeffery and Bleasdale, 2017). However, countries who offer similar products are fast becoming more open to price cutting in order to win over the competition. To further encourage the influx of the Chinese market, the Tunisian government eased visa requirements for the Chinese tourists. In addition, they made trips to meet officials in China to further cement their new relationship (OBG, 2018). These steps yielded an 11.3% increase in the number of Chinese tourists to Tunisia in 2016 (OBG, 2018). Another challenge is the costly adaptation of supply and promotion. Adjusting to the needs of new markets can be very costly. Countries looking to diversify have had to invest heavily in new infrastructure (e.g. luxury accommodation) and alternative attractions to attract and cater to new target markets. As part of this, language barriers can prove to be a major challenge. Consequently, countries such as Egypt and Tunisia have had to adapt their promotional campaigns to accommodate other languages (e.g. Mandarin, Japanese) by developing websites in the target market's language (OBG, 2018).

Relaxing of visa requirements

The mobility of people within and across borders is central to the development of travel and tourism (Cohen and Cohen, 2015). With greater interaction and integration between people, organisations and countries worldwide, fuelled by improvements in transportation and communication technology, the physical movement of people across spaces has increased considerably. People's ability to travel has further increased due to lower travel cost, increases in paid holidays, improved standards of living and the blurring of communication boundaries between work and leisure time (Coles, 2015). In addition, the introduction of various visa policies (e.g. relaxation of visa requirements, which many countries have adopted as a tool to enhance visitor number growth), have also greatly aided intra-regional and cross-border mobility (Cohen and Cohen, 2015).

This strategy (i.e. visa relaxations) has been employed by several countries, not just during crisis recovery, to promote tourism. The relaxing of visa requirements includes visa exemption for certain nationalities who wish to visit the destination. This strategy has been employed by countries during or after crises to promote their tourism industry or attract a specific target audience. For example, Egypt and Tunisia, after a series of terrorism crises in 2011 and 2015, exempted Chinese and Russian tourists from visa requirements upon entry (HON, 2015). Not long after the policy was passed, they recorded an increase in the number of Chinese and Russian tourist arrivals (France-Presse, 2018). Visitor numbers from China and Russia to Tunisia increased by 57% and 46% in 2017 respectively and are expected to increase in the coming years (France-Presse, 2018).

However, it is important to note that although transnational mobility has been on the increase, visa policies have been used by many countries as a major instrument of mobility restriction for economic and/or political reasons (Mau, Gulzau, Laube, and Zaun, 2015). Various studies (e.g. Neumayer, 2010; Mau, Gülzau, Laube, and Zaun, 2015) have pointed out the damaging effect of visa restrictions on travel. For instance, a study by Neumayer (2010) suggests that visa restrictions can reduce bilateral travel by on average 52%. Mau et al. (2015) argued that countries with positive attitudes to mobility and simple visa processes have proven to have a competitive advantage concerning foreign investment, trade flows and tourism over those that do not. Hence, many countries face the challenge of encouraging mobility and controlling unwanted travellers. Thus, the ongoing debate on the criteria for the selection of those who fall into the category of 'unwanted travelers' – whether it is based on the economic value generated from an originating destination, security or political reasons or a mixture of all of these (Neumayer, 2010; Mau et al., 2015).

Conclusion

This chapter has discussed terrorism crises in Tunisia and Egypt and the recovery strategies that were employed to re-attract tourists in the aftermath of terrorism events. These strategies could be adopted by other countries facing terrorism crises. However, what strategy a country facing similar terrorism crises chooses depends on the specific circumstances surrounding the country. Countries with one-off cases of terrorism may not necessarily adopt the 'acknowledging the negative image' technique, as new events and the passing of time may cause tourists to forget about the crisis. This could also depend on the severity of the one-off attack. The September 11 attack was a one-off but difficult to get over, despite it occurring over a decade ago. However, for countries that receive constant international media coverage concerning terrorism, acknowledging the negative image may be a beneficial strategy. It must be remembered that making tangible and meaningful change is more important than launching campaigns. In other words, if a country is perceived as unsafe for tourists due to terrorism, the best way to handle this image is to significantly improve security.

References

Adeloye, D., and Brown, L. (2018). Terrorism and domestic tourist risk perceptions. *Journal of Tourism and Cultural Change*, *16*(3), 217–233.

Aly, H. Y., and Stazicich, M. C. (2004). *Terrorism and tourism: Is the impact permanent or transitory? Time series evidence from some MENA countries*. Cairo: Economic Research Forum.

Amara, T. (2018). Tunisia sees record tourist numbers in 2018 as attack effect fades. *Reuters*, February 21, 2018. Retrieved from https://af.reuters.com/article/tunisiaNews/idAFL8N1QB1TX

Avraham, E., and Ketter, E. (2006). Media strategies for improving national images during tourism crises. In M. Kozak and L. Andreu (Eds.), *Progress in tourism marketing* (pp. 115–125). Oxford: Elsevier.

Avraham, E., and Ketter, E. (2016). *Tourism marketing for developing countries: Battling stereotypes and crisis in Asia, Africa and the Middle East*. New York: Palgrave Macmillan.

Baker, K., and Coulter, A. (2007). Terrorism and tourism: The vulnerability of beach vendors' livelihoods in Bali. *Journal of Sustainable Tourism*, *15*(3), 249–266.

Butscher, S. A., Vidal, D., and Dimier, C. (2009). Managing hotels in downturn: Smart revenue growth through pricing optimization. *Journal of Revenue and Pricing Management*, *8*(5), 405–409.

Cohen, E., and Cohen, S. A. (2015). A mobilities approach to tourism from emerging world regions. *Current Issues in Tourism*, *18*(1), 11–43.

Coles, T. (2015). Tourism mobilities: Still a current issue in tourism? *Current Issues in Tourism*, *18*(1), 62–67.

Crawford, D. (2012). Tourism and terrorism: Conflicts and commonalities. *Worldwide Hospitality and Tourism Themes*, *4*(1), 8–25.

Essouaid, D., and Rejeb, H. (2017). An approach to Tunisian tourism according to the political changes between 2011 and 2016. *American Journal of Applied Psychology*, *5*(2), 45–49.

eTurbo News (eTN). Various dates. Retrieved from www.eturbonews.com

France-Presse, A. (2018). Tunisia tourism rebounds after 2015 attacks. *The National*, May 23. Retrieved from www.thenational.ae/world/mena/tunisia-tourism-rebounds-after-2015-attacks-1.733411

Hansen, R. H. (2010). The narrative nature of place branding. *Place Branding and Public Diplomacy*, *6*(4), 268–279.

Helm, T. (2002). Synagogue explosion 'no accident'. *The Telegraph*, April 15, 2002. Retrieved from www.telegraph.co.uk/news/worldnews/africaandindianocean/tunisia/1390998/Synagogue-explosion-no-accident.html

HON. (2015). Tunisia relaxes visa procedures for Chinese and Indian tourists. *Hospitality-ON*. Retrieved from https://hospitality-on.com/en/reglementation/tunisia-relaxes-visa-procedures-chinese-and-indian-tourists

Jeffery, H., and Bleasdale, S. (2017). Tunisia- mass tourism in crisis? In D. Harrison and R. Sharpley (Eds.), *Mass tourism in a small world* (pp. 191–199). Oxfordshire: CABI.

Laqueur, W. (2012). *A history of terrorism* (7th ed.). New Brunswick, NJ: Transaction Publishers.

Lepp, A., and Gibson, H. (2003). Tourist roles, perceived risk and international tourism. *Annals of Tourism Research*, *30*(3), 606–624.

Macdonald, G., and Waggoner, L. (2018). *IRI experts look at drivers of terrorism in Tunisia in the journal of democracy*. Washington, DC: International Republican Institute.

Matiza, T., and Oni, O. A. (2014). Managing the tourist destination image: The case of Africa. *Tourism Review*, *62*(4), 397–406.

Mau, S., Gülzau, F., Laube, L., and Zaun, N. (2015). The global mobility divide: How visa policies have evolved over time. *Journal of Ethnic and Migration Studies*, *41*(8), 1192–1213.

Monks, K. (2017). Tourists return to Tunisia after terror. *CNN*, August 15, 2017. Retrieved from https://edition.cnn.com/2017/08/15/africa/tunisian-tourism-terror/index.html

Morgan, M. J. (2009). *The impact of 9/11 on politics and war: The day that changed everything?* London: Palgrave Macmillan, p. 222.

Neumayer, E. (2010). Visa restrictions and bilateral travel. *Professional Geographer*, *62*(2), 171–181.

Oxford Business Group (OBG). (2018). *Tunisian tourism focuses on increased security and new segments*. London: United Kingdom.

Press Association. (2017). Timeline of European terror attacks since 2015. *The Telegraph*, May 23, 2017. Retrieved from www.telegraph.co.uk/news/2017/05/23/timeline-european-terror-attacks-since-2015/

Saleh, H. (2016). Egypt's tourism industry dealt body blow by air crash. *Financial Times*, May 21, 2018. Retrieved from www.ft.com/content/e40729a0-1e94-11e6-b286-cddde55ca122

Saleh, H. (2018). Tourists return to Egypt as prices fall and security improves. *Financial Times*, May 20, 2018. Retrieved from www.ft.com/content/7553fce6-5451-11e8-b3ee-41e0209208ec

Shapiro, E. (2015). Metrojet plane crash: Egyptian authorities say bomb is most plausible scenario as Russia halts flights. *ABC News*, November 6, 2015. Retrieved from https://abcnews.go.com/International/putin-suspend-russian-flights-egypt-deadly-jet-crash/story?id=35019367

Stafford, G., Yu, L., and Armoo, A. K. (2002, October). Crisis management and recovery: How hotels responded to terrorism. In *Cornell hotel and restaurant administration quarterly*. Washington, DC: Cornell University.

Tarlow, P. E. (2014). *Tourism security: Strategies for effectively managing travel risk and safety*. Oxford: Butterworth–Heinemann.

Trading Economics. (2018a). *Egypt tourist arrivals*. Retrieved from https://trading economics.com/egypt/tourist-arrivals

Trading Economics. (2018b). *Tunisia tourist arrivals*. Retrieved from https://trading economics.com/tunisia/tourist-arrivals

Tunisia Online. (2018). *How the Tunisian tourism industry is staging a recovery*. Retrieved from www.tunisiaonline.com/tourism-industry-staging-a-recovery/

World Travel and Tourism Council (WTTC). (2018a). *Travel and tourism economic impact 2018: Egypt*. London: World Travel and Tourism Council.

World Travel and Tourism Council (WTTC). (2018b). *Travel and tourism economic impact 2018: Tunisia*. London: World Travel and Tourism Council.

18 The trophy hunting controversy

How hunters rationalise their pastime in social media

Mucha Mkono

Introduction

The last few years have witnessed what might be described as a moral panic over trophy hunting, most notably in the aftermath of 'Cecilgate' in 2015 (Macdonald, Jacobsen, Burnham, Johnson, and Loveridge, 2016; Mkono, 2018; Nelson, Bruskotter, Vucetich, and Chapron, 2016). When Cecil, a famous 'celebrity' lion was shot in Zimbabwe by the American tourist-trophy hunter, Walter Palmer, the story was hailed as a teachable moment which brought trophy hunting back into the public consciousness. Across traditional and social media, the 'sport' was widely criticised as gratuitous violence, which, for a civilised society, had become morally indefensible. Subsequently, Cecil's cub was shot under roughly similar circumstances in July 2017 (Mkono, 2018). A number of studies have since been published on the subject of trophy hunting, from a variety of angles, including sustainability and conservation imperatives, social movement impacts and human-animal ethics (Lindsey, Balme, Funston, Henschel, and Hunter, 2016; Macdonald, Jacobsen et al., 2016; Mkono, 2018; Nelson et al., 2016). In the moral debate which has ensued, scholars have also highlighted the unpalatable elitist, political and racial overtones – rich white Western men shooting charismatic megafauna in impoverished Africa (Macdonald, Jacobsen et al., 2016). Surprisingly, the debate has not received much attention in tourism studies, even though big game hunting is typically enacted as a form of wildlife tourism.

In the majority of previous studies, too, the hunter's perspective has largely been overlooked, or at best, hunters have been surveyed and categorised according to motivations, satisfactions and other such reductionist dimensions (for example, Decker, Brown, and Gutierrez, 1980; Harper, Shaw, Fly, and Beaver, 2012; Suni and Pesonen, 2017). In contrast, this chapter seeks to understand the trophy hunter's mindset and reasoning discursively, with particular (but not exclusive) reference to big game hunting in African contexts, where the hunters are almost always rich Western tourists. Indeed, the hunter's perspective is an object of enduring curiosity for many people, which lends us to the research question: How do hunters justify their act? The study objectives which flow from that research question are threefold: (i) to identify and interrogate hunters' online discourses, with a view to (ii) understanding how hunters frame and rationalise their controversial pastime in response to their critics and (iii) to consider the implications for animal ethics in (wildlife) tourism.

The discursive social media approach is timely in the digital era, as it taps into naturally occurring exchanges that shed new light on the elusive trophy hunter mindset. The digital method also circumvented the low response rate associated with soliciting interviews or other forms of participation from reticent hunters under the recent onslaught of public criticism. It should be noted here that the social media posts that are quoted in this study are not anonymised, being already in the public domain, with the respective figures having self-styled public profiles in which they present as proud, unapologetic hunters. Furthermore, it is fair to state that their narratives are inseparable from their identities, and, given that posts can be reverse-searched online, anonymising the hunters is futile. For this reason, prominent hunters such as Corey Knowlton and Walter Palmer are named in other recent studies (Macdonald, Jacobsen et al., 2016; Spivey, 2016). I return to this research ethics matter in the method section.

The chapter is organised as follows. First, a brief overview of relevant existing literature is provided, followed by an outline of the ontological positioning, namely moral relativism, and the study method. The main section presents the findings, detailing and critiquing the various ways in which hunters argue for the continuation of trophy hunting, and how they characterise the controversial pastime to make it more palatable to their social media audiences. The chapter concludes with a summary of the key contributions to theory and practice.

Literature review

Moral/ethical perspectives on trophy hunting

In recent years, trophy hunting has become highly topical in the public discourse, particularly in the three years since 'Cecilgate' (Macdonald, Jacobsen et al., 2016; Nelson et al., 2016). The resulting scholarly debate has focused on human-animal ethics in a range of tourism and other recreational contexts (Macdonald, Jacobsen et al., 2016; Mkono, 2018). However, moral concerns have been part of tourism academic theorising for decades (for example, Carr, 2009; Fennell, 2014; Fennell and Malloy, 1999; Holden, 2003; Lea, 1993). Within tourism studies, though, very little attention has been paid to the subject of trophy hunting, with only a handful of studies in the last decade (Cohen, 2014; Descubes, McNamara, and Claasen, 2018; Mkono, 2018; Nordbø, Turdumambetov, and Gulcan, 2018; Suni and Pesonen, 2017). The few existing studies also tend to focus on North American and European hunting settings (for example, Suni and Pesonen, 2017).

Within and outside the domain of tourism studies, the ethicality of trophy hunting lends itself to complex philosophical moral arguments and schools of thought: moral relativism, moral absolutism, consequentialism, utilitarianism, deontological ethics, pragmatic ethics – the list goes on. Then there are more specific theories within those that relate specifically to human-animal ethics, including speciesism, anthropocentrism, animal rights, ecocentrism, critical animal studies and animal liberation, among others. This fraught nature of trophy hunting morality is perhaps in part responsible for the limited research on the subject emerging from tourism scholars.

Helpfully, Macdonald, Johnson, et al. (2016) provide a useful distillation of the underlying factions within the debate, identifying two main camps. First, the Kantian camp opposes trophy hunting regardless of any positive outcomes. There is for them an absolute moral imperative not to hunt for recreation. The second camp are the consequentialists, or more specifically, the utilitarian view traceable to the philosophy of Jeremy Bentham, wherein the morality of an action is judged on its outcomes (as opposed to motive or nature of the action) (Macdonald, Jacobsen, et al., 2016).

Interestingly, until recently, conservation scientists have sided with the consequentialists, arguing that the biodiversity gain from legally controlled trophy hunting far outweighed the loss of individual fauna (Heffelfinger, Geist, and Wishart, 2013; Lindsey, Frank, Alexander, Mathieson, and Romanach, 2007). However, following Cecilgate, a number of scholars have adopted a more Kantian view that takes note of changing attitudes and a higher moral benchmark for the treatment of animals (for example, Nelson et al., 2016). MacDonald, Johnson, et al. (2016, p. 308), however, caution, 'Those in the Kantian camp on trophy hunting might reassure themselves with the knowledge that they occupy the moral high ground, but if they hold sway, there may be rather less African wildlife for them to see from that lofty position'. Whatever side of the debate is more persuasive, it is clear that morality is evolving social construction, and tourism studies benefits from engaging with the global conservation debate as it unfolds.

Philosophical viewpoints aside, studies show that attitudes towards hunting vary with the composition of the population and its traditions, among other factors. For example, Gamborg et al. (2018) note, in many parts of the United States, hunting enjoys high levels of acceptance. Furthermore, they observe, recreational hunting enjoys much lower public support than subsistence hunting, in general. It is therefore important to understand hunters' views in the context of their background and socio-cultural socialisation.

Hunters' perspectives and experiences

The views of trophy hunters are relatively scanty across the literature on hunting, conservation and wildlife tourism (Creel et al., 2016; Descubes et al., 2018; Di Minin, Leader-Williams, and Bradshaw, 2016; Lindsey, Roulet, and Romanach, 2007; Mkono, 2018). Furthermore, while some studies have analysed the motivations and experiences of hunters (for example, Decker and Connelly, 1989; Ebeling-Schuld and Darimont, 2017; Harper et al., 2012; Hayslette, Armstrong, and Mirarchi, 2001), they have rarely focused on African contexts. As already indicated, by far, the most popular contexts for studying hunters are North American and European. For example, Ebeling-Schuld and Darimont (2017) studied hunting forums from British Columbia, Texas and North America to assess how hunter satisfactions might vary with target species. Similarly, Kalof and Fitzgerald

(2003) explored the display of dead animals in American hunting magazines and observed that, instead of love and respect for nature and wildlife, the photographs showed extreme objectification and marginalisation of animal bodies (trophies).

There are some exceptions, however, to this contextual pattern. For example, Rader and Bech-Larsen (2009) studied hunters in the South African case and found that motivations included male identity, escape, appreciation of nature and bonding with family and friends, thus refuting, they argue, perceptions that biltong hunters primarily hunt for the meat or for the sake of killing an animal. Radder (2005) also conducted a survey with 600 international trophy hunters who hunted in the Eastern Cape, South Africa, between 1999 and 2003, and identified six motivator categories, namely spiritual, emotional, intellectual, self-directed, biological and social.

There is also a methodological bias in existing research which has epistemological implications: the vast majority of studies on hunters and their experiences are based on broad survey 'tick-box' data, which, while providing a large-scale description of hunters, often fail to capture their complex reasoning and mindsets in pursuing hunting and how they rationalise their pursuits in light of growing criticism against the trophy hunting industry in particular. The output of most of these survey studies is typically in the form of categorisations of hunters' motivations (for example, Decker and Connelly, 1989), dimensions for satisfaction and goal orientations (for example, Child and Darimont, 2015; Hayslette et al., 2001; Hendee, 1974). The present study instead engages with hunters on a discursive level, creating an alternative conceptualisation and reading of the tourist-hunter.

A notable study by Peterson (2014) investigated how wildlife management agencies and hunting organisations frame ethical hunting in the United States. Peterson found that non-governmental organisations placed significantly more emphasis on being skilled and being motivated by experiencing nature, whereas government agencies placed more emphasis on respecting landowners. However, like other existing studies on hunters and hunting organisations, the question of how hunters respond to their critics in recent times remains largely unaddressed.

Another interesting contribution is Von Essen's (2018) study of Swedish hunters to determine their hunting ethics in response to modernisation and its associated socio-cultural values, including those towards wildlife. She found new lines of moral demarcation that define taboos and what constitutes right and wrong hunting. She further observed a shift from individualistic orientations to more holistic and self-imposed standards of how to hunt in ways that would be socially, aesthetically and morally defensible. Von Essen worries that ethical relativism produces a scenario where hunters become 'moral islands' unto themselves, because, if there is no right or wrong, everyone is entitled to their own subjective position. It can be submitted in response, however, that this is not warranted worry, as people do get exposed to moral frameworks that are different from their own, especially in this digital social media age, and can be convinced through reason and/or evidence to revise their views.

Study method

Discourse analysis

Discourse and discourse analysis are interpreted variously in research, and as Cheek (2004) observes, there is confusion around what, exactly, they mean. For the purposes of this study, a Foucauldian approach is adopted, where discourse refers to ways of thinking and speaking about aspects of reality, and discourse analysis is

> more than analysing the content of texts for the ways in which they have been structured in terms of syntax, semantics, and so forth. Rather, discourse analysis is concerned with the way in which texts themselves have been constructed in terms of their social and historical "situatedness".
>
> (Cheek, 2004, p. 1144)

At any one point in time, certain discourses will be favoured by particular groups over others, and they may operate to the exclusion of competing frames. Furthermore, which discursive frame is favoured is a function of power-knowledge relations (Alvesson and Karreman, 2000; Cheek, 2004; van Dijk, 1993). Therefore, to fully understand how discourses order reality in a certain way, they must be studied in consideration of their broader context. Thus, researchers must go beyond the actual text to arrive at a contextualised interpretation.

Discourse analyses therefore refer to situated reality; they view texts as constructed by understandings of reality rather than as describing *a* or *the* reality (Cheek, 2004; Shaw and Bailey, 2009). They do not seek to produce the only possible reading; that is, the results are not static or generalisable as descriptions of *how things are*, but as explanations of how a phenomenon can be seen or interpreted (Cheek, 2004). As such, discourse analysts view research 'findings' as socially constructed and as influenced by the researchers themselves; discursive findings 'are therefore seen as rigorously produced interpretations rather than "discoveries"' (Shaw and Bailey, 2009, p. 418).

Discourse analysis allows the researcher to delve into people's subjective and social worlds through their use of language (Blommaert and Bulcaen, 2000; Shaw and Bailey, 2009), an affordance which is particularly useful for the present study goal: to understand hunters' rationalisations and characterisations of their controversial 'sport'. By opening up of the subjective worlds of participants, discourse analysis creates pathways for interrogating how people justify their actions, which is especially useful for understanding deviant behaviours, or behaviours which violate societal norms or which represent a minority worldview, as is apparent with trophy hunting. However, before detailing the process of discourse analysis, it is necessary to outline the ontological positioning and moral assumptions of the study. This is essential given the morally fraught nature of the trophy hunting debate, as already noted. It is also important for clarifying what the chapter is *not* seeking to accomplish.

The ontology of moral relativism

The study is underpinned by a moral relativist ontology. Moral relativism is a philosophical position that holds the truth or falsity of moral beliefs as products of our traditions and cultural histories, rather than as objective statements based on logic, or facts about the state of the world independent of our own opinions or perspectives (Rai and Holyoak, 2013). Put differently, moral relativism is the position that moral submissions do not reflect objective or universal truths; rather, the claims they make are relative to social, cultural, historical and personal circumstances (Demuijnck, 2015; Rai and Holyoak, 2013; Sarkissian, Park, Tien, Wright, and Knobe, 2011). Moral relativism is the opposite of moral absolutism, which holds that some moral beliefs are objectively right and reflect facts that are independent of any social group's preferences (Rai and Holyoak, 2013). Thus, for a moral relativist, moral claims can only be judged relative to a particular set of values, meaning that different moral claims could be right when asserted by different individuals (Sarkissian et al., 2011).

Moral relativism allows for differences in culture and context: there are no absolute standards binding all people at all times. Such a lens is appropriate for the present study because the goal is not to make claims about which side in the trophy hunting controversy is *morally* right or wrong – this would not be very useful – but rather to understand and contextualise hunters' perspectives. In other words, the goal is to glean what hunters' own standard of morality entails. By understanding that standard, they can be critiqued on their own terms. Such a critique is much more useful for progressing the debate and moving towards pragmatic solutions that address wildlife conservation challenges and other human-animal issues in tourism and beyond. Of course, the merits of hunters' arguments and claims about trophy hunting can be undermined with counter-arguments and evidence to the contrary, but that is separate from making normative moral judgements about right and wrong.

Moral relativism also works well with discourse analysis as it allows individual interpretations of reality to be examined in their cultural and moral context. Thus, for example, an American hunter in Texas might have a different moral framework and attitudes towards trophy hunting from those of a Maasai hunter in a remote Kenyan village. It would be problematic if their experiences and ideas of hunting were to be evaluated regardless of context, that is, by applying some universal moral standard (according to moral absolutism) or by projecting the standard of one hunter on the practices of the other.

For completeness, three kinds of moral relativism can be distinguished in the literature (Demuijnck, 2015; Quintelier and Fessler, 2012). *Descriptive moral relativism* is simply the observation that different cultures have different moral standards. *Meta-ethical moral relativism* on the other hand goes further and holds that in these disagreements, no one is objectively right or wrong. *Normative moral relativism* goes even further and holds that since nobody is right or wrong, we ought to tolerate or accommodate the behaviour of others, even when we consider it to be wrong. All three are compatible with the goals of the study, in that it is argued, in order to make progress towards pragmatic solutions for sustainable wildlife tourism and conservation, all sides must strive to understand the perspectives of those who disagree with them, and then reason with them from an informed yet respectful position. It is not useful for any side of that debate simply to insult and shame opposing sides. I-am-right-and-you-wrong style claims have not brought consensus over the decades that the matter has been in debate, which suggests the existence of a fundamental disagreement, not just a lack of facts, for example.

Research ethics considerations

As already indicated, all of the hunters' narratives (and identities) studied in this chapter were already in the public domain online. In addition, the narratives are associated with personalities and individuals who enjoy a self-styled public reputation as proud hunters. As such, the hunters are not 'outed' here, nor are they 'named and shamed' in this study. As the data were already publicly available, and no further information was solicited from any of the participants, no consent was sought for their use in the study. This meets the protocol for online 'lurker' format studies (see Björk and Kauppinen-Räisänen, 2012; Kozinets, 1998, 2015; Mkono, 2011; Mkono, Markwell, and Wilson, 2013).

Data

Data sources were identified through a keyword search on Google, Facebook, YouTube, Twitter and TripAdvisor, using terms 'hunter', 'hunting' and 'trophy hunting'. Following an initial perusal of the hundreds of results pages (over 1000), the most relevant content was selected for detailed analysis. A diversity of sources in the sample ensured that a wide range of hunters' perspectives would be captured. All sources were accessed between May 2018 and October 2018.

The following sources were included in the final sample:

i   Facebook pages of six hunters who have public profiles as proud, unapologetic hunters, many of whom pursue recreational hunting as a career: Jim Shockey (American 'celebrity' hunter), Diggory Hadoke (British big game hunter), Melissa Bachman (American big game hunter), Rebecca Francis (American big game hunter), Brett Maffenbeier (Canadian sport hunter) and Craig Boddington (American 'celebrity' hunter). On their Facebook pages, the hunters share their hunting philosophy and experiences.
ii   Public Twitter pages of two American hunters, namely Walter Palmer (of the Cecilgate infame) and Philip Glass (big game hunter).
iii   Interviews with big game hunters (accessed from YouTube), American Corey Knowlton and British Diggory Hadoke.
iv   TripAdvisor discussion forums: 'Trophy hunting in the Timbavati Game Reserve' and 'News re: Trophy hunting in the Timbavati game reserve'.
v   Personal hunting blog, 'The Will to Hunt', by Will Jenkins.
vi   YouTube videos of a lion hunt and a rhino hunt.

Once the sources were identified, the collation of data involved cutting and pasting text onto a word document. Next, the interviews were transcribed verbatim from YouTube. The combined data were then subjected to a process of discourse analysis. It should be noted that the data were not edited for typographical or other errors, to preserve their raw authenticity.

Analysis

Once the data were collated, the goal of discourse analysis was to glean the ways in which hunters, through deliberate language choices, characterise (or frame) and rationalise trophy hunting in their narratives. The analysis proceeded in three iterative steps or layers (that is, going back and forth, rather than in a linear fashion), as outlined in Smets and Struyven (2018):

1 Description (text analysis): The online narratives were read carefully to gain deep familiarity with their content, focusing on identifying hunters' *semantic choices* and *argumentation*, in relation to their responses to anti-hunting critics, or their justification of hunting. Relevant segments of data or semantic units (for example, 'generates revenue for general conservation') were highlighted for further interpretation, in this particular example noting the *discourse* of *conservation* as an *argument for hunting*.

2 Interpretation (identifying themes): This step identified and interrogated the most common patterns in hunters' discursive frames and arguments, which were then grouped into themes. Themes were labelled interpretively (rather than descriptively), to draw out the underlying assumptions, meanings and interpretations of reality from the hunters' perspectives, as revealed by the discourses they deployed.

3 Broad contextualisation (social analysis): Once the themes were identified and labelled, the next step was to review and synthesise them in their socio-political context. This involved considering, for example, the social location of trophy hunters and the socio-political and cultural context of the hunt, as well other geopolitical considerations, where available and relevant.

It is important to stress that the moral relativist underpinning meant that the hunters' discourses would be scrutinised without making moral judgments of right or wrong. In other words, the goal was to illuminate and understand the mindset of hunters, rather than to make normative judgments.

Rigour

Cheek (2004) explains that for a discourse analysis to be rigorous, it is crucial to form and present a decision trail, detailing what theoretical understandings of discourse and discourse analysis are in use, the theoretical/philosophical underpinning, which texts were analysed, why they were chosen and how they were generated. These criteria have been met in the preceding sections. Rigour was further enhanced in three ways:

Data audit trail: A reverse-search of any of the online narratives quoted in this chapter will reveal the origin of the content and therefore the identity of the respective hunter. This provides an audit trail for readers who wish to check the authenticity of the narratives cited here, as well as the context in which they were generated. This is important for research accountability and reproducibility.

Triangulation: The triangulation of data formats, through the combination of YouTube interviews, Facebook narratives, Twitter posts, TripAdvisor discussion forums and personal blog content, qualitatively enriches the study and optimises the opportunity to understand multiple facets of the hunter's reasoning.

The lurker format: The data used for the study were *not* generated by soliciting input from hunters. As such, the limitations resulting from 'researcher bias' (for example, biases that result from framing 'leading questions' in traditional data gathering) are minimised.

Findings

Altruisation: discourses of doing good for animals[1]

The most recurrent pattern of rationalisation among hunters was the *altruistic framing* of trophy hunting as a conservation and sustainability tool – that is, the characterisation of hunting as driven by the desire to save animals from the threats of extinction, poaching and other such undesirable possibilities. The discourses of *conservation* and *sustainability* were deployed variously, built around the claim that hunting fees, in many instances in the tens of thousands of dollars in the case of African big game hunting, were the key source of conservation funding. It was this economic rationale for African countries in particular, they claimed, which guaranteed the preservation of wildlife habitats and ensured the survival of Africa's megafauna: in other words, if wildlife drew income, it would be protected from competing interests such as agriculture. This consequentialist argument, where the ends (are supposed to) justify the means, was expressed in a range of ways, for example: 'Took this pic in South Africa. Magnificent . . . and only alive today, along with thousands of other lions, because the hunters give real economic value to the wild animals of the world'. In another extensive post, a hunter writes, 'This is the ugly reality when "Trophy" hunting is banned. Lions die . . . all of them. Read this repost and cry if you are a hunter . . . feel shame if you support this reality'. The hunter relates a story from Tanzania, which for him demonstrated the value of trophy hunting for wildlife survival:

When income is derived by local communities from wildlife, the locals not only tolerate these predators, but actually protect them. When the value of lions is lost, the local communities totally eradicate the felines. Local herds-man are now poisoning predators, including lion with pesticides such as Furadan (Carbofuran).

Similarly, in an interview with British broadcaster Piers Morgan, well-known big game hunter Diggory Hadoke argues that the public distaste for trophy hunting was: 'an uninformed view which doesn't take into account the key thing which is areas which are managed for hunting there are more animals than there are in areas which are not managed for hunting'. Hadoke adds that 'hunting, it may not be to everybody's taste, but it works for *conservation*'. On his Facebook page, Hadoke suggests that without the intervention of hunters, old lions face painful natural deaths, following inevitable starvation.

In a TripAdvisor discussion forum, the chairman of the Timbavati Private Game Reserve in South Africa uses the same consequentialist argument, as well as the *sustainability* discourse, to argue for rhino hunting: '*Sustainable* hunting of rhino is legal, and encouraged by environmental legislation and policy, generates revenue for general *conservation* activities and rhino protection and, probably most importantly, results in the expansion of rhino habitat and numbers'. He further dismisses alternatives such as photographic tourism, arguing that they do not generate sufficient income to sustain conservation:

> It is generally accepted by reputable scientists that photographic tourism operations are more damaging to the environment than *sustainable*, well managed hunting operations . . . it takes approximately 18,000 guest nights in lodges . . . to generate the same revenue that the Timbavati Association receives from one hunter shooting one rhino.

He then challenges anti-hunting lobbyists to provide viable alternatives:

> If you do not accept controlled, *sustainable* hunting as part of the solution (which it already is and has been for many years) you need to provide alter-natives to hunting revenue. Ecotourism is only part of the funding solution and cannot always replace hunting revenue and is an ecologically damaging activity. What do you propose? Philanthropy? Extra tax?.

Again, in the one of the most publicised trophy hunting incidents in recent years, where Corey Knowlton, an American big game hunter who gained infamy after winning an auction for which he paid $350,000 to shoot a black rhino in Namibia in 2014, argues in an interview posted on YouTube that his hunt had a genetic and financial rationale which would help stop inbreeding in the rhino population:

> I have a belief system in *sustainable* use. . . . It's not about killing it. . . . It's a genetic argument as well as a financial reasoning behind it. . . . He's [the rhino] his own daughters, that's inbreeding, and by all genetic arguments, that's not good.

Knowlton further asserts,

> *We care about animals* and the world's animals and I believe that by hunting them and being involved in that I will know more about the animal than almost anybody will by the time I do it.

Other hunters pointed out the role of trophy hunting in *population control*:

> People fail to understand how *conservation* works, it's not always about saving the pandas. It can be about *population control* and saving certain animals from starvation. The majority of my hunting is for the purpose of *conservation*. The animals I kill will die from starvation, so I *save them*'.

In all of these scenarios, the tourist-hunters profess to care and love animals, a paradox, which, as Cohen (2014) argues, is hard to resolve. It is indeed difficult to reconcile images of dead animals with statements such as, 'we are not killers we love the animals we hunt and do a ton for all the wildlife we help keep a *healthy population*!!' Cohen opines that this paradox of killing a loved animal in recreational hunting is irresolvable on the ethical sphere, 'but can be interpreted as an antinomian but exalted ritual, resembling sacrifice in the religious sphere' (2014, p. 3).

Nonetheless, by framing trophy hunting variously as ultimately benefiting the animals and communities (rather than as merely a hedonistic indulgence for hunters), the activity is elevated to virtue. It ceases to be about ending the life of an animal, and becomes about concern for a species or population of animals and about bettering the livelihoods of local communities. Hunters can then enjoy the 'warm glow' of having 'saved' animals from the various threats they cite; having contributed money and other resources for local communities and the like.

However, philosophically and practically, there are problems with the hunters' consequentialism. Abiding by the relativist premise that hunters' actions must be viewed in the context of their own moral standards, which means we accept their rationale (the ends justify the means; we can kill a few to save the rest), then it is morally incumbent on us, as Zamir and Medina (2006) put it, to chop up one person and harvest her organs to save the lives of five other people; to torture the baby daughter of a terrorist to force him to reveal information that may save lives; and so forth.

For many, consequentialism simply does not suffice. As Nelson et al. (2016) argue, even if we grant that trophy hunting does bring in significant funds for conservation, we would still need to address the question, is the killing justified? Taking on the alternative Kantian view, they add further that it is not enough to appeal to the beneficial consequences of the killing, as indeed, in many other human scenarios we condemn actions even where there are benefits obtained:

> For example, trafficking humans is taken to be a wrong way to treat humans even if doing so generates revenue that would be used for philanthropic

purposes. The revenue that could be generated is not sufficient to override the wrong that is done when we condone human trafficking. The analogous questions need to be asked of trophy hunting in the name of conservation.

(Nelson et al., 2016, p. 303)

Euphemisation: discourses of 'not killing'

By euphemisation, I refer to the hunters' *discursive choice* to substitute the word *kill* with more palatable terms such as *harvesting, taking,* and so on. For instance, Walter Palmer, the infamous American hunter who shot Cecil in Zimbabwe, issued a statement in response to the criticism directed at him in the aftermath of the incident: 'To my knowledge, everything about this trip was legal and properly handled and conducted. I had no idea that the lion I *took* was a known, local favourite, was collared and part of a study until the end of the hunt'. In similar fashion, the chairman of the Timbavati Game Reserve uses the term 'harvesting' in a rebuttal of anti-hunting posts in a TripAdvisor discussion forum: 'The Timbavati regards itself as one of the few examples in Africa where photographic tourism and sustainable utilisation through *harvesting* are conducted within the same environment'.

Harvest and *take* do not conjure up images of blood, guns or dead animals. Instead, they equalise hunting with the gathering of grain crops and other non-violent farming activities. In the imagery produced, hunters are then not too different from farmers performing ordinary farming tasks. The semantic and discursive choices of hunters here are not accidental; conscious of the public scrutiny and moral panic that accompanies reports of trophy hunting, hunters' language choices constitute efforts to sanitise hunting and achieve a degree of political correctness. As Graham (2015) asserts, 'management' or 'harvesting' are

> politically correct words that allow the speaker to avoid using the word 'kill' when he or she is talking about culling a group of animals or birds. Graham views this discursive construction by hunters as covering up the reality of killing in recreational hunting.

Wheeler (2012) likewise views this euphemisation as orchestrated to create a fuzzier, more nostalgic imagery, wherein 'Grandpa' is 'mowing the hay or rustic villagers picking grapes'.

In his personal blog, proud hunter Will Jenkins laments this political correctness trend among his colleagues, and expresses that hunters should instead own that they are killers without shame:

> We can use fancy words or long winded explanations but ultimately we are killers. . . . You can use whatever word to describe your successful hunts but I think I'm ok with just killing. Harvesting sounds boring anyway.

Jenkins' frankness and unapologetic attitude is notable in the context of the backlash hunters have faced in recent times.

Thus, discursive frames are not just about the words that are used, but also about words that are avoided. From a moral relativist standpoint, however, it is important to recognise how different language choices reflect the differences in social acceptability across cultures. Whereas the term hunting would be used without reservation in connection with the Bushmen hunters of Botswana, for example, it clearly carries negative connotations in the Western public discourse, as the above narratives suggest. Thus while there is no objective standard of right and wrong on the moral status of hunting, language serves as an indicator of the political correctness or incorrectness of the moral positions of the majority versus the minority, at any one given time. In this case, hunters are the deviants who must alter their language to suit the norms of the majority.

Scientifising and anti-emotionality: discourses of 'science' and 'logic'

Anti-emotionality captures the observed tendency among hunters to discount the public outrage against trophy hunting as fuelled by emotion rather than reason. Thus hunters portrayed themselves using the discourses of *science* and *logic* ('scientifising'), the opposite of the public's emotionality. For example, big game hunter Diggory Hadoke states in an interview on Good Morning Britain, 'You don't seem to be able to get over your *emotional* distaste for hunting, which you are very entitled to', adding that journalist Piers Morgan's criticism had 'a very sensationalist focus on a very small part of the conservation management of, for example, lions'. In another example, Walter Palmer argues on his Twitter account: 'The problem is, all the hateful animal "lovers" base their judgements solely on *emotion and nothing more*', adding, 'Anyone that wants to have a discussion based on *logic* and *facts* rather than *emotion*, let's talk alternative solutions'.

Thomas Hancock, the chairman of Timbavati Game Reserve, observes that trophy hunting is a consistently emotional subject, advocating actions based on *science*:

> When it comes to hunting, we will always encounter *emotive* arguments. Our management team have a duty to put emotion aside to make the best decisions based on the best *scientific information* . . . to ensure we uphold our objective to 'promote the conservation of biodiversity for the sake of posterity'.

Hancock expresses further that he fears that uninformed anti-hunting activists' '*sentimentality* for individual species, or even for individual specimens within a species, will have the unintended consequence of the decline or even destruction of certain species in the wild'.

The de-emotionalising attempts in these instances fail to recognise that emotions cannot be eliminated or suspended from situations involving human judgements. However, the idea that emotion is antithetical to reason is a longstanding assumption (Nelson et al., 2016). Nelson et al. (2016) concede that while emotional outrage is sometimes no more than irrational lunacy, often emotional outrage is a reasonable, sometimes even 'reasoned', response to injustice and unfairness. Thus, they add, the eruption of emotion in response to trophy hunting incidents could be regarded as a call for closer inspection for signs of injustice.

The hunter's dismissal of emotion points to the 'politics of emotional expression', as Campbell (1994) puts it. The individual or group showing emotion is dismissed as weak, hysterical, irrational and so forth, while the stoic, calm, composed (male) is viewed as more reliable and reasonable. By applying this politics, it may be argued, hunters avoid engaging with the substance of the arguments put forward by their opponents. The *emotional* public are portrayed as akin to the tantrum-throwing child who the parent instructs to go away and return after they have calmed down.

Discussion

A moral relativist framework implies that when one considers an act to be wrong, one should *accommodate*, meaning, as Wong (2006) puts it, that one should attempt to understand and tolerate the other's viewpoint. Thus, the findings were presented from a position of seeking to understand and illuminate hunters' perspectives, rather than imposing 'absolutist' right and wrong value judgments. The findings show hunters deploying a range of discourses to frame trophy hunting positively and thus justify its continuation. Using their economic power, they were able assert a hegemonic privilege available only to rich elites, namely the right to shoot precious and even endangered megafauna for recreation.

The hunters' key discourses converge around a consequentialist argument, where the claimed benefits to wildlife conservation justify trophy hunting. It is worthwhile noting that there is no conclusive evidence to support the claims, nor is there consensus among conservationists that trophy hunting has created net benefits for conservation (Lindsey, Alexander, Frank, Mathieson, and Romanach, 2006; Lindsey, Balme, Booth, and Midlane, 2012). Thus, it can be argued, according to hunters' own consequentialist standard, trophy hunting is not morally defensible where no benefits to conservation have been demonstrated.

Aside from debating the benefits of hunting, another problem with consequentialism is that it ignores the motive of an action, focusing instead on its results (Nelson et al., 2016). In that sense, no distinction is made between killing for fun and killing for food, and for most people in the anti-hunting camp, that distinction is material. In the latter case, hunting may be justified as part of the natural order (for example, it could be argued that people need meat to survive), whereas in the former case, the hunting act is not necessary for survival. Indeed, the last few years have shown consequentialist arguments to be unsatisfactory for the anti-hunting public (Clemens, 2017; Macdonald, Jacobsen et al., 2016; Nelson et al., 2016). A more humane approach has been advocated more passionately, creating a precarious future for Africa's hunting industry in particular (Mkono, 2018; Nelson et al., 2016). Furthermore, the impossibility and impracticability of determining and weighing the totality of consequences of trophy hunting, including unintended outcomes, undermine hunters' consequentialist reasoning. For example, it is impossible to predict what the full impact of killing one male lion would be on the entire pride and on the rest of the lion population in the relevant habitat.

Consequentialism is also problematic because actors take a strictly impersonal view of all actions, since it is only the consequences, and not who produces them, that are said to matter (Berker, 2013). In the trophy hunting scenario, the 'who' is very significant and cannot be minimised. Rich, white, mostly male-tourist-Westerner-elites are the participants, re-enacting the power imbalances of the colonial past. Hunters' altruisation of big game hunting may thus also be viewed through the colonialist tropes of elitism and a white saviour mentality (Edwards, 2013). Thus, by relying on a consequentialist rationale alone, hunters are rendered oblivious to many of the nuances that were behind the public outrage against trophy hunting in recent years.

From a tourism and animal ethics perspective, consequentialism is problematic because it takes the focus away from the treatment and welfare of animals. The manner of the killing is discounted – trophy hunting takes many arguably inhumane forms, including the use of bow and arrows that do not kill in the first shot, often leading to the animal suffering for an extended period before it is tracked and finished off, as in the Cecil case (Mkono, 2018; Nelson et al., 2016). Furthermore, trophy hunters also often purport to uphold the highest levels of ethical practice, yet the evidence often suggests otherwise. For instance, in many instances, hunters have been reported to use a bait to lure the animal out of a non-hunting zone (Macdonald, Jacobsen et al., 2016). It becomes irrelevant in that situation that the hunter paid sums of money which might be used for whatever noble purpose.

Conclusion

This chapter sought to (i) explore the ways in which hunters (especially big game, rich Western tourist-hunters), discursively frame and rationalise their pastime and to (ii) consider the implications for human-animal ethics in tourism. On a theoretical level, the discourse analysis lays a conceptual foundation for dissecting hunters' interpretations of reality, without minimising, as previous studies have tended to do, the role of political, social and cultural situatedness. The moral relativist underpinning allowed hunters' discourses and arguments to emerge free from normative judgments of right and wrong.

Three kinds of discourses were identified from the analysis: (i) altruisation discourses, which rationalise hunting on the grounds of supposed good outcomes for animal conservation (for example, discourses of *conservation, sustainability, population control*); (ii) euphemisation discourses, which attempt to create a more palatable imagery of hunting, divorced from the reality of violent killing (using terms such as *taking* or *harvesting* animals, rather than *killing* animals); and (iii) anti-emotionality discourses, where hunters portray their critics as irrational, emotional and sentimental, and view themselves as the reasonable and responsible actors who make decisions based on 'facts' (for example, using discourses of *science* and *logic*).

The most recurrent discourses were underpinned by a consequentialist moral philosophy, where the (claimed) ends justify the means, even where the means involve the killing of endangered megafauna. The discussion has shown the consequentialist basis to be flawed on several levels. First, hunters' claims that hunting benefits conservation have not been conclusively substantiated. Second, consequentialism ignores the motive of an action. Third, by taking an impersonal view of actions, the political and historical dimensions of hunting in African contexts are minimised. Fourth, from an animal ethics perspective, consequentialism is problematic because it takes the focus away from the treatment of animals.

It is clear also from the above that hunters fail to engage meaningfully and empathise with their critics' moral discourses which prioritise the sentience of animals over economic or other benefits they may claim for hunting. What hunters do have in their favour though is a pro-hunting African tourism geopolitical system – with very few exceptions, such as Botswana – which continues to resist pressures to ban big game hunting. Until an alternative conservation funding model is found, big game hunter-tourists can count on the economic imperatives for African governments to compel them to continue to sanction and protect trophy hunting as a sustainable form of wildlife tourism (Mkono, 2018). The animal welfare arguments appear to hold little persuasion for these money-poor governments, who need the tourist dollar in all its forms and from all possible streams. To put it simply, for them trophy hunting, and indeed tourism activity more broadly, are fundamentally domains of economics, rather than of moral philosophies.

But while the anti-hunting movement has so far failed to lobby successfully for a ban on trophy hunting, the events of the last few years have undoubtedly brought animal welfare in tourism contexts into the spotlight, with possible ramifications for other human-animal contexts (for example, zoos). Further, with the international community's recent moves to deter hunters, such as trophy transportation and importation bans by airlines and some Western countries respectively (Mkono, 2018; Spivey, 2016), the hunting community faces an ever increasing challenge to maintain its moral-environmental legitimacy, even though their activities are legally sanctioned in the contexts where they hunt.

Note

1 Emphasis added to highlight discourses.

References

Alvesson, M., and Karreman, D. (2000). Varieties of discourse: On the study of organizations through discourse analysis. *Human Relations, 53*(9), 1125–1149.
Berker, S. (2013). The rejection of epistemic consequentialism. *Philosophical Issues, 23*(1), 363–387.
Björk, P., and Kauppinen-Räisänen, H. (2012). A netnographic examination of travelers' online discussions of risks. *Tourism Management Perspectives, 2–3*(0), 65–71.

Blommaert, J., and Bulcaen, C. (2000). Critical discourse analysis. *Annual Review of Anthropology, 29*(1), 447–466.

Campbell, S. (1994). Being dismissed: The politics of emotional expression. *Hypatia, 9*(3), 46–65.

Carr, N. (2009). Animals in the tourism and leisure experience. *Current Issues in Tourism, 12*(5–6), 409–411.

Cheek, J. (2004). At the margins? Discourse analysis and qualitative research. *Qualitative Health Research, 14*(8), 1140–1150.

Child, K., and Darimont, C. (2015). Hunting for trophies: Online hunting photographs reveal achievement satisfaction with large and dangerous prey. *Human Dimensions of Wildlife, 20*(6), 531–541.

Clemens, M. (2017). Cecil the Lion: The everlasting impact on the conservation and protection of the king of the Jungle. *Villanova Environmental Law Journal, 28*, 51.

Cohen, E. (2014). Recreational hunting: Ethics, experiences and commoditization. *Tourism Recreation Research, 39*(1), 3–17.

Creel, S., M'soka, J., Dröge, E., Rosenblatt, E., Becker, M. S., Matandiko, W., and Simpamba, T. (2016). Assessing the sustainability of African lion trophy hunting, with recommendations for policy. *Ecological Applications, 26*(7), 2347–2357.

Decker, D. J., Brown, T. L., and Gutierrez, R. J. (1980). Further insights into the multiple-satisfactions approach for hunter management. *Wildlife Society Bulletin*, 323–331.

Decker, D. J., and Connelly, N. A. (1989). Motivations for deer hunting: Implications for antlerless deer harvest as a management tool. *Wildlife Society Bulletin (1973–2006), 17*(4), 455–463.

Demuijnck, G. (2015). Universal values and virtues in management versus cross-cultural moral relativism: An educational strategy to clear the ground for business ethics. *Journal of Business Ethics, 128*(4), 817–835.

Descubes, I., McNamara, T., and Claasen, C. (2018). E-Marketing communications of trophy hunting providers in Namibia: Evidence of ethics and fairness in an apparently unethical and unfair industry? *Current Issues in Tourism, 21*(12), 1349–1354.

Di Minin, E., Leader-Williams, N., and Bradshaw, C. J. (2016). Banning trophy hunting will exacerbate biodiversity loss. *Trends in Ecology and Evolution, 31*(2), 99–102.

Ebeling-Schuld, A. M., and Darimont, C. T. (2017). Online hunting forums identify achievement as prominent among multiple satisfactions. *Wildlife Society Bulletin, 41*(3), 523–529.

Edwards, K. T. (2013). White activism and social justice in educational leadership: The work of Jean-Charles Houzeau. *International Journal of Leadership in Education, 16*(3), 263–278.

Fennell, D. A. (2014). Exploring the boundaries of a new moral order for tourism's global code of ethics: An opinion piece on the position of animals in the tourism industry. *Journal of Sustainable Tourism, 22*(7), 983–996.

Fennell, D. A., and Malloy, D. C. (1999). Measuring the ethical nature of tourism operators. *Annals of Tourism Research, 26*(4), 928–943.

Gamborg, C., Jensen, F. S., and Sandøe, P. (2018). Killing animals for recreation? A quantitative study of hunters' motives and their perceived moral relevance. *Society and Natural Resources, 31*(4), 489–502.

Graham, W. (2015). *When people kill wild animals they now call it 'harvesting'*. Retrieved from www.freshvista.com/2015/patterns-in-nature-when-people-kill-wild-animals-they-now-call-it-harvesting/

Harper, C. A., Shaw, C. E., Fly, J. M., and Beaver, J. T. (2012). Attitudes and motivations of Tennessee deer hunters toward quality deer management. *Wildlife Society Bulletin*, *36*(2), 277–285.

Hayslette, S. E., Armstrong, J. B., and Mirarchi, R. E. (2001). Mourning dove hunting in Alabama: Motivations, satisfactions, and sociocultural influences. *Human Dimensions of Wildlife*, *6*(2), 81–95.

Heffelfinger, J. R., Geist, V., and Wishart, W. (2013). The role of hunting in North American wildlife conservation. *International Journal of Environmental Studies*, *70*(3), 399–413.

Hendee, J. C. (1974). A multiple-satisfaction approach to game management. *Wildlife Society Bulletin*, 104–113.

Holden, A. (2003). In need of new environmental ethics for tourism? *Annals of Tourism Research*, *30*(1), 94–108.

Kalof, L., and Fitzgerald, A. (2003). Reading the trophy: Exploring the display of dead animals in hunting magazines. *Visual Studies*, *18*(2), 112–122.

Kozinets, R. V. (1998). On netnography: Initial reflections on consumer research in investigations of cyberculture. *Advances in Consumer Research*, *25*, 366–371.

Kozinets, R. V. (2015). *Netnography: Redefined.* London: Sage Publications.

Lea, J. P. (1993). Tourism development ethics in the third world. *Annals of Tourism Research*, *20*(4), 701–715.

Lindsey, P. A., Alexander, R., Frank, L., Mathieson, A., and Romanach, S. (2006). Potential of trophy hunting to create incentives for wildlife conservation in Africa where alternative wildlife-based land uses may not be viable. *Animal Conservation*, *9*(3), 283–291.

Lindsey, P. A., Balme, G. A., Booth, V. R., and Midlane, N. (2012). The significance of African lions for the financial viability of trophy hunting and the maintenance of wild land. *Plos One*, *7*(1), e29332.

Lindsey, P. A., Balme, G. A., Funston, P. J., Henschel, P. H., and Hunter, L. T. (2016). Life after Cecil: Channelling global outrage into funding for conservation in Africa. *Conservation Letters*, *9*(4), 296–301.

Lindsey, P. A., Frank, L., Alexander, R., Mathieson, A., and Romanach, S. (2007). Trophy hunting and conservation in Africa: Problems and one potential solution. *Conservation Biology*, *21*(3), 880–883.

Lindsey, P., Roulet, P., and Romanach, S. (2007). Economic and conservation significance of the trophy hunting industry in sub-Saharan Africa. *Biological Conservation*, *134*(4), 455–469.

Macdonald, D. W., Jacobsen, K. S., Burnham, D., Johnson, P. J., and Loveridge, A. J. (2016). Cecil: A moment or a movement? Analysis of media coverage of the death of a lion, Panthera leo. *Animals*, *6*(5), 26.

Macdonald, D. W., Johnson, P. J., Loveridge, A. J., Burnham, D., and Dickman, A. J. (2016). Conservation or the moral high ground: Siding with Bentham or Kant. *Conservation Letters*, *9*(4), 307–308.

Mkono, M. (2011). The othering of food in touristic eatertainment: A netnography. *Tourist Studies*, *11*(3), 253–270.

Mkono, M. (2018). The age of digital activism in tourism: Evaluating the legacy and limitations of the Cecil anti-trophy hunting movement. *Journal of Sustainable Tourism*, 1–17.

Mkono, M., Markwell, K., and Wilson, E. (2013). Applying Quan and Wang's structural model of the tourist experience: A Zimbabwean netnography of food tourism. *Tourism Management Perspectives*, *5*, 68–74.

Nelson, M. P., Bruskotter, J. T., Vucetich, J. A., and Chapron, G. (2016). Emotions and the ethics of consequence in conservation decisions: Lessons from Cecil the lion. *Conservation Letters*, *9*, 302–306.

Nordbø, I., Turdumambetov, B., and Gulcan, B. (2018). Local opinions on trophy hunting in Kyrgyzstan. *Journal of Sustainable Tourism*, *26*(1), 68–84.

Peterson, M. N. (2014). How wildlife management agencies and hunting organizations frame ethical hunting in the United States. *Human Dimensions of Wildlife*, *19*(6), 523–531.

Quintelier, K. J., and Fessler, D. M. (2012). Varying versions of moral relativism: The philosophy and psychology of normative relativism. *Biology and Philosophy*, *27*(1), 95–113.

Radder, L. (2005). Motives of international trophy hunters. *Annals of Tourism Research*, *32*(4), 1141–1144.

Radder, L., and Bech-Larsen, T. (2009). Hunters' motivations and values: A South African perspective. *Human Dimensions of Wildlife*, *13*(4), 252–262.

Rai, T. S., and Holyoak, K. J. (2013). Exposure to moral relativism compromises moral behavior. *Journal of Experimental Social Psychology*, *49*(6), 995–1001.

Sarkissian, H., Park, J., Tien, D., Wright, J. C., and Knobe, J. (2011). Folk moral relativism. *Mind and Language*, *26*(4), 482–505.

Shaw, S., and Bailey, J. (2009). Discourse analysis: What is it and why is it relevant to family practice? *Family Practice*, *26*(5), 413–419.

Smets, W., and Struyven, K. (2018). Power relations in educational scientific communication – a critical analysis of discourse on learning styles. *Cogent Education*, *5*(1), 1429722.

Spivey, D. (2016). Conservation force Et Al. v. Delta air lines: The legality of an airline ban on big game hunting trophies. *DePaul J. Sports L. and Contemp. DePaul Journal of Sports Law*, *12*, 108.

Suni, J., and Pesonen, J. (2017). Hunters as tourists – an exploratory study of push – pull motivations. *Scandinavian Journal of Hospitality and Tourism*, 1–17.

Van Dijk, T. A. (1993). Principles of critical discourse analysis. *Discourse and Society*, *4*(2), 249–283.

Von Essen, E. (2018). The impact of modernization on hunting ethics: Emerging taboos among contemporary Swedish hunters. *Human Dimensions of Wildlife*, *23*(1), 21–38.

Wheeler, J. (2012). *Harvesting versus hunting*. Retrieved from www.hcn.org/blogs/range/harvesting-versus-hunting

Wong, D. (2006). *Natural moralities: A defense of moral pluralism*. New York: Oxford University Press.

Zamir, Eyal and Medina, Barak (2006). *Incorporating moral constraints into economic analysis*. Downloaded from: https://ssrn.com/abstract=931988 or http://dx.doi.org/10.2139/ssrn.931988

19 Management of a mature destination

Kruger National Park, South Africa

Sanette Ferreira

Introduction

> *A national park is not merely a physical entity, a geographical area, or a suite of ecosystems and species, but a mirror of society and a vigorous symbol.*
> — (Carruthers, 1995, 12)

The Kruger National Park (KNP), South Africa's flagship park, is one of the success stories of southern African tourism, offering a wildlife experience that ranks among the best in the world (Beekwilder, 2018). Tourism development in the park has always played a significant role in the success and resilience of the KNP and SANParks[1] as a whole. In a developing economy, a national park that conserves two million hectares of wilderness area, provides employment to 3400 people, received 1.8 million visitors in 2017 and earned a net income of R 911 million (USD 66 million) (SANParks, 2017) in the same year is perceived as the goose that lays the golden egg. The resilience of the park is, therefore, crucial to South Africa's ecological conservation and economic development (Ferreira and Harmse, 2014).

The KNP's success story can be traced back more than 100 years during which it shared important milestones with other national parks. However, its challenge to maintain its good reputation and success for the next 100 years is daunting. In addition, the park faces political pressure to provide benefits and opportunities to neighbouring communities, to be more accessible to the local population and to attract larger numbers of visitors (Morais, Bunn, Hoogendoorn, and Birendra, 2018; Novelli, 2015). Other challenges include coping with climate change (Venter, Naiman, Biggs, and Pienaar, 2008); the poaching of wild animals (Griffiths, 2017); tourist traffic congestion during high days and holidays (Ferreira and Harmse, 2014); service-level issues of housekeeping staff (Ferreira and Van Zyl, 2016); accommodation maintenance (Engelbrecght and Kruger, 2014); the refurbishment (or replacement) of old accommodation structures (SANParks, 2018) and the upgrade of public ablution and outdoor facilities (Tourism Facility Manager, Skukuza, Personal communication, May 2018).

The aim of this chapter is to provide a brief discussion on the evolution and milestones of the KNP and to evaluate the current state of the tourism plant, especially the tourist accommodation (main rest camps excluding private concessions), the public picnic sites and the public ablution facilities in the pioneer rest camps of the Marula region. The chapter is divided into five sections. First, a brief review of the relevant literature on the life cycle of tourist destinations, the importance of service levels, the maintenance of accommodation facilities and resilience planning is presented. Second, the mixed-method research approach is explained, followed by an outline of the evolution, milestones and challenges of the KNP. Fourth, the tourism contexts and tourism plant of the Marula-South region are introduced, whereafter the state of the rest camps is discussed. Finally, managerial implications are presented and recommendations made.

Life cycles of destinations, quality of accommodation and resilience planning

Most destinations follow a predictable but uncontrolled development pattern from birth to maturity and finally to old age and decline. At each stage, the destination appeals to a different group of visitors who determine the destination's character and success. Several models have been used to describe the evolution of tourism destinations. The first is provided by Plog (1974), who states that destinations appeal to specific types of people and typically follow a relatively predictable pattern of growth and decline in popularity over time. This is due to character changes of most destinations because of the growth and development of tourist-orientated facilities. As the destinations change, they lose the audience or market segment that made them popular, and they only appeal to an ever-shrinking group of visitors (Plog, 2001).

Butler's (1980) tourism area life cycle model (TALC model) is the most widely accepted tool for analysing the historical path and expected future development trends of destinations. The TALC model involves a six-stage evolution of tourism, namely exploration, involvement, development, consolidation (mature), stagnation and post stagnation. The last stage is further characterised by a period of decline, rejuvenation or stabilisation. The TALC model highlights the importance of long-term planning and control to maintain the competitiveness of destinations (Rodriquez, Parra-Lopez, and Yanes-Estevez, 2008). Butler (1980, p. 9) further argues that 'only in the case of the truly unique area could one anticipate an almost timeless attractiveness'.

However, tourism is a service-intensive industry that is dependent on the quality of customers' experiences, and therefore the constant assessment of satisfaction is required (Filieri, McLeay, and Tsu, 2017; Saha and Theingi, 2009). There is usually a positive association between tourist satisfaction and the destination's long-term economic success (Akama and Kieti, 2003), as tourist satisfaction contributes to increased retention rates of tourists' patronage, loyalty and acquisition, which in turn helps in realising economic goals, such as increased numbers of tourists and revenue (Cooper and Hall, 2008; Augustyn and Ho, 1998). Nature-based destinations offer experiences that include services and activities such as accommodation, dining, wildlife activities, entertainment and educational opportunities (Sortiriadis and Nduna, 2014; Merkesdal, 2013).

According to Rodger, Taplin, and Moore (2015, p. 172), 'understanding the relationships between service quality, satisfaction and loyalty continues to both intrigue and frustrate researchers and the managers of protected areas'. Many protected-area agencies face decreasing levels of public funding and an increasing dependence on internal capital generation. As a result, many of these bodies have changed their management structure from that of a traditional government agency to a parastatal structure that retains its revenues. This scenario has created an increased managerial focus and reliance on client satisfaction (Wade and Eagles, 2003; Vaske, Donnelly, and Williamson, 1991). A World Bank study (2014) isolated the key determining factors for African countries' tourism development for maintaining and enhancing their competitiveness as tourism destinations. The study found that human resource capacities and the availability and quality of accommodation services are some of these most important determining factors. Overall, this reality has to be embraced and carefully managed to ensure that the existing accommodation stock stays fresh and welcoming, and to make sure that the destination maintains its appeal (Plog, 1974, 2001).

Resilience planning has recently emerged as a more effective approach to destination planning and development than the sustainability paradigm (Butler, 2018; Lew, 2014). A tourist destination needs to manage the persistent changes associated with the predictable deterioration of facilities, from the entropy of gradual wear and tear over time to the need to upgrade or otherwise modify services to meet the less predictable changing tastes of tourists (Lew, 2014). Protected areas' fundamental approach is to conserve ecosystems, but they are also social-ecological systems whose ecological management and sustainability are heavily influenced by people. The management of national parks as social-ecological systems (SES) seems to be the most appropriate approach (Cummings and Allen, 2017). Societal support for national parks has always been critical to their survival, but this support is particularly important in times of uncertainty and rapid change, both of which are fundamental features of this century (Weiler, Moore, and Moyle, 2013; Rosenberger, Bergeson, and Kline, 2009). Weiler et al. (2013) compare national parks with species in danger of extinction, as the benefits they provide to visitors and society in general are not understood and valued. A conflict of interest can arise when some national parks serve as important nodes of economic growth (Ryan, Shih Shuo, and Huan, 2010), where they play critical roles as catalysts and drivers of local economic development (Ferreira and Harmse, 2014), but also act as vehicles of political transformation, as is the case with South African National Parks (SANParks, 2017).

Case study: Kruger National Park

Research methodology

A mixed-methods approach was used in this research. Primary data were collected from the written comments on the customer care database[2] of the KNP

(2010–2017), 10 interviews with managers of different sections in the park (planning and development, conservation services, traffic and roads, maintenance of superstructures, catering services and retail, tourist services, crime prevention and savannah research unit) and site visits to the rest camps of the Marula region. Secondary data and information were distilled from the SANParks annual reports, relevant websites and blogs, newspaper articles on the KNP and unpublished data sets provided by SANParks' administrative head office in Pretoria. The pioneer rest camps in the Marula region (Pretoriuskop, Crocodile Bridge, Lower Sabie, Malelane, Skukuza and Satara) were visited to evaluate the aesthetic appeal and functional state of the superstructures and supporting facilities.

The written comments on the customer database (2010–2017) were analysed using a qualitative framework presenting different components of the visitor experience (online booking system, ease of access at the gates of the park, check-in and check-out at rest camps, aesthetic appeal and maintenance of accommodation, state of picnic spots and lookout points, cleanliness of ablution facilities, traffic congestion on certain roads and the standard of restaurants in the Marula region). From the repetition (at least 20 mentions) of the same type of complaints linked to a specific component of the visitor experience to KNP, insights could be distilled to enable a narrative report on the state of the tourism plant and if the expectations of visitors were met during their stays in the park. Interviews with managers in the park were used to confirm or clarify insights drawn from the customer's point of view and to ascertain the park management's stance on these complaints.

Relative location and geography

The KNP stretches for 350 km from south to north along the border between South African and Mozambique. It is divided into two large regions for management purposes (Figure 19.1). The northern part, the Nxanatseni region, is more wilderness oriented and boasts fewer tourism superstructures. The Marula region, the southern part, boasts a highly developed tourism plant, and some tourism experts see this region as already over-developed (Figure 19.2) (Ferreira and Harmse, 2014). The Marula region, situated next to the Sabie and Crocodile Rivers, is water rich and offers many opportunities to view the best of the African fauna. The Marula-South's magnetism is embedded in particular geographical contexts (specific fauna, trees, grass cover, rivers and easy access from Gauteng province), although congestion of tourists in the area is exacerbated by infrastructural and superstructural fixity deriving from earlier planning (Hoek, 1953) and the more recent tourism developments outside the park (on the south and south-western borders) (Ferreira and Harmse, 2014). Marula-South constitutes 22% (419,264 ha) of the area of KNP but contains more than 50% of the park's total infrastructure. This region provides 66% of all staff accommodation, and the clustering of tourist superstructure is directly responsible for the dense traffic on the southern ring roads.

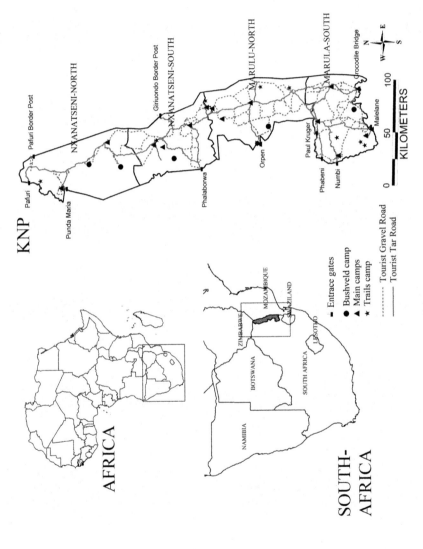

Figure 19.1 Relative location and management regions of KNP

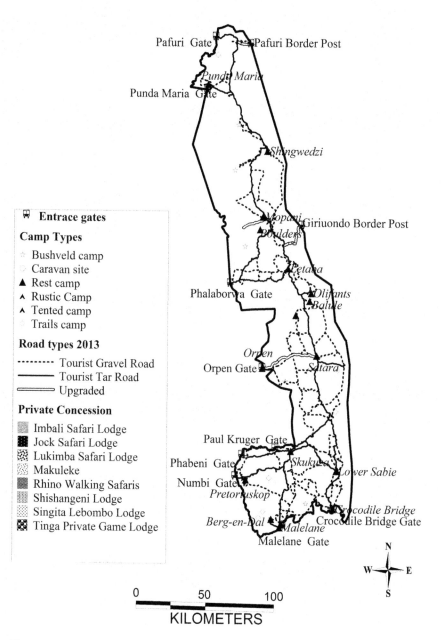

Pafuri Gate
Pafuri Border Post
Punda Maria
Punda Maria Gate
Shingwedzi
Mopani
Giriuondo Border Post
Boulders
Petana
Phalaborwa Gate
Olifants
Balule
Orpen
Orpen Gate
Satara
Paul Kruger Gate
Phabeni Gate
Skukuza
Lower Sabie
Numbi Gate
Pretoriuskop
Crocodile Bridge
Berg-en-Dal
Malelane
Crocodile Bridge Gate
Malelane Gate

N
W — E
S

0   50   100
KILOMETERS

Figure 19.2 Tourism plant of KNP

Evolution, milestones and challenges

Evolution

Although established in 1889, the KNP only opened its gates to tourists in 1928. Over the last 90 years, the tourism plant of the KNP has developed organism-like, boasting 22 rest camps, 15 private lodges, camping sites in most of the rest camps, several picnic sites and one conference facility in Skukuza. Visitor numbers to KNP have grown from approximately 600 in 1928 to 1.8 million in 2017 (SANParks, 2018) (Table 19.1), of which two-thirds are day visitors. Currently (2018), the overnight bed capacity is approximately 4400 (excluding camping facilities) – that has the potential to secure 1,584,000 bed nights per year. Although the total number of visitors is growing each year, the number of overnight visitors has stabilised, with an average occupancy of between 62% and 80%. Measured against the variety of tourist products and experiences offered, as well as the general management of the park, the KNP is certainly not a 'paper park'.[3] When the tourism infrastructure, superstructures and the number of visitors are considered in the context of Butler's (1980) tourism area life cycle model, the Marula region of KNP has reached its mature (or consolidation) life cycle phase and the first signs of stagnation are visible. With the exception of the new Skukuza Conference Lodge that will be opened in 2019, no new additions to the current accommodation stock are envisioned. The overall focus is on upgrading and maintaining the existing stock.

Tourism development milestones

Many milestones characterise the tourism development of the KNP over the past more than 100 years, but the discussion in this section is limited to changes in management philosophy, social responsibility and broader access for the South African tourist. The management philosophy of the KNP has changed from being a 'fortress' park – preservation to the exclusion of people on the periphery of the park (pre-1994) (Carruthers, 1995) – to working towards being integrated with

Table 19.1 Number of tourists to KNP (1928–2018)

YEAR	TOTAL NUMBER OF GUESTS
1928	650
1938	38,014
1948	58,739
1958	122,227
1968	306,347
1978	391,512
1988	625,772
1998	948,732
2008	1,326,054
2017	1,800,000

society (SANParks, 2018). Since 2002, the zonation plans of the KNP have been acknowledging that the park is inextricably linked to the neighbouring communities that it serves, and it is therefore no longer an island in a 'sea of poverty' (Mabunda, 2003). Consistent with this new thrust, the KNP is now reaching out to its bordering communities, and its social responsibility projects confirm this change in philosophy (SANParks, 2018). Much-needed facilities are provided to communities adjacent to the park. Through a 1% levy on tourism income, a number of social legacy projects are provided annually (amongst other projects are computers and e-learning facilities for primary and high schools, science laboratories in schools, environmental education and awareness programmes).

These changes have also resulted in a 'softer' or permeable-border approach, where certain communities have been given access to the park to deploy their own tourism operators for the socioeconomic development of the communities. To provide broader access to the KNP and all other national parks, a Wildcard membership was introduced in 2003, which functions as a subsidised access card for all South Africans. In 2017 there were 85,912 Wildcard members, of which 38% were 60 years and older – a concerning statistic when considering indicators for resilience. Almost 60% of the loyal members were found to be 50 years and older. Weiler et al. (2013) have strongly argued that the future of national parks rests on the support of the younger generations of society.

Key challenges

The need for financial sustainability is a strong motivator for change in the KNP. SANParks estimates that its profit from tourism will exceed R 800 million (USD 61 million) by 2022, but running costs are projected to be around R 1.4 billion per year (USD 105,883,008) (Blaine, 2013). Tourism is the primary and preferred internal mechanism for attaining financial sustainability (SANParks, 2017). Although SANParks admitted earlier that 'the financial driver should never become an end in itself and should never erode the conservation values' (SANParks, 2009, p. 22), the commercialisation strategy of 2012 contradicts the latter statement. Over the last six years, more tourism products (e.g. morning and night safari drives, guided hiking trails, guided 4×4 trails, bush braais, mountain biking events, conferences and weddings) were developed to add to the revenue streams of the park. The change in management philosophy has affected the number of visitors to the park, specifically the visitors to the Marula-South area. The excess of tourists which has resulted, especially day visitors, in specific areas at certain times is directly affecting visitor experiences (Ferreira and Harmse, 2014) and has already changed the profile of current visitors to people who are more tolerant of crowded situations (Manager Tourism Business Unit KNP, June 2018). Ultimately, this will have a long-term effect on the sustainability of the wildlife-viewing product. Wildlife viewing in an undisturbed context, where tourists can take their time to enjoy a wildlife spectacle, is the main draw card to the KNP. In particular, the heavy traffic over Easter and Christmas long weekends on the ring roads around Skukuza has been observed to interfere with the wildlife-viewing experience.

The poaching of rhinos, as well as elephants and cycads, inside the KNP necessitated the establishment of anti-poaching units, estimated at a cost of more than R 25,000 per rhino per year (South African Wildlife College, 2018). This clearly has a direct impact on the KNP's financial sustainability. KNP is at the heart of the illicit and licit wildlife economy. Rates of rhino poaching have ballooned since 2007, causing alarm among both conservationists and concerned citizens. As a custodian of iconic species, the decimation of one of the iconic Big Five species has potentially dire consequences for the regional economy. Since the country's economy relies on wildlife tourism as one of its sources of income, poaching has significant economic consequences. The negative impact, however, extends into the cultural sphere too. Some fear that extinction will rob future generations of the chance to experience wildlife, thus depriving them of their rightful cultural heritage (Griffiths, 2017). Fortunately, the fight against rhino poaching has been greatly enabled through the assistance of a range of donors.[4]

Deterioration of the superstructure and tourist facilities

SANParks' guest feedback analysis for the 12 months ending on March 31, 2017, showed a 68% negative response from customers. The accommodation services category received the most negative comments, with recurrent references to 'poorly maintained accommodation' (23.4%), followed by unsatisfactory cleaning services (16.1%). In addition, the condition of the inventory and supplies was determined to be at 15.6% of expectations. Table 19.2 provides a snapshot of tourist comments in relation to their overnight stay at Skukuza, Pretoriuiskop, Lower Sabie, Crocodile Bridge, Berg-en-Dal and Satara (2010–2018). Site visits to these rest camps confirmed that the overnight visitors' responses were not unwarranted – the visible aging of the superstructures (accommodation, public ablutions and picnic sites) was obvious. On a five-point Likert scale (weak, lower than what is expected, reasonable, good, better than what is expected), all the rest camps ranked, according to the visitor feedback, as 'reasonable' to 'lower than what is expected'.

As seen from the negative responses of overnight visitors (Table 19.2), many visitors felt that they do not receive value for money and that the park continues to deteriorate. Some respondents indicated they would no longer be staying in the park's accommodation and instead visit as day excursionists in future.

A senior manager in the maintenance section shed light on the deterioration of facilities; the problematic time frames for refurbishment of accommodation structures; the limited budget for maintenance; and the subpar quality of the medium-term contractors responsible for this work. Due to this combination of factors, he observed, it was almost impossible to maintain superstructures at the level that is expected by contemporary tourists. He lamented that the management team were not optimistic about the future in this regard.

Nonetheless, to address some of these concerns and broader strategic directions, KNP implemented a medium-term strategic framework (MTSF) in 2017 that consists of four strategic goals (SANParks, 2017). The first goal focuses on

Table 19.2 Negative responses of overnight guests (2010–2017)

Accommodation aesthetic appeal	Picnic spots and lookout points
Rest camps are a bit worn down, chalets need a makeover; camps are all tired and run down.	General maintenance of picnic sites not on standard.
Tiles missing from the roof, leaked badly on the Veranda. The old reception block at Lower Sabi looks like Albasini's ruins.	Pity about some of the picnic sites especially Tshokwane not being tidy.
It seems that the varnish of the chalets has disappeared, very disappointed with accommodation's appearance.	Nkulu picnic site was a disgrace.
Unit is neglected, value proposition becomes less and less.	Facilities at Afslaan pathetic, tables were disgusting.
Facilities not up to standard – no value for money.	Toilets at Nwanetsi were not clean.
Accommodation is expensive and needs an upgrade.	Radios and day visitors have to be forbidden at picnic spots.
Pretoriuskop not on standard especially furniture.	Overcrowding, had to queue to use a toilet.
Lower Sabie rest camp is disgusting.	Filthy and dirty.
Too expensive . . . for the same price as a basic bungalow in the park we could sleep outside the park in Hippo Hotel including a full breakfast.	Not well maintained.
Satara camp bungalows need a serious upgrade. . . . I will not take international visitors there.	Very disappointed with picnic places.
Skukuza was a shocker, superstructures old and neglected.	Gas braai rusted and not cleaned properly.
Cupboards for groceries must be upgraded.	Tables and chair dilapidated.
Lower Sabie looks like a glorified squatter camp.	Toilets could not flush.
Bungalows need a serious revamp, public areas shabby, especially Skukuza.	Garbage bins not cleaned regularly.
Patio furniture very scruffy.	

Accommodation equipment and maintenance	Cleanliness of ablution facilities
Stoves without heat control indicators, unsteady furniture, heating and cooling system not working, leaking taps, pipes, roofs etc.	Bath mats have to be provided in the showers and bathrooms for the camping visitors to prevent one standing on the wet floor in another person's water.
Equipment such as braai tongs, salad bowls, plates, pots, cutlery and crockery are limited and not in good shape.	The ablution blocks are not as neat and clean as even a few years ago.
Cobwebs, dust, dirty walls, mildew in the shower, park gets more expensive and more unkept.	During the six days we stayed in the camp there were never paper towels in the bathroom.
Braai stand was not cleaned after previous usage; maintenance is falling with every visit.	Lower Sabie can surely do something about the urine smell in the urinals!

(Continued)

Table 19.2 (Continued)

Accommodation equipment and maintenance	Cleanliness of ablution facilities
Problem with air conditioner . . . have to sweat in December. . . . It is so sad, can see that park is going down every year.	Bath mats have to be provided in the showers and bathrooms for the camping visitors to prevent one standing on the wet floor in another person's water.
At Skukuza the stench of the drains is terrible.	Toilets at reception display bad image
For the price you pay, you have to step up cleaning of accommodation and maintenance.	Maintenance is bad – blocked drains – I will stay outside the park in future.
Luxury tents were leaking without any compensation.	Toilets at Malelane gate a shame for SANParks.
Rhino house disgusting, oven dirty, no plates of the stove in working condition.	Showers not clean and no hooks for towels.
Mosquito screen at windows are broken.	Ablutions in Malelane camp not adequate.
Laundry facilities poor and not adequate for the number of visitors.	Camp sites ablution facilities need a face lift.

Standard of towels and Linen	Pools
Towels and linen have to be donated to a charity.	NO day visitors to go into Pretoriuskop's swimming pool like it was before . . . the pool was too full to use on the 25 and the 26 of December.
Linen is old and thin from all the use.	Green and dirty, ablutions at pools not adequate.
Towels were stained and I would not use it for my dog.	Landscaping around pool neglected.

the sustainable management of the conservation asset. The second goal is linked to diverse and responsible ecotourism that is designed to enhance the tourism plant and to maximise economic returns and social and environmental benefits, by creating diversified and better tourism products for visitors to enjoy. The third strategic goal relates to progressive, equitable and fair socioeconomic transformation, while the fourth goal deals with effective resource utilisation and good governance (SANParks, 2017). It remains to be seen whether these strategic directions will yield the desired outcomes.

Key issues and imperatives

KNP is embedded in a socio-ecological system where the poverty of neighbouring communities will dictate the future of certain wildlife species. Poaching of wildlife within the borders of the park unfortunately forms part of the livelihoods (or survival strategies) of some of the households residing in proximity to the borders of the park. Structural limitations also prevent members of neighbouring communities from experiencing wildlife in the way that tourists are able to do. The absence or presence of certain iconic species will in turn affect tourists' attraction to the KNP. Crimes against wildlife may have a severe impact on tourism, the economy and national security. 'It is speculated that tourists may become reluctant to visit the country due to violence involved in poaching incidents, which may consequently exacerbate socio-economic problems, such as employment' (Griffiths, 2015, p. 66). Thus, future strategies of conserving biodiversity in parks should focus as much on the socioeconomic human dimension of biodiversity conservation as on the scientific study of species and habitats in national parks.

Urgent action is also needed from SANParks to mitigate the aging of its superstructures (tourism plant). The ability to understand the diversity of tourists in any source market, their underlying motives and the type of products that may appeal to them (Plog, 1974) is of utmost importance. It is important too to note that the KNP's main market is the domestic market, consisting of very loyal, middle-class families who have been visiting the Kruger for decades. A considerable proportion of these repeat tourists have left South Africa but are returning every year to KNP because of the spectacular wildlife viewing.

The SANParks management is particularly focused on surviving the rhino poaching war; however, to play an important role in the socioeconomic circumstances of its neighbouring communities, they need to prioritise the more than 100 years of investment in the tourism plant – to sustain the existing jobs and businesses in the park. Income generated from selling tourism products (especially bed nights) will also provide the finance to realise two of the other strategic goals, namely, to manage and protect the natural and heritage assets of the park, as well as to progressively contribute to equitable and fair economic transformation in South Africa.

Although the day visitor numbers are still increasing (year on year), the negative responses of overnight visitors to the accommodation facilities, general maintenance, cleanliness of ablution facilities and picnic sites are revealing the story of a fading jewel. Furthermore, visible signs of stagnation of the Marula-South region are evident: superstructures look old and tired, gardens are not well kept, garbage bins are overflowing and the public ablutions in camps are in dire need for upgrading. The camping facilities need major renovation. The deterioration of the tourism plant could be detrimental to the long-term resilience of the park (Table 19.3). The largest part of the income raised from tourism (more than 80%) comes from the accommodation component (SANParks, 2015). It is therefore

Table 19.3 Traffic light resilience indicators

Green	Red
Integration of KNP in to the greater social-ecological system of the neighbouring region	Poverty of neighbouring communities (high unemployment)
Embargo on tourism development south of the Sabie River	Poor maintenance of rest camps
	People prefer to stay outside the park, more value for money

critical that the overnight customers' expectations are met, as a matter of priority. Overall, KNP will need to focus on protecting their supply (in the broadest sense) rather than relying on creating demand (Butler, 2018).

Conclusion

The KNP is a notable success story of tourism development in southern Africa. Attracting huge volumes of tourists from all over the world, this attraction has offered the definitive wildlife safari experience in the SADC region for decades. However, among other issues that have been highlighted, the over-development of the Marula-South section has demonstrably led to undesirable outcomes for visitors, ultimately threatening the resilience of the park.

The KNP story offers a lesson in long-term destination management: when destination managers become complacent about the success of their efforts to grow the tourism base year after year, unseen forces emerge gradually and upset the status quo. In the case of the KNP, this complacency is evident in the lack of maintenance of superstructures and the deterioration in accommodation facilities, which have a direct and negative impact on the visitor experience. If the trajectory does not change, it is likely that the number of overnight visitors will continue to decrease, with significant implications for KNP's revenues. Without drastic action in this regard, the decline of this African jewel is unfortunately almost certain. Still, there are opportunities yet to reinvigorate the park and reaffirm its position as one of the best in the world.

Notes

1 SANParks is a semi-state managing agency of 19 national parks in South Africa.
2 An online platform where visitors can post comments on their positive and/or negative experiences about their visit to the KNP.
3 'Paper parks' exist on a map but when you visit these parks, you have to use your imagination to see them, as there is limited wildlife resources and tourist services, no controlled access and no accommodation inside the borders of these parks.
4 Donors including but not limited to the GEF, the Peace Parks Foundation, the WWF, various US government agencies and government departments.

References

Akama, J. S., and Kieti, M. K. (2003). Measuring tourist satisfaction with Kenya's wildlife safari: A case study of Tsavo West National Park. *Tourism Management, 24,* 73–81. doi:10.1016/S0261-5177(02)00044-4

Augustyn, M., and Ho, S. K. (1998). Service quality and tourism. *Journal of Travel Research, 37,* 71–75. doi:10.1177/004728759803700110

Beekwilder, J. (2018). *Serengeti National Park voted best African park in 2018.* Retrieved from www.safaribookings.com/blog/serengeti-national-park-voted-best-african-safari-park-2018

Blaine, S. (2013, March 28). *SANParks funding plan 'will stand up to scrutiny.* Business Day Live. Retrieved from www.bdlive.co.za/national/science/2013/03/28/sanparks-funding-plan-will-stand-up-to-scrutiny

Butler, R. W. (1980). The concept of a tourist area of life cycle of evolution: Implications for management of resources. *Canadian Geographer, 19*(1), 5–12. doi:10.1111/j.1541-0064.1980.tb00970.x

Butler, R. W. (2018). Sustainable tourism in sensitive environments: A wolf in sheep's clothing? *Sustainability, 10*(6), 1–11. doi:10.3390/su10061789

Carruthers, J. (1995). *The Kruger national park: A social and political history*. Pietermaritzburg: University of Natal Press.

Cooper, C., and Hall, C. M. (2008). *Contemporary tourism: An International Approach.* London: Butterworth-Heinemann.

Cumming, G. S., and Allen, C. R. (2017). Protected areas as social-ecological systems: Perspectives from resilience and social-ecological systems theory. *Ecological Applications, 27*(6), 1709–1717. doi:10.1002/eap.1584

Engelbrecght, W. H., and Kruger, M. (2014). An analysis of critical success factors in managing the tourist experience at Kruger national park. *Tourism Review International, 17*(4), 237–251. doi:10.3727/154427214X13910101597120

Ferreira, S. L. A., and Harmse, A. C. (2014). Kruger National Park: Tourism development and issues around the management of large numbers of tourists *Journal of Ecotourism, 13*(1), 16–34. doi:10.1080/14724049.2014.925907

Ferreira, S. L. A., and Van Zyl, G. (2016). Catering for a large number of tourists: The McDonaldisation of casual dining in Kruger National Park. *Geography Bulletin Socioeconomic Series, 33*, 39–53. doi:10.1515/bog-2016-0023.

Filieri, R., McLeay, F., and Tsu, B. (2017). Antecedents of travellers' satisfaction and purchase intention from social commerce websites. In R. Schegg and B. Stangl (Eds.), *Information and communication technologies in tourism* (pp. 517–528). London: Springer International Publishing. doi:10.1007/978-3-319-51168-9_37

Griffiths, M (2015) *The illegal trade in endangered animals in KwaZulu-Natal, with an emphasis on rhino poaching*. Unpublished MA (Criminology) dissertation, University of South Africa. Retrieved on January 24, 2018 from http://www.rhinoresourcecenter.com/index.php?s=1&act=refs&CODE=ref_detail&id=1461162420

Griffiths, M. L. (2017). Heritage lost: The cultural impact of wildlife crime in South Africa. *SA Crime Quarterly, 60*, 1–6. doi:10.17159/2413-3108/2017/v0n60a1728

Hoek, Anon. (1953). *Die organisasie en administrasie van die Nasionale Parkeraad [The organisation and administration of the National Parks Board]* (Unpublished report), National Parks Board.

Lew, A. (2014). Scale, change and resilience planning. *Tourism Geographies, 16*(1), 14–22. doi:10.1080/14616688.2013.864325

Mabunda, M. D. (2003). *An integrated tourism management framework for the Kruger National Park, South Africa* (Ph.D. Thesis), University of Pretoria. Retrieved from https://repository.up.ac.za/bitstream/handle/2263/27523/00front.pdf?sequence=1

Merkesdal, C. (2013). *Green experience value: An investigation whether thoroughly green service providers enhance the value for the customer experience* (Unpublished Thesis), Frederiksberg, Denmark. Retrieved from http://hdl.handle.net/10417/4009

Morais, D. B., Bunn, D., Hoogendoorn, G., and Birendra, K. C. (2018). The potential role of tourism microentrepreneurship in the prevention of rhino poaching. *International Development Planning Review, 40*(3), 1–20. doi:10.3828/idpr.2018.21

Novelli, M. (2015). *Tourism development in Sub-Saharan Africa: Current issues and local realities*. London: Routledge.

Plog, S. C. (1974). Why destinations areas rise and fall in popularity. *Cornel University Hotel and Restaurant Administration Quarterly, 14*(4), 55–58. doi.org/10.1177%2F001088047401400409

Plog, S. C. (2001). Why destinations areas rise and fall in popularity: An update of a Cornell quarterly classic. *Hotel and Restaurant Administration Quarterly, 42*(3), 13–24. doi:10.1177/0010880401423001

Rodger, K., Taplin, R. H., and Moore, S. A. (2015). Using a randomized experiment to test the causal effect of service quality on visitor satisfaction and loyalty in a remote national park. *Tourism Management, 50,* 172–183.

Rodriquez, J. R. O., Parra-Lopez, E., and Yanes-Estevez, V. (2008). The sustainability of island destinations: Tourism area life cycle and teleological perspectives. The case of Tenerife. *Tourism Management, 29*(1), 53–65. doi/10.1016/j.tourman.2007.04.007

Rosenberger, R. S., Bergeson, T. R., and Kline, J. D. (2009). Macro-Linkages between health and outdoor recreation: The role of parks and recreation providers. *Journal of Park and Recreation Administration, 27*(3), 8–20.

Ryan, C., Shih Shuo, Y., and Huan, T. (2010). Theme parks and a structural equation model of determinants of visitor satisfaction – Janfusan Fancy world, Taiwan. *Journal of Vacation Marketing, 16*(3), 185–199.

Saha, G. C., and Theingi, A. (2009). Service quality, satisfaction, and behavioural intentions: A study of low-cost airline carriers in Thailand. *Managing Service Quality, 19*(3), 350–372. doi:10.1108/09604520910955348

Sortiriadis, M. D., and Nduna, L. (2014). Market segmentation of nature-based attractions: A framework for experience and activity-orientated segmentation. *Journal of Human Ecology, 46*(1), 63–71.

South African National Parks. (SANParks). (2009). *Strategic environmental assessment for the Marula Region of the Kruger National Park* (Unpublished report), Final analysis report. Project No.9235. Prepared by INVEST.

South African National Parks. (SANParks). (2015). *Annual performance plan 2017–2018.* Retrieved from http://pmg-assets.s3-website-eu-west-1.amazonaws.com/170502 sanparks.pdf

South African National Parks. (SANParks). (2017). *SANParks annual report.* Retrieved from http//www.sanparks.co.za/assets/docs/general/annual-report-2017.pdf

South African National Parks. (SANParks). (2018). *Kruger Park management plan – 2018–2028.* Retrieved from www.sanparks.org/assets/docs/conservation/park_man/knp/draft-plan.pdf

South African Wildlife College. (2018). *Rhino poaching statistics – June 2018.* Retrieved from http://wildlifecollege.org.za/news-media/articles/rhino-poaching-statistics/

Vaske, J. J., Donnelly, M. P., and Williamson, B. N. (1991). Monitoring for quality control in state park management. *Journal of Park and Recreation Administration, 9*(2), 59–72.

Venter, F. J., Naiman, R. J., Biggs, H. C., and Pienaar, D. J. (2008). The evolution of conservation management philosophy: Science, environmental change and social adjustments in Kruger national park. *Ecosystems, 11,* 173–192. doi:10.1007/s10021-007-9116-x

Wade, D., and Eagles, P. (2003). The use of importance-performance analysis and market segmentation for tourism management in parks and protected areas: An application to Tanzania's National Parks. *Journal of Ecotourism, 2,* 196–212.

Weiler, B., Moore, S. A., and Moyle, B. (2013). Building and sustaining support for national parks in 21st century: Why and how to save the national park experience from extinction. *Journal of Park and Recreation Administration, 31,* 110–126.

World Bank. (2014). *Tourism in Africa: Harnessing tourism for growth and improved Livelihoods.* Washington, DC: World Bank.

20 The future of tourism in Africa

Optimism in a changing environment

Mucha Mkono

Contemplating the future

Africa's tourism stories are best explained and understood, not in comparison to the 'first world' – that would be comparing oranges with apples – but in terms of the continent's unique histories and dynamics that require localised contextualisation. The varied chapters in this book have demonstrated the diversity of Africa's tourism environments within regions and individual countries. As such, there is no one umbrella narrative about the future of tourism in Africa. Nonetheless, it is useful to identify critical issues that must be contended with as African countries continue on their trajectories of harnessing their tourism potential.

In this concluding chapter, the future of tourism is contemplated within a growing optimistic sentiment, *Africa rising*, under which it is argued that Africa has turned a new corner, 'and talk of "the hopeless continent," as *The Economist* called Africa in 2000, has been dropped in favour of names such as "a hopeful continent" '(Taylor, 2014, p. 144). Studies have pointed to a number of trends in some parts of Africa: increased democratisation, a growing middle class, relative peace, greater availability of mobile phones and access to the internet, growth in African consumer spending and domestic entrepreneurship (Bunce, Franks, and Paterson, 2016; Hofmeyr, 2013; Pillay, 2015; Schroeder, 1999; Taylor, 2014). This macro-environment provides a promising setting for Africa's tourism performance in the 21st century. From this, we can conceive of an 'Afro-positive turn' in scholarship and on the ground.

The preceding chapters have indeed demonstrated tourism's actual and potential contribution to livelihoods, communities and economies in Africa, as well as to the millions of tourists who visit the continent each year. The picture painted is not all doom and gloom, but one of potential, growth and the various modalities thereof. In the next section I discuss some of the critical issues for Africa's tourism in the 21st century, namely, wildlife conservation and animal ethics (particularly in relation to trophy hunting and its controversy in the last few years); climate change; politics, governance and leadership; and terrorism. In this respect, it is important to be realistic about the continent's performance and prospects. Taylor (2016) states that when discussing the narrative surrounding the idea of 'Africa rising', it is also crucial to note the deep structural problems that remain, even though superficial features of Africa's economies might be promising. The re-imaging and re-imagining of Africa that is spurred by the positive developments should therefore be balanced with critical reflection.

Critical issues for Africa's tourism in the 21st century

Wildlife conservation and animal ethics

There is no doubt that wildlife is at the heart of Africa's tourism product. Therefore, conservation should always be monitored closely to ensure that risks to wild animal populations are minimised. In particular, more resources are needed to reduce poaching, which remains a major issue in many parts of Africa (Büscher and Ramutsindela, 2015). Dwindling lion numbers and the threat of extinction for rhinos must be kept at the top of conservation agendas around the world.

Also worth noting, with the recent controversy following the much publicised shooting of the lion, Cecil, in Zimbabwe, trophy hunting is under the spotlight (Mkono, 2018). African governments will need to acknowledge the importance of ethics in wildlife tourism and the shift in public sentiment in that regard. Consequentialist arguments where sport hunting is justified on the grounds of funding conservation no longer suffice. Therefore, alternatives to trophy hunting must be sought. At the same time, diversifying the tourism product so that it is not overly reliant on wildlife will be important. Jim Ayorekire, Joseph Obua and Michael Bruce Byaruhanga's analysis (Chapter 7) of potential innovative cultural tourism for Uganda experiences shows that diversification is possible with creative use of indigenous resources, for example. Tom Kwanya (Chapter 10) argues similarly in the Kenyan case.

Managing climate change risks

African countries are particularly vulnerable to climate change due to their comparatively lower adaptive capacity, as a result in part of their lack of capital and technological flexibility (Hoogendoorn and Fitchett, 2018). Adaptation is also slow because climate change is not considered a priority, in the face of other urgent issues such as poverty reduction, housing and disease (Hoogendoorn and Fitchett, 2018). Climate change impacts are nevertheless already being felt, as the following examples will demonstrate.

In the case of the Okavango Delta in Botswana, studies show that excessively warm temperatures have had a negative impact on tourist operators as outdoor activities which could not be climate controlled, such as boat and canoe rides, were often cancelled (Hambira, Saarinen, Manwa, and Atlhopheng, 2013). In northern Tunisia, during summer and autumn, the climate is increasingly becoming too hot for sightseeing activities (Köberl, Prettenthaler, and Bird, 2016). Temperature increases also threaten to interfere with wildlife migration patterns in countries such as Botswana, Namibia, Kenya and Tanzania, thus compromising wildlife tourism activities there (Agnew and Viner, 2001; Hambira et al., 2013;

Hoogendoorn and Fitchett, 2018). In South Africa, it is reported that storm surges have become recurrent, and the recent drought in Cape Town has been attributed in part to climate change effects (Hoogendoorn and Fitchett, 2018). Furthermore, as a result of droughts, animals are affected by the reduction of vegetation, which provides both habitat and food, as in the case of the Kruger National Park in South Africa (Steyn and Spencer, 2012). In addition, a reduction in rainfall threatens to reduce bird-watching in Botswana (Hambira and Saarinen, 2015).

Even more concerning is the threat of sea level rise, which is already impacting parts of Africa's coastline. For exaple, empirical studies have highlighted concerns regarding the impacts of sea level rise to tourism in Kenya (Awuor, Orindi, and Ochieng Adwera, 2008), Morocco (Snoussi, Ouchani, and Niazi, 2008), and South Africa (Fitchett, Grant, and Hoogendoorn, 2016; Hoogendoorn, Grant, and Fitchett, 2016; Steyn and Spencer, 2012). All of these provide a compelling case for international cooperation to help African countries achieve more comprehensive climate change adaptions. After all, Africa's tourism resources are enjoyed by tourists from all over the globe.

Politics, governance and leadership

It is a fact that corruption is endemic across Africa, although it is worse in some parts than in others, enabled by African countries' weak governance institutions (Gyimah-Brempong, 2002). This means that tourism governance suffers, and tourism funds are often misused. Zimbabwe offers a good example of the impact of political leadership on a country's tourism performance, where the Mugabe-led land invasions of the early 2000s resulted in the dwindling of tourist arrivals and the loss of game reserves to illegal occupations. The Mugabe government's Look-East response failed to generate volumes that could make up for the reduction in Western arrivals. To regain its market share, Zimbabwe will require a new political image that will inspire goodwill from the international community.

Beyond politics, as Shepherd Nyaruwata, Takaruza Munyanyiwa and Cleopas Njekerai demonstrate in their chapter (Chapter 5), African governments have an important role to play in ensuring that communities reap optimal benefits from tourism projects. By collaborating with communities, governments can leverage the synergies between tourism and poverty alleviation. African governments will also advance their tourism development by strengthening cooperation and collaboration with their counterparts across national borders, as in the case of Transfrontier National Parks, as discussed in Zibanai Zhou's chapter. Binaswaree Bolaky's contribution (Chapter 11) also makes a strong case for regional integration and cooperation.

Terrorism

In the post-2011 Arab Spring era, Africa has been experiencing a surge in terrorist attacks (Asongu, Tchamyou, Asongu, and Tchamyou, 2018), as exemplified by the 2015 Garissa University and the 2013 Westgate shopping mall killings in Kenya. The terrorist group, Boko Haram, continues to extend its sphere of activity in Nigeria and neighbouring Chad, Cameroon and Niger (Asongu et al., 2018; Oyewole, 2015). Terrorism activity makes destinations less appealing as travellers worry about their safety. Buigut and Amendah (2016, p. 937) found that 'terrorism, proxied by the number of fatalities, negatively and significantly affects the number of visitors to Kenya. A 1% increase in fatalities decreases the arrivals by about 0.132%'. It is therefore incumbent on African governments, in cooperation with the international community, to find ways to mitigate terrorism risks and guarantee, as far as possible, the safety of tourists. But where terror has occurred, there is still hope for tourism recovery, with the right strategy. David Adeloye and Neil Carr's analysis (Chapter 17) of post-terror recovery strategies adopted by Egypt and Tunisia provides useful guidelines for other terror-prone destinations both within and outside Africa.

Future research directions – realising the 'Afro-positive turn'

This book sought to present a more balanced representation of tourism in Africa, one that uses the frame of *positive tourism* to recognise the progress made, while acknowledging the many challenges that remain. The book is therefore intended to signal an 'Afro-positive turn'. How then, can tourism studies embrace this Afro-positive turn in the future?

Crucially, it is important to recognise the power of plural stories and *the danger of a single story*, as Nigerian author Chimamanda Ngozi puts it. In simple terms, the Afro-positive turn is about affirming that the continent of Africa is not all doom and gloom. Thus, a more balanced representation of Africa can be achieved if an appropriate level of complexity is conveyed when presenting findings, and the accompanying context is detailed in full, while resisting generalisations. When context and specificity are lost, African stories are reduced to generalities (Fair, 1993). Consistently focusing on the continent's shortcomings creates a sense of hopelessness. For hybrid intellectual spaces that ensure inclusion of diverse Others to thrive, tourism scholars also need to be reflective and reflexive about their biases regarding Africa.

Further, it is important to observe that the status quo partly results from the relatively limited tourism research coming from African tertiary institutions. As a result, knowledge on Africa in tourism is constructed through the lens of mostly Western scholars. However, as more tourism research emerges from African institutions, it is hoped that more complex representations of Africa will follow.

In this postcolonial era, it is critical for academics in all disciplines to critically engage with culture and recognise their own cultural embeddedness, in order to transform colonial relations instead of reproducing them (Grant, Djomo, and Krause, 2016). In practical terms, researchers embracing the Afro-positive turn would need to:

1   frame research questions that allow them to *seek out* and foreground positive stories of Africa pertaining to tourism and other spheres of inquiry;

2   advance more balanced analyses of diverse African tourism contexts, celebrating successes along with failures;
3   involve more African scholars (for example through strategic collaborations) to ensure more complex representations of Africa; and
4   demonstrate awareness of the heterogeneity of African countries' tourism industries, that is, moving away from treating Africa as a country or as a homogeneous 'dark continent'.

Furthermore, through strategic initiatives such as special issues of journals focusing on Afro-positive studies and similarly themed conference streams and keynotes, these postcolonial representations may become more equitable. Postgraduate students, African and otherwise, could also be encouraged to take up this thrust in their research as a way of encouraging a new generation of balanced African theorisations. The resultant body of work, it is hoped, will constitute an important step towards the epistemological emancipation of African images.

I will stress again that Afro-positivism does not ignore the real challenges that Africa faces. It does not seek to misrepresent Africa as a land of untainted beauty and progress. Rather, it seeks to challenge assumptions that the pessimistic perspectives are the complete story. It calls for diverse and plural representations that will also uplift and inspire African peoples. But the new narrative of Africa not only needs to be more nuanced and balanced; it should also be evolving and dynamic, that is, capable of capturing how Africa is transforming and progressing.

Academics have a responsibility not only to tell stories that interest them, but to be conscious of any unfair representations, intentional or unintentional, covert or overt. They also have a moral duty to actively advance representational, social and cultural justice in the way they tell stories about places and peoples. In particular, this applies to tourism scholars working in the critical studies framework, and especially in light of the critical turn (Ateljevic, Harris, Wilson, and Collins, 2005; Hollinshead, 2006).

In this digital era, there has emerged an opportunity to tap into social media narratives that offer an alternative view of Africa as a dynamic cultural space and as a site of tourist experiences. As Africans increasingly gain access to these digital platforms, we will likely see more stories told by Africans themselves. The more voices about Africa we hear, the more we will discover Africa in all its facets.

References

Agnew, M. D., and Viner, D. (2001). Potential impacts of climate change on international tourism. *Tourism and Hospitality Research*, *3*(1), 37–60.
Asongu, S. A., Tchamyou, V. S., Asongu, N., and Tchamyou, N. P. (2018). Fighting terrorism in Africa: Benchmarking policy harmonization. *Physica A: Statistical Mechanics and Its Applications*, *492*, 1931–1957.
Ateljevic, I., Harris, C., Wilson, E., and Collins, F. L. (2005). Getting 'entangled': Reflexivity and the 'critical turn' in tourism studies. *Tourism Recreation Research*, *30*(2), 9–21.
Awuor, C. B., Orindi, V. A., and Ochieng Adwera, A. (2008). Climate change and coastal cities: The case of Mombasa, Kenya. *Environment and Urbanization*, *20*(1), 231–242.

Buigut, S., and Amendah, D. D. (2016). Effect of terrorism on demand for tourism in Kenya. *Tourism Economics*, *22*(5), 928–938.

Bunce, M., Franks, S., and Paterson, C. (2016). *Africa's media image in the 21st century: From the 'heart of darkness' to 'Africa rising'*. New York: Routledge.

Büscher, B., and Ramutsindela, M. (2015). Green violence: Rhino poaching and the war to save Southern Africa's peace parks. *African Affairs*, *115*(458), 1–22.

Fair, J. E. (1993). War, famine, and poverty: Race in the construction of Africa's media image. *Journal of Communication Inquiry*, *17*(2), 5–22.

Fitchett, J. M., Grant, B., and Hoogendoorn, G. (2016). Climate change threats to two low-lying South African coastal towns: Risks and perceptions. *South African Journal of Science*, *112*(5–6), 1–9.

Grant, J. A., Djomo, A. N., and Krause, M. G. (2016). Afro-optimism reinvigorated? Reflections on the glocal networks of sexual identity, health, and natural resources in Africa. *Global Change, Peace and Security*, *28*(3), 317–328.

Gyimah-Brempong, K. (2002). Corruption, economic growth, and income inequality in Africa. *Economics of Governance*, *3*(3), 183–209.

Hambira, W. L., and Saarinen, J. (2015). Policy-makers' perceptions of the tourism – climate change nexus: Policy needs and constraints in Botswana. *Development Southern Africa*, *32*(3), 350–362.

Hambira, W. L., Saarinen, J., Manwa, H., and Atlhopheng, J. R. (2013). Climate change adaptation practices in nature-based tourism in Maun in the Okavango Delta area, Botswana: How prepared are the tourism businesses? *Tourism Review International*, *17*(1), 19–29.

Hofmeyr, J. (2013). Africa rising? Popular dissatisfaction with economic management despite a decade of growth. *Afrobarometer Policy Brief*, *2*.

Hollinshead, K. (2006). The shift to constructivism in social inquiry: Some pointers for tourism studies. *Tourism Recreation Research*, *31*(2), 43–58.

Hoogendoorn, G., and Fitchett, J. M. (2018). Tourism and climate change: A review of threats and adaptation strategies for Africa. *Current Issues in Tourism*, *21*(7), 742–759.

Hoogendoorn, G., Grant, B., and Fitchett, J. M. (2016). Disjunct perceptions? Climate change threats in two-low lying South African coastal towns. *Bulletin of Geography. Socio-economic Series*, *31*(31), 59–71.

Köberl, J., Prettenthaler, F., and Bird, D. N. (2016). Modelling climate change impacts on tourism demand: A comparative study from Sardinia (Italy) and Cap Bon (Tunisia). *Science of the Total Environment*, *543*, 1039–1053.

Mkono, M. (2018, In Press). The age of digital activism in tourism: Evaluating the legacy and limitations of the Cecil anti-trophy hunting movement. *Journal of Sustainable Tourism*, *26*(9), 1608–1624. doi:10.1080/09669582.2018.1489399

Oyewole, S. (2015). Boko Haram: Insurgency and the war against terrorism in the Lake Chad region. *Strategic Analysis*, *39*(4), 428–432.

Pillay, D. (2015). The global economic crisis and the Africa rising narrative. *Africa Development*, *40*(3), 59–75.

Schroeder, R. A. (1999). Geographies of environmental intervention in Africa. *Progress in Human Geography*, *23*(3), 359–378. doi:10.1177/030913259902300302

Snoussi, M., Ouchani, T., and Niazi, S. (2008). Vulnerability assessment of the impact of sea-level rise and flooding on the Moroccan coast: The case of the Mediterranean eastern zone. *Estuarine, Coastal and Shelf Science*, *77*(2), 206–213.

Steyn, J., and Spencer, J. (2012). Climate change and tourism: Implications for South Africa: Tourism and adventure. *African Journal for Physical Health Education, Recreation and Dance, 18*(1), 1–19.

Taylor, I. (2014). Is Africa rising? *Brown Journal of World Affairs, 21,* 143–161.

Taylor, I. (2016). Dependency redux: Why Africa is not rising. *Review of African Political Economy, 43*(147), 8–25.

Index

Note: Page numbers in *italic* indicate figures, and page numbers in **bold** indicate tables on the corresponding page.